BE YOUR FINEST ART

Joanne Miller
&
Dorsey McHugh

Awaken your creative self

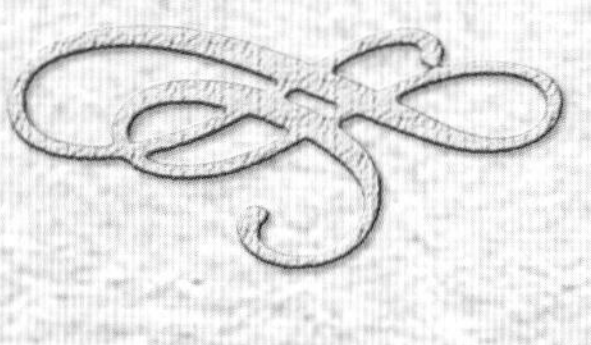

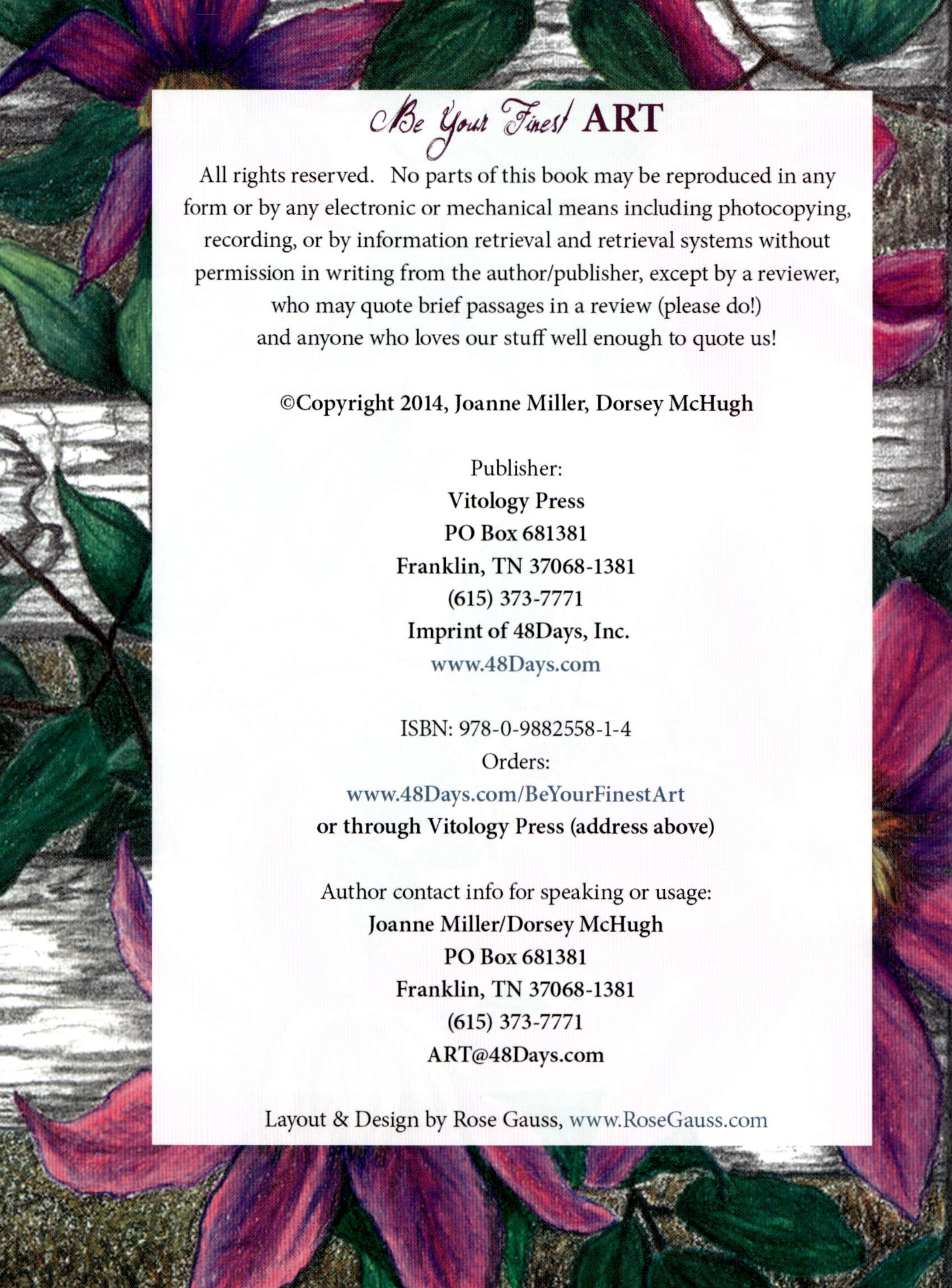

Be Your Finest **ART**

Publisher:
Vitology Press
PO Box 681381
Franklin, TN 37068-1381
(615) 373-7771
Imprint of 48Days, Inc.
www.48Days.com

ISBN: 978-0-9882558-1-4
Orders:
www.48Days.com/BeYourFinestArt
or through Vitology Press (address above)

Author contact info for speaking or usage:
Joanne Miller/Dorsey McHugh
PO Box 681381
Franklin, TN 37068-1381
(615) 373-7771
ART@48Days.com

Layout & Design by Rose Gauss, www.RoseGauss.com

If you really want to, you can seize the day
Only if you want to, will you fly away.

Enya, If Only

Dedicated To:

Daniel from us both: Your love, support and encouragement provided the impetus for our writing this book. We thank you for believing in us; for validating our gifts and pushing us to completion.

Robin from Dorsey: A whole book could be written about how precious my sister, Robin has been to me in this creative journey. Thank you, dear, for your love, your prayers and your unflagging support.

Acknowledgments:

Many people have helped us with this project. This is not just a book of words but is also a work of art, interviews, quotes and examples. We want to thank each of you for taking time to share how you embrace creativity in your daily life. You have blessed us. We hope you take pride in sharing a little of yourself with other readers in hopes your story will be an encouragement and light to their lives.

We want to give abundant thanks to all our proofers and editors who helped make us look like rock stars! Caleb Miller, Jan Mosher, Judith Hibbard, Dan Miller, Ilea Angaza and Doak Turner. Bless you all! *(If you find any typos, it's their fault!)*

A big thank you to Susan Macke Miller, Dorsey's partner in crime in the world of art. Susan keeps her on the straight and narrow *(often saving her from embarrassment)* and takes care of all the registration for the private and group class students, does PR and sales for Dorsey.

Rose Gauss has illustrated and done layout for four children's books for me (Joanne). She can see my words as pictures in her head. I love that. She is amazing. I am so proud of her and so blessed by her talent in being versatile enough to do this grown up book. We have history and together we will continue to learn and grow more in future projects. Love you, girlfriend!

We give love and kudos to Candy Richey for instinctively knowing Dorsey and I would appreciate and enjoy each other. Little did she know what would develop from this friendship she orchestrated. You never know the power of networking people and she is a master! Bless you, Candy. You are a forever friend.

And we certainly want to mention the Sanctuary Sessions art classes. The students in that class have given us so much fodder for this project. Can't say enough about how they add excitement to our lives. Wish every reader could get involved in a wellspring of creativity such as we have here in Franklin, TN. *(but we aren't sharing with you, we are possessive of this group!)*

Our amazing lay-out artist, Rose Gauss, has created a work of art in these pages and to avoid confusion you will know when I am speaking by the fancy JM at the beginning of my words. Rose has incorporated a fade out from one of my drawings called Peaceful Perch that will be the background for my "voice". Dorsey, being the colorful personality that she is, will have her artistic Dorsey McHugh she uses on her paintings to indicate her "voice". Rose has incorporated a colorful border for Dorsey that is a collage of pieces from Dorsey's original art. How cool is that!?

Introduction

JM Did you ever meet someone with whom you were instantly drawn in a way you knew would enhance your life and you simply had to know more?

I met Dorsey McHugh at a Christmas party in 2011 at the home of a mutual friend and was immediately drawn to her. We had instant rapport. Instinctively, I knew I was going to make the effort to get to know her. After being introduced, it wasn't any time at all before Dorsey and I found ourselves steeped in a lively, couldn't-get-a-word-in-edgewise, conversation. It was as if two old friends were reuniting after a long separation. I knew I had just met a person who would enhance my life in ways I was eager to discover.

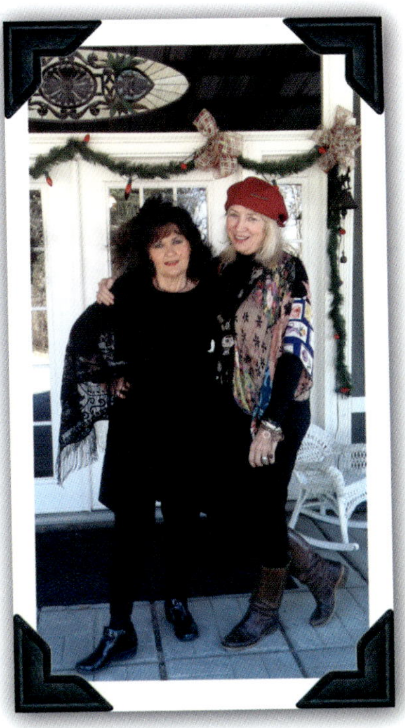

Joanne and Dorsey dressed up for the first art class Christmas party, December, 2012; we were to come dressed as our Finest Art!

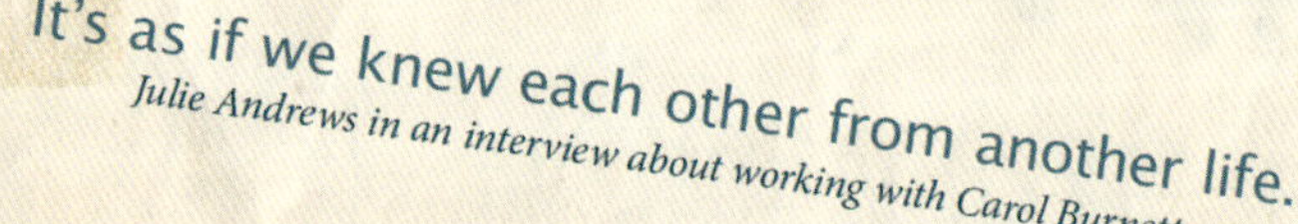

In that first conversation, Dorsey shared her desire to teach art and how she had been working with a few students privately. I asked if she had ever thought about teaching a group class and she said no, but might be open to the idea. Before we left the Christmas party that night, we exchanged contact information and promised to get together soon. It wasn't too many days later she and her assistant, Susan Macke Miller, were sitting at my kitchen table eating quiche and discussing a group class at our Sanctuary. Thus our journey began.

Dorsey McHugh

I had the same initial interest in Joanne. She has the ability to make one feel instantly comfortable. She has experienced enough pain in her life to be very compassionate.

All of us need to be in touch with a mysterious, tantalizing source of inspiration that teases our sense of wonder and goads us on to life's next adventure.

Rob Brezsny, Astrologer, Author, Poet, Musician

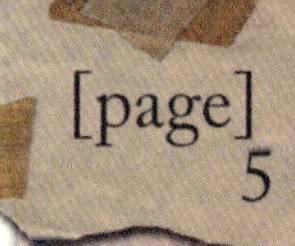

She tells the truth while exercising a love of fantasy. I was immediately drawn to her great imagination, and her ability to communicate well.

She is a loving, multitalented woman who knows who she is and is courageous about sharing her wisdom. I am always drawn to wisdom and humor. When she speaks she makes sense to me. She also makes fun of the same things I think are funny. Her sense of justice is, in my opinion, right on. In short, she is a woman I knew, in the first few moments of our meeting, I could respect and learn from.

I felt Joanne had lived so many of the same emotional realities I had. We had similar mountains to climb in order to become who we are today. My intuition told me this was going to be a lovely opportunity for growth. I was eager to put my toes in the waters of teaching. Another draw for me was the desire to learn what I could from Joanne about writing. She was exactly the right person for me to meet in that particular season of my life. She has encouraged me, listened quietly at times, and spoken many words of wisdom into my heart. She has become a dear friend.

We all have an opportunity to paint a beautiful picture on the canvas of life if we choose to take the reins and be deliberate about it.

Jared Miller Angaza, ***Wisdom Meets Passion***

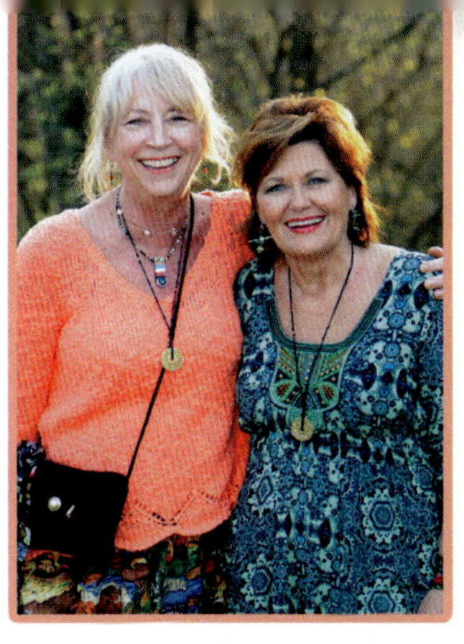

All about us, an unlikely collaboration

We joked about titling this part "Stevie Nix meets June Cleaver" OR "Lawrence Welk meets The Rolling Stones" but thought it might be a little over the top. However, that is a not-too-far-out description of the dissimilar backgrounds Dorsey and I come from. Even though we are both Baby Boomers, products of the wild and crazy sixties, our early years were vastly different. Maybe that's what makes this collaboration, and our unlikely friendship, so full of adventure—we come from different worlds. Yet we have discovered priceless truths in the forging of our friendship and our journey into creativity.

My kids have always referred to me as June Cleaver in my continual quest to create an organized, clean and aesthetically beautiful home. Now, I don't dance around the house with my feather duster, pearls and high heels, but you will never see me in blue jeans and rarely without my 'face' on and my hair 'just so'.

Dorsey was definitely a hippie. Still a free spirit, she fondly remembers living in her VW van with her son, Todd, roaming from place to place, in her quest for meaning and adventure. I can't even conceive of that kind of life but I love hearing her talk about it. She once said, while discussing one of our class sessions, *"I think we were all high! Art is way better than drugs!"* (And legal, too!)

Dorsey is an artist who has been painting professionally for twenty-five years. Her work is in galleries across the nation. I am a writer and artist. We have developed a great friendship, and over the course of that lovely journey, we have deposited a wealth of laughter, compassion, inspiration and wisdom into each other's lives. We have come to the belief that this kind of friendship will only get better when enriched with creativity. So, it is our hope that you will find this book to be a rousing fusion of our distinct personalities, talents and humor. By working together, we generate a unique blend of creative energy that we want to share with you, and in so doing, we believe it will:

-Inspire you
-Make you laugh
-Encourage you to want more
-Help you 'see' with new eyes
-Teach you to play

Be Your Finest Art is intended to be your creative friend. Read it, write in it, and highlight passages that resonate and make you go *"Oh, yeah!"* Periodically review it for inspiration and encouragement; consider it mental nutrition and motivation. Begin feeding and acting upon your creative impulses. Wonderful things will happen. Your life will not be the same from here forward.

Introduction

Every child is an artist.
The problem is how to remain an artist
once he grows up.

Pablo Picasso, (1881-1973) Spanish painter, sculptor

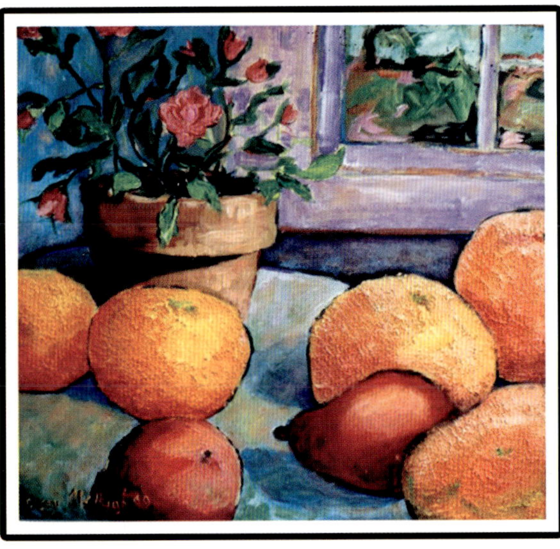

"Oranges"
16"x16"
Acrylics
by
Dorsey

Scattered throughout this book you will read about some very special people who have discovered the power in tapping into their creativity—a power that brings them joy, a sense of adventure and increased confidence in their abilities and problem solving skills. We thank them for taking the time to open up and share their insight and experiences. We hope they will serve as a guiding light as you embark upon your own daring journey into creativity! ***Happy reading***!

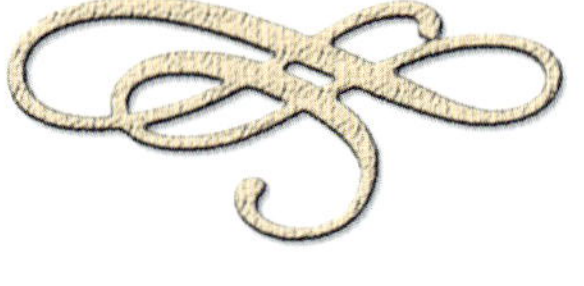

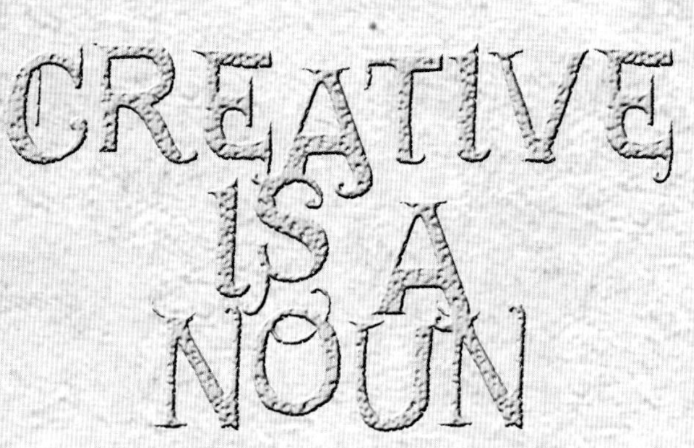

(We give you permission
to use it that way)

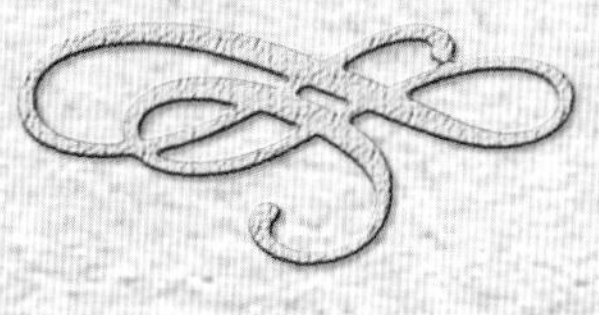

The Sanctuary Sessions

My husband is Dan Miller, career coach and author of many books and products centered around **48 Days to The Work You Love**. Just to clarify I have always called him Daniel, so when you see that name crop up in my writing you get the picture. Dan is simply too mundane a name for my imaginative brain to grab hold of. And Miller…well, can Miller be any more common?

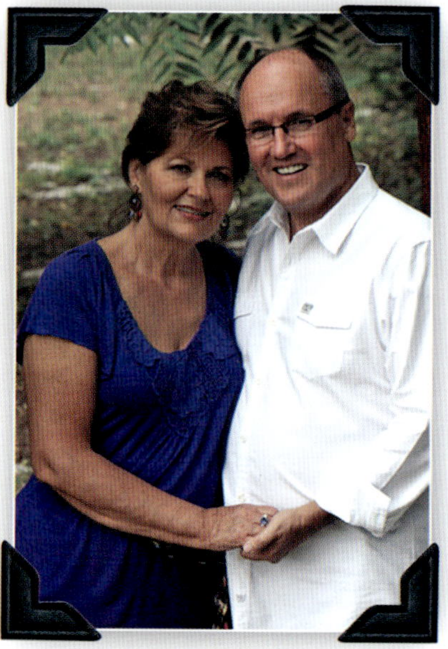

photo of Dan and Joanne by Deby Dearman

Daniel and I have been married since 1968. You do the math... ...it's a very long time.

In 2005 we bought a piece of property behind our house that included five acres and a rather plain grey barn where the former owner did automotive repairs on one side and lived in an apartment on the other. About 1000 sq. feet on each side. We painted and put in new windows and doors and made that old barn into what we now call **The Sanctuary.** It has evolved from a product fulfillment center to a place where we now hold live events, classes and parties as well as Daniel's office, and guest quarters.

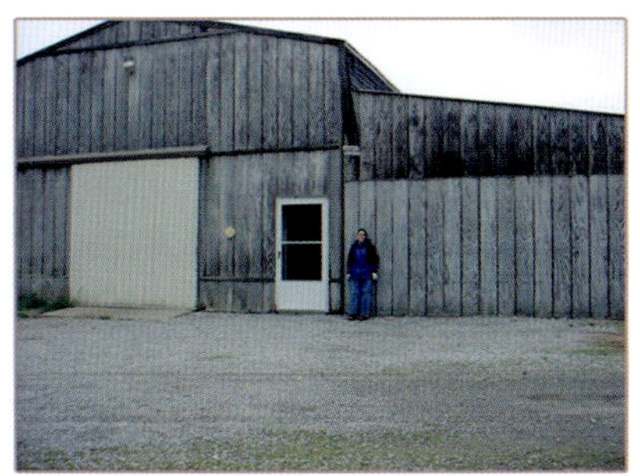

***The Sanctuary**, above 2005*
below 2013

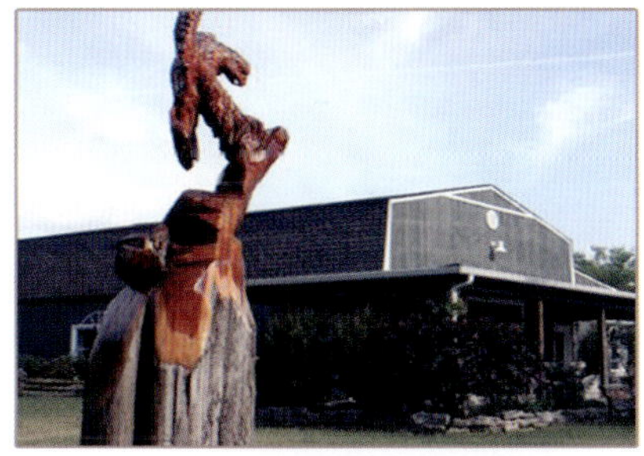

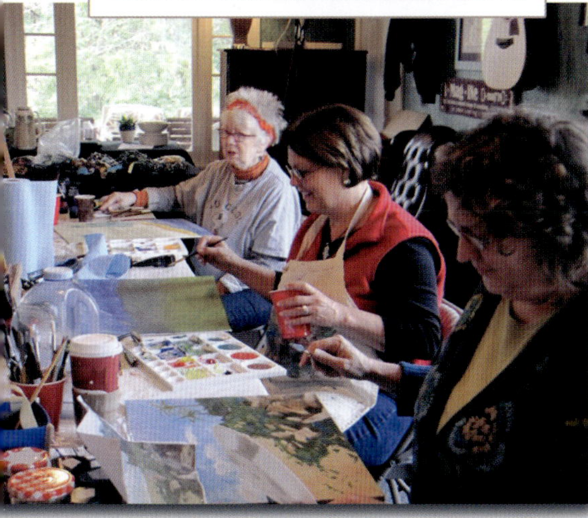

Photo from art class.
Right top is Patsy Clairmont, middle is Gail Hyatt and left front is Melanie Riekena

Because we have made it a goal in our home to create a haven of peace, the name **Sanctuary** seemed appropriate for our place of work, fun and enrichment.

Dorsey and Susan loved the idea of classes at our place so we put out the word to our various centers of influence and began what has become **The Sanctuary Sessions** *(Thanks, Susan for the name).*

We meet for two and a half hours or so each Wednesday morning. There currently seems to be a core group of about eight students but at least a dozen more (male and female) come and go as their time permits.

Dorsey McHugh Discovering art in my life has been the most exciting adventure I could imagine. It has given me new meaning, tools and insight. It has removed from me any doubt that I will do what I am designed for. I am so crazy in love with this adventure that I want to write a book to shout about it. Developing your artistic side is to bring a wealth of new awareness into your everyday moments. It is not about money, though it can be. It is about seeing yourself in a new way. It is about giving yourself a new kind of confidence, and has the side effect of making you a more interesting individual.

This book is intended to point you in that direction. When I met Joanne, we discovered we had experienced a similar awakening to art. In getting to know her, I have found a kindred spirit and a dear friend. Between the two of us, there is a lot to share with you.

We have art in every cell of our being. We are designed by a Master Designer. Nothing has been left out. There are no mistakes made by this Sculptor. The enemy of beauty (chaos), is out to destroy our confidence. We don't follow our hearts if we never learn to have confidence in our intuition. I have found that the best way to develop confidence is to do what is fun for us. So, Joanne and I want to encourage you with practical instruction and a lot of reminders to play. PLAY! Let yourself have a lot of fun while your artist wakes up.

Life Mimics Art

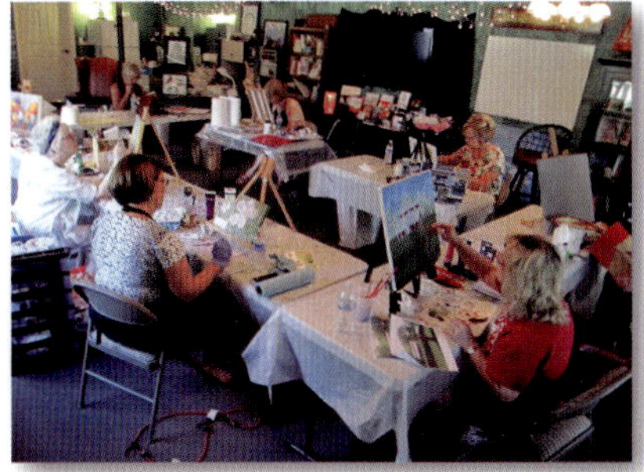

Art class June 19, 2013

Daniel is usually in his office doing his weekly podcast when we are in class but some times he comes out of his cave to ask our collective opinion about a question one of his listeners has sent in concerning their creative journey. He knows, by listening to our group, that ours is not "just" an art class but has become a part of each student's search for inner meaning, peace and for finding one's own voice. I truly believe Wednesday mornings has become "church" to many of us. A time for inspiration, healing and spiritual renewal.

I keep a journal with me in class where I write down "Dorsey-isms" that are worth mulling over and using in this book. I write down great comments and conversations from others in the class and from other resources I think might enhance our creative awakening. Rarely does an art session go by that we don't hear an art principle that mimics life. I am always quick to capture it on paper.

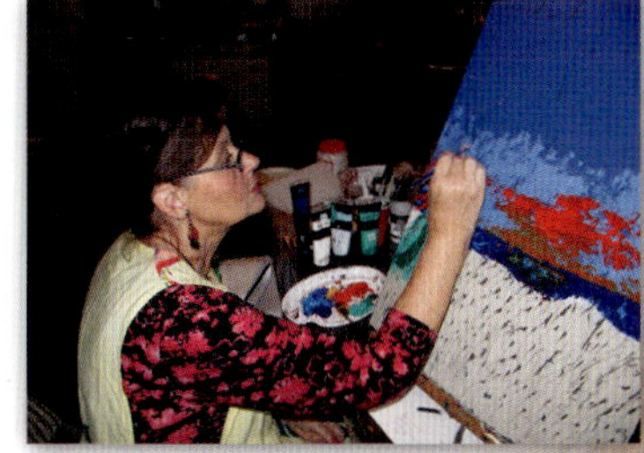

Joanne in art class

Art teaches you to tell a better story.
Dorsey

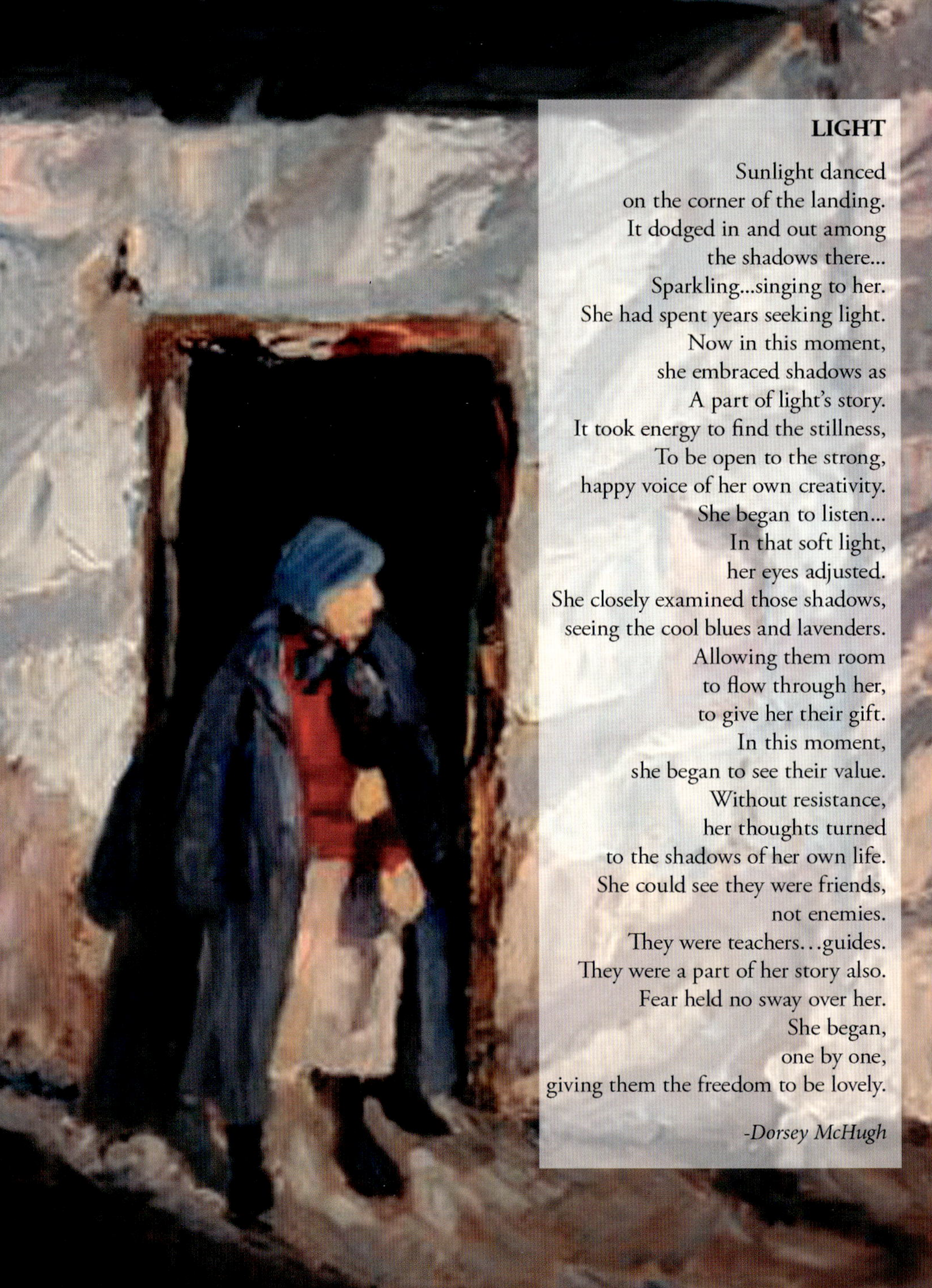

LIGHT

Sunlight danced
on the corner of the landing.
It dodged in and out among
the shadows there...
Sparkling...singing to her.
She had spent years seeking light.
Now in this moment,
she embraced shadows as
A part of light's story.
It took energy to find the stillness,
To be open to the strong,
happy voice of her own creativity.
She began to listen...
In that soft light,
her eyes adjusted.
She closely examined those shadows,
seeing the cool blues and lavenders.
Allowing them room
to flow through her,
to give her their gift.
In this moment,
she began to see their value.
Without resistance,
her thoughts turned
to the shadows of her own life.
She could see they were friends,
not enemies.
They were teachers. . .guides.
They were a part of her story also.
Fear held no sway over her.
She began,
one by one,
giving them the freedom to be lovely.

-Dorsey McHugh

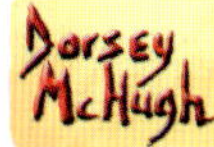

We are learning to paint light

There is always light even in the darkest shadows. Giving form to an image is done by observing and recording light's journey across its surface. We retrain our eyes and brains to see what light is doing. This takes a new kind of seeing. No color exists apart from light.

We have to be willing to do it badly even in public

It takes courage and discipline to do art. Our motivation needs to be greater than our fear of not being good enough. The artist lays aside fear for the joy of creating. An artist often feels his art is bad for a time before it gets better. A life principle that rings true.

Artists are modern day prophets

We tell a better story when we recognize where we are in the story. An artist learns to tell her story and knows she is part of the on-going story of the centuries.

We are playing, not failing

An artist learns that creating is play and in playing, there is no failing. It is simply learning to play better through trial and error. There is also a release of creativity as you relax and learn to play without trying to impress someone else. Play helps lift you out of yourself.

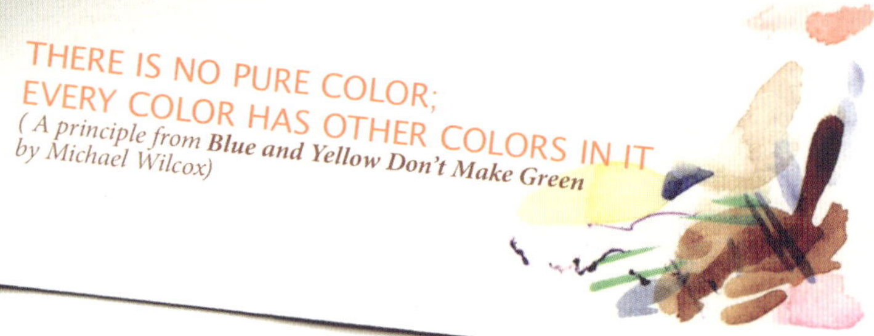

A broken line is a more beautiful line

Dorsey McHugh

This is a principle my teacher, Juanita Green Parks used many times a day. I repeat it to my students often. I have read that gardeners and nature lovers say "nature abhors a straight line". They love meandering, serpentine and undulating lines in their work and in their travels. There is so much more character in a broken path, a broken horizon, a twisted tree or crooked fence. There is no better life principle than to recognize it is the person who has, at some point, been broken, who is more authentic and more appealing to be around. We learn from what we perceive as our failures (our brokenness) and move on to be richer for them. Broken people have more to give in rich experience.

A great analogy of our lives; we are the sum of all that goes into us, and we are richer for it.

A great analogy of our lives. We are the sum of all that goes into us. And we are richer for it.

Dorsey

A great example of learning life principles happened to me one day in class when I had to stop mid-painting and write in my journal...

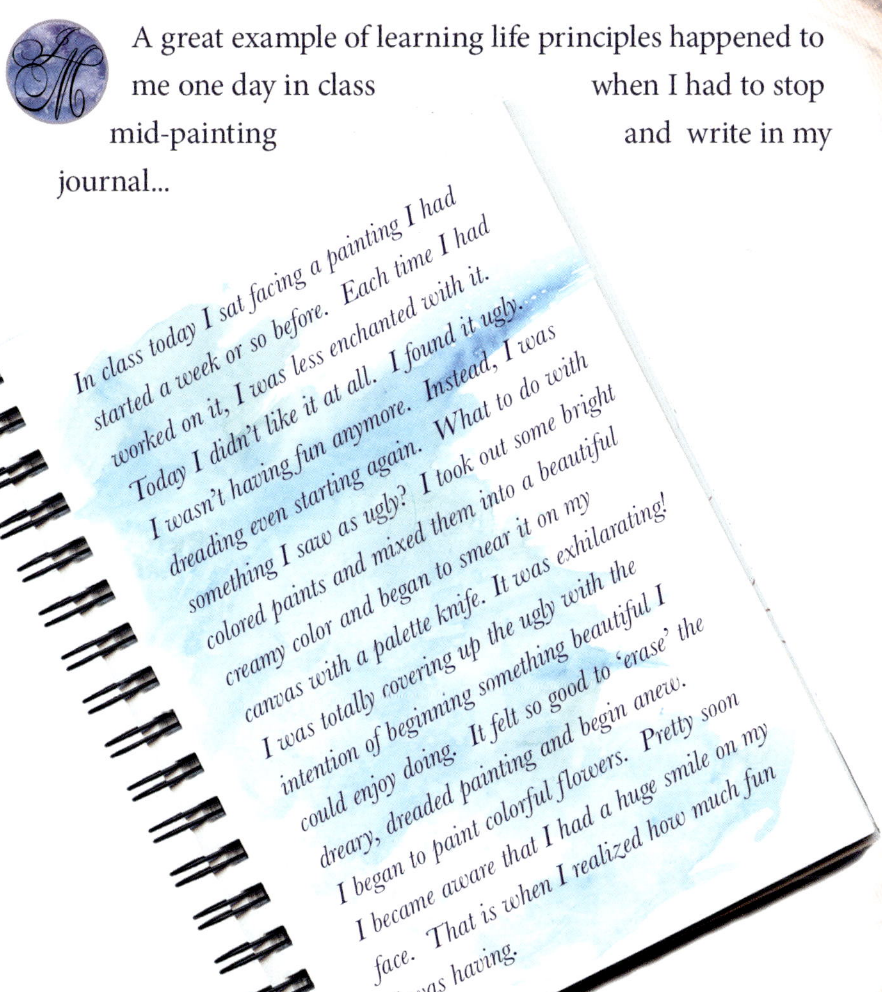

I stopped for a moment to capture the experience on paper while it was fresh in my mind.

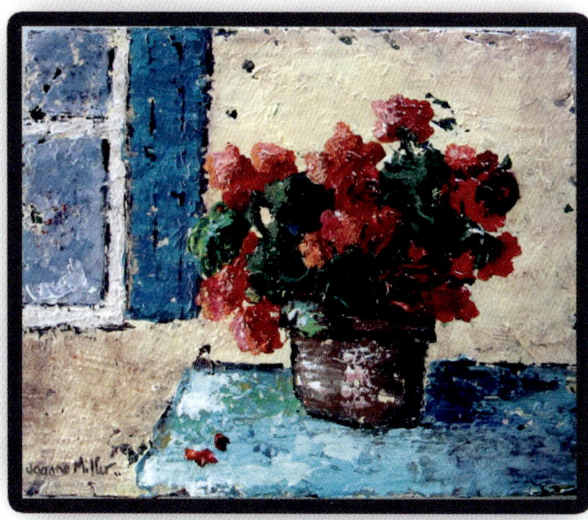

Acrylic on board, Oh Happy Day! by Joanne

As I was discussing this with my classmate and friend, Gail Hyatt, she said, *"Why do we stick with something for so long when we can so easily change it?"* A good life principle we can apply in so many areas of our lives. I hope you will find many creative ways to bring joy into your life while reading the pages of this book.

I shared this story of the "ugly painting" with Caleb, my 18-year-old grandson. He wrote back some profound words that I felt needed to be included on this page. Wise words from a young mind:

"You wrote about how it felt so good to 'erase' what you got tired of and to start something new. This made me think...You were doing something you didn't enjoy, and finally decided to start over. But you didn't completely start over. You didn't use a new canvas. You didn't even take the paint you disliked off the canvas; you just covered it and made it unnoticeable...even though it was still there. There's a good life principle in that: When we're living without meaning and passion, feeling purposeless and resentful of our current situation, we have the power to immediately start changing how we're living. The memories and scars of our past are still there. However, we can cover them and let them have no part in the future we are pursuing and longing for. When we cover the hardship of our past, and make it invisible, there's a good chance it will make us stronger and give our future character it wouldn't have otherwise."

In the movie **Girl With A Pearl Earring,** based on the fictional/historical representation of the Dutch artist, Johannes Vermeer's (1632-1675) life there is a scene that so clearly depicts this concept. Vermeer (Colin Firth) enters his studio and sees Griet (Scarlett Johansson), his maid and eventual protégé, looking skeptically at his work in progress. Here is the scene:

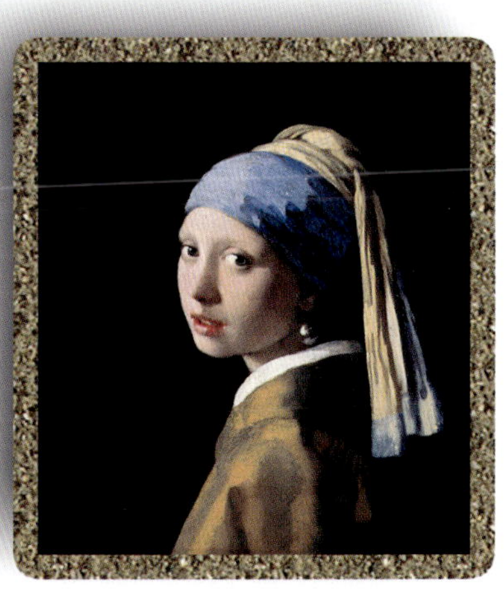

Vermeer: *" (Are)you looking at it? Well?"*

Griet: *"Nothing's the right color."*

Vermeer: *"This is the base color (as he points to parts of his painting). It gives it tone; shadow and the light. And when it's dry I glaze over it with blue...but, thinly so that the black shows through..." He walks to the window and opens it and she follows. They gaze outside.*

Vermeer: *"Look Griet...Look at the clouds. What color are they?"*

Griet: *"White. No. No, not white. Yellow. Blue. And grey. There are colors in the clouds"*

Vermeer: *"Now you understand."*

It's one of my favorites... the painting, the book and the movie. Vermeer taught Griet to really see what is beneath the surface. To look beyond the obvious and see the depth. That is a lot of what we learn in our art classes. Life truly does mimic art.

Dorsey McHugh Doing art, painting, sketching, story, has owned my heart for as long as I can remember. I think all children have the seeds of art in their souls. Some are never encouraged to imagine deeply or to recognize the value of their own thoughts. My own art is a reflection of the relationships, and experiences I have been given.

In my work there is a story of a little girl who grew up on the South Dakota prairie. I have heard it said artists are driven by their own search for "meaning". I don't know if this is true for every artist. It is certainly true for me. I look closely at my memories, to define their significance. I love conversations when they carry in them some form of real meaning. I love movies and books and poetry, which transmit some truth of the mystery we all live in.

The first time I saw a Van Gogh original painting, I was at the National Gallery of Art in Washington D.C. My reaction to it was instantaneous. I saw the artist's "Little Peasant Girl", and with my heart I felt a little bit, I think, of what Van Gogh felt about her. Her life, her courage, her hope was in his rendition of her image. I began to cry, unselfconsciously, in the center of the room, in front of his painting. This experience is now part of my history. In one moment, I submitted to Van Gogh's amazing ability to tell the little peasant girl's story. I understood a little of what he felt as he painted her. He told her story with color, with the expression on her face, with his brush strokes. It is my own desire to tell stories in this way. This is for me, a life worth living.

Find Your Voice

The more one creates, the clearer he becomes in finding his own voice. When a beginning painter first confronts a canvas, he copies other artists he likes. At some point he begins to expand on what he sees and makes little changes and additions to his copying till he finds his own voice and his art becomes truly, authentically his own. It is a process and rarely is accomplished without trial and error and the copying of other creatives.

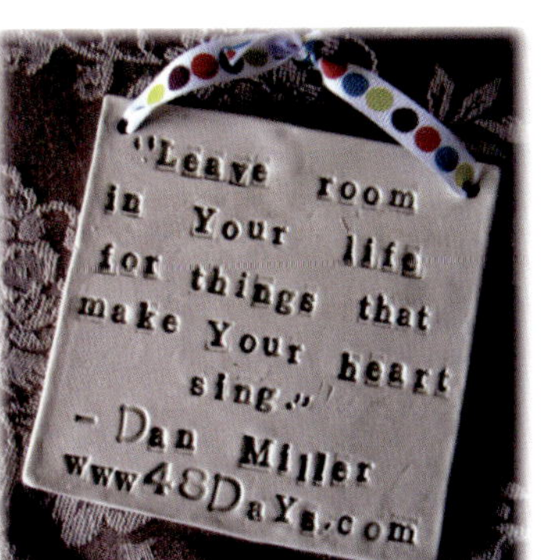

The trick is to find where your heart sings and what appeals most to you and make it your own voice.

Finding your own artistic voice is a little like drilling for oil, or discovering a vein of gold or silver. It is dangerous (synonymous with adventurous), sometimes dark, often exciting and interesting. The labor is all done on the inside. In the depths of our own souls.

It is difficult to be honest with yourself, not to mention with others. An artist puts his heart out for everyone to see. He learns to value his critics. If someone knows his language, they relate to and enjoy it. In art, the conversation is in the language of image. Symbols. What does a color mean to you? What does line say in its simplest form? We have to do the work it takes to become our finest, most honest, selves.

We can do what is safe. Paint pretty pictures. We can become brilliant at copying other artists' work. Or we can tell our own story. We can find out what colors we are. We learn to mix the colors, to exaggerate where the composition needs the intensity. We learn to take risks, to experiment. And we go on from one frame to the next. People say to me all the time that my art is happy. I'm surely not happy all the time. I have learned to live with a glass that is half full, not half empty. But, I am also dark at times. I have chosen to paint night scenes a lot. Darkness holds mysteries and magic and secrets. I love what it holds. I embrace it.

When I paint I get into the feeling of what I am painting. I like to breathe the air, to imagine the sounds of the scene. I long to be where I am imagining. So I paint happy, positive. Because this is where I want to be and believe that if I visualize it well enough, I will be. This is my story.

The experiences I have had in life have all contributed in one way or another to a positive point of view. We only have so much time here. We can choose to make the best possible use of it.

Is it work or play?

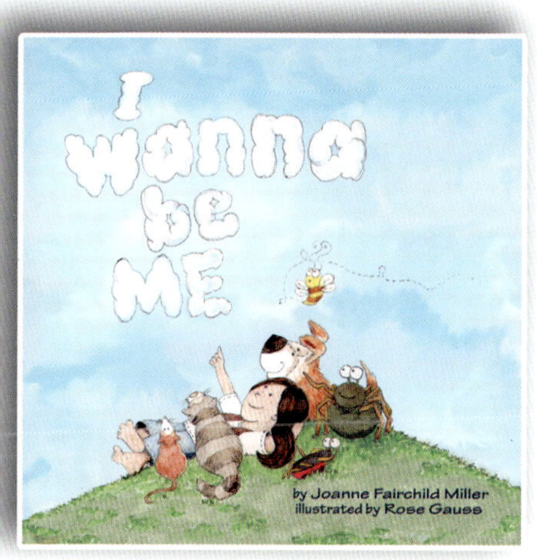

My own creative journey took a big leap when I was inspired in 2008 to write a poem. It came to me in the middle of the night in a hotel room in Florida. I jumped out of bed and jotted it down on scrap paper so I wouldn't forget it. I think it was a nudge from God to do something with my creative talents and it was the beginning of what has led to the writing of this book.

The poem was for my granddaughter, Autumn Grace. When she received it, she called to say, *"Nana, that needs to be a book!"* It had never crossed my mind, but it stuck there like a piece of gum! I mulled it over for months and in 2009 I contacted Rose Gauss in Pennsylvania to see if she would be interested in illustrating for me. Our son, Kevin, was familiar with her work and thought she might be just the person I was looking for. Now before you join many others in asking, *"You are an artist. Why didn't you illustrate your own book?"* you need to understand that illustrating is a lot different from what I do. I needed someone who could convey motion, expression, and action. I want my subjects quiet, submissive and inanimate!

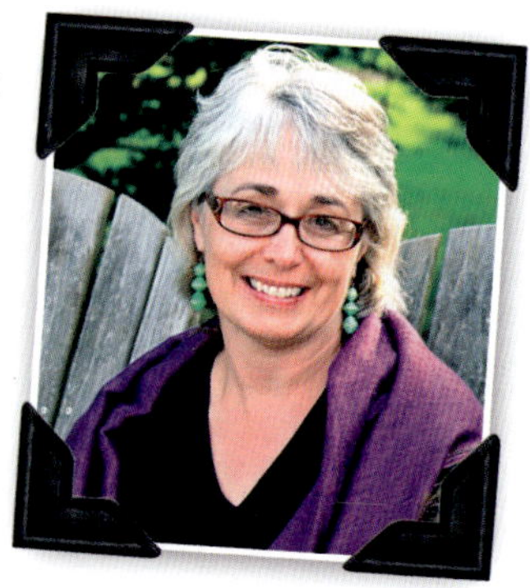

Rose was an excellent choice. Check out her website at www.RoseGauss.com. We work well together and both of us have grown our passion for creativity through the hard work of writing, illustrating and publishing. Each time gets easier but that first book made us feel pretty stupid. We have published four in the **I Wanna Be©** Series. Each story portrays a different personality style and I use my grandchildren as the models.

Rose has a great website to help you 'create' with your children/grandchildren/students. It is colorful, engaging and has FREE drawing lessons. I have had a lot of fun teaching art to my grandkids with the help of these pages. Go to her site at:

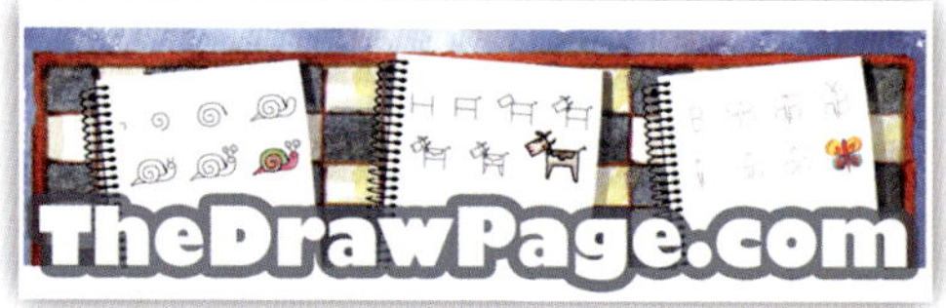

We Are Artists whether you believe it or not!

One of the hardest confessions I ever made was to admit to being an artist. It sounds crazy, but even after taking drawing classes for many years, poetry and writing workshops, teaching and learning everything I could about art and creativity, I still, to this day, feel awkward calling myself an artist.

> To be an artist is to believe in life.
> *Henry Moore (1898-1986) English sculptor and artist*

By definition an artist is a person who exhibits exceptional skill in one of the fine or performing arts. Dorsey and I believe that definition to be very limiting and for that reason we prefer to make the adjective *creative* into a noun. Throughout this book you will read about ***Creatives*** and ***Creative Thinkers*** who have found a new lease on life by doing what inspires them. We hope by the time you finish reading this book you will recognize we all have the potential to be artists in ways that go beyond the paint and performing. We believe everyone has the power to be creative.

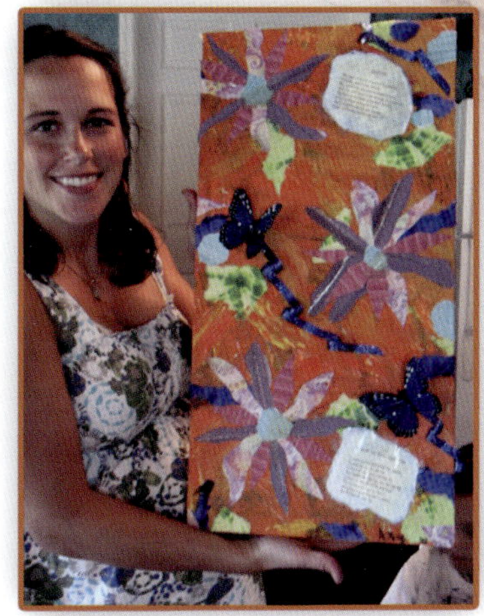
Photo of student Ashley Miller Logsdon with mixed media painting

A Show-and-Tell Life

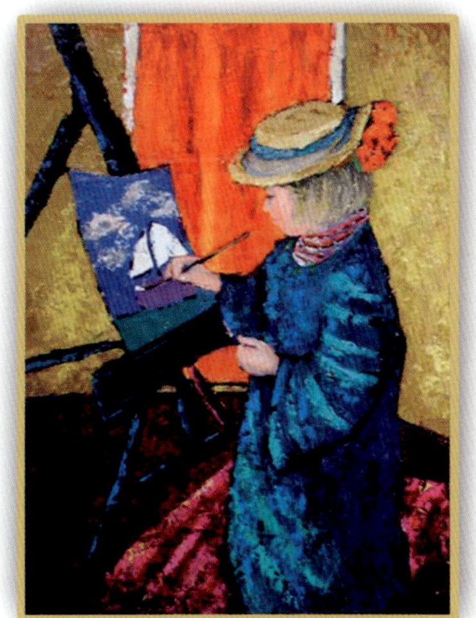
acrylic on board, ***Betsy's Art Day*** *by Dorsey*

Jan Mosher taught high school English for 21 years, working also in speech and drama. Then for 14 years she worked in Social Services. Both areas of employment depended on creative communication. We asked Jan to tell how her creativity played into her career.

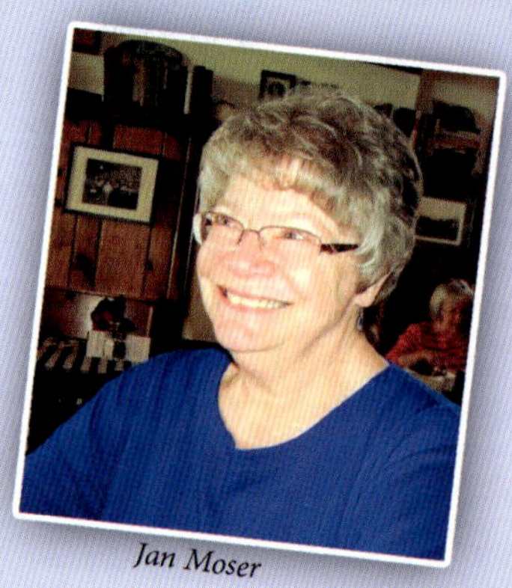

Jan Moser

"As a recently retired high school English teacher, it seems that I can now switch gears and claim the role of life-long learner! Even though I spent over twenty years enthusiastically guiding students to develop skills and appreciate the value and the power of writing, my own creative efforts historically depended strictly on the spoken word. Only recently am I learning the personal joy of using pen and camera to recreate the power and mood of a moment from my own experience; only recently am I finding new excitement in the opportunity to touch others' hearts and minds with my own unique perspective and creative efforts.

We all remember a life moment reaching out in a way never experienced before, a moment that almost forced us to write about it in a journal, to take a picture of it, or to draw it in a sketch book. I remember the moment I first understood the impact of child abuse by reading a memoir, and when I simply had to snap a travel photo of that amazing waterfall in Norway, and when I sat in awe before a Monet. In each of those moments, I experienced an almost palpable need to interact in some way.

I also remember the best show-and-tells, those that included something tactile and visual to help tell the story. The ability to hold a prop helped me reconnect with the passion of the original moment, but also helped classmates connect and interact in a more engaged manner than simply hearing might allow. In a similar tactile and interactive manner, creative artistic expressions allow us to connect with others in ways that share diverse and dynamic perceptions of life.

Over time, I came to understand creativity as any original expression, whether using a pen, a camera, or a paintbrush; to understand art as any interactive show-and-tell, any sharing of a meaningful image which encourages reflection and response, whether I take the role of creator or audience.I now see living a creative life as gathering and sharing meaning-filled moments, much like we did in those early show-and-tell experiences of kindergarten! I see I can no longer remain content in the comfort of intellectual understanding, rather the joy of this new creative life challenges and sends me to imaginative expression…and, if lucky, sharing with others.

Continuing in this life-long learning experience, I predict personal joy in the creation process, acknowledging any appreciation by others as an extra gift of sharing the artistic conversation with open hearts and minds, always expecting and accepting new insight. The experience deserves great respect and love, since each effort holds potential for all experiencing the show-and-tell."

Living out Her Gift

Patti Mead is my favorite hairdresser. She's the kind of hairdresser women love because she really cares about how you look. Being a hairdresser is not just a job to Patti and it shows in her work. She is a great example of someone passionate about their creativity and because she adds so much value….and love….to what she does, she stands out from the norm.

*"I have always loved playing with hair. And I do consider it play. Your hair tells me a story of where it has been, what it has been through, and where it wants to go. Once I figure that out, I can create something beautiful and **healthy**.*

I love my creative tool box which isn't just a pair of scissors. It is gels, mousse, clays, glazes, colors, sprays and oils, changing frequently with current trends. It is fun to try a new color or product and see my work come to life in a way I have not seen before. I love taking classes or going to shows to see what the best artists in our country are doing. They inspire me.

*When I highlight hair, I get so relaxed; it is as if I am doing needlepoint. I can create looks I haven't tried before and I am a little girl again...playing in the tub with bubbles on my head. My poor doll babies all had haircuts when I was a little girl. My love of hair began that long ago. I am so thankful for my hairdresser friend who saw my gift and said, **"You should be a hairdresser".** I am privileged to be around talented women and play every day. I love my clients. I get to know people in such a personal way. I hear about their lives. I give them their first hair cut, fix their hair for prom, weddings and special days and sad days. I know their story and enjoy their company. I don't have a job; I get to live out my gift."*

Know Your Heart

Scott Stearman is a gifted sculptor, a dear friend and god-father to our Colorado grandkids. Scott loves telling stories through bronze. His website www.scottstearmanstudio.com tells of this man's love of people translated into clay, bronze and remembrance. Much as a ghost-writer gets into the head of the person he is writing about, Scott gets into his pieces through educating himself and expressing each detail accurately whether he is sculpting nature or a military memorial. He feels bronze sculptures are timeless containers for our collective stories. What sculptures capture in the present, they continue to speak long into the ages. Bronzes outlive the generations that birth them. They preside over public places and whisper their history into the present. Like no other art form, they withstand the weather of time, and tirelessly ask the future to pause and remember.

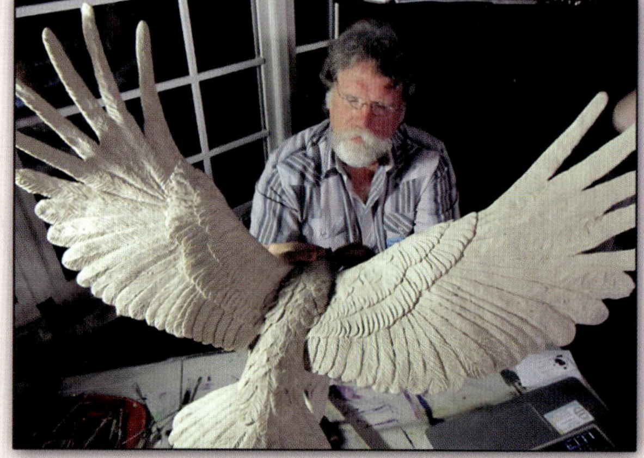

In a blog Scott wrote on listening to your heart, he talked about the conflict of embracing that you love and feeding your family. A common concern for Creatives. He says,

"If you find yourself conflicted between what you do to feed your family and what your heart longs for, embrace that conflict and the passion it reveals because in it you have been given the gift of seeing and knowing what is in your heart...while many never know." March 7, 2013 Blog

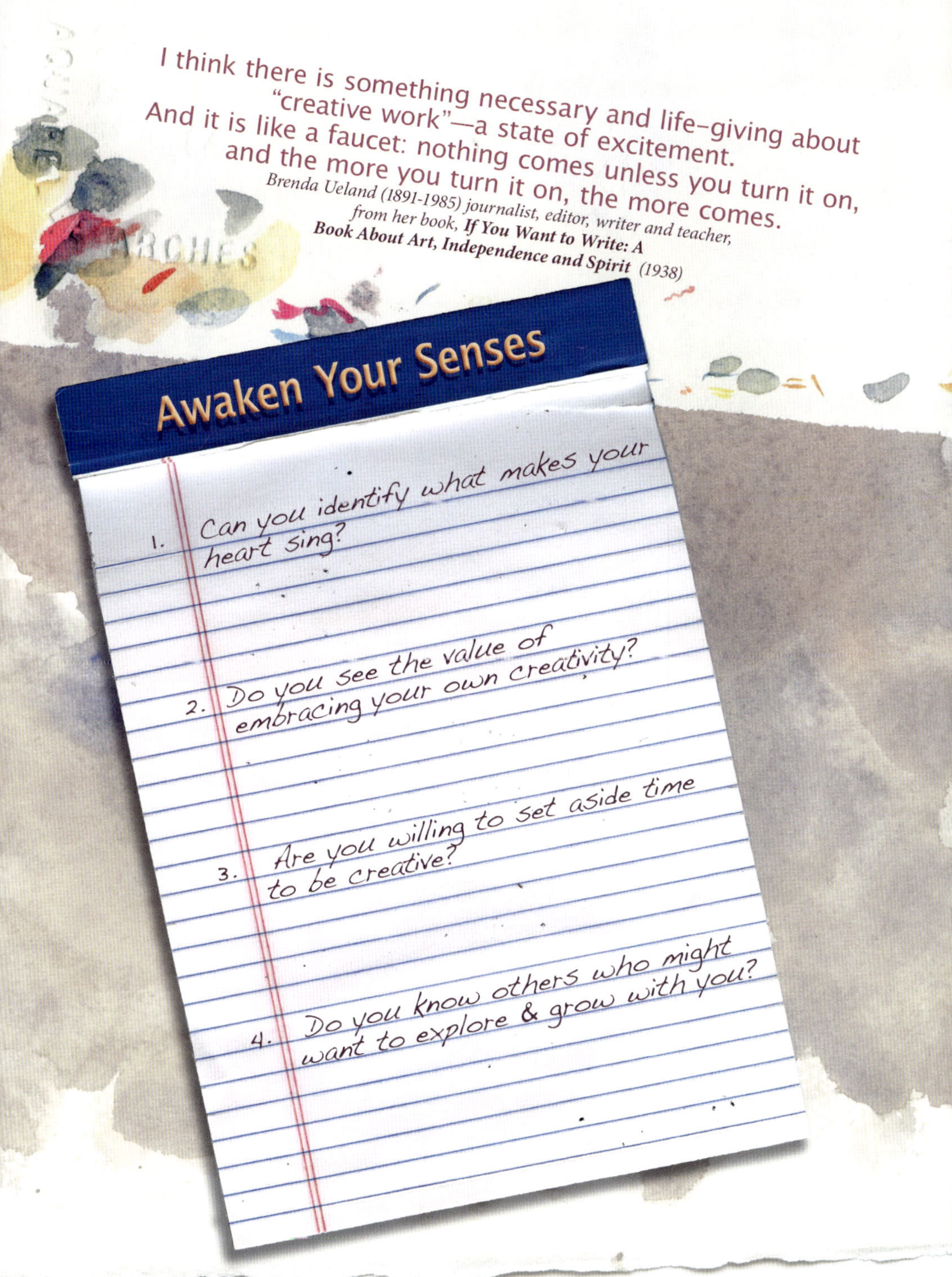
I think there is something necessary and life-giving about "creative work"—a state of excitement.
And it is like a faucet: nothing comes unless you turn it on, and the more you turn it on, the more comes.
Brenda Ueland (1891-1985) journalist, editor, writer and teacher, from her book, **If You Want to Write: A Book About Art, Independence and Spirit** (1938)
Awaken Your Senses
1. Can you identify what makes your heart sing?
2. Do you see the value of embracing your own creativity?
3. Are you willing to set aside time to be creative?
4. Do you know others who might want to explore & grow with you?

WHY?

Dorsey McHugh

Creative thinkers ask more questions. Children enter into a period of asking "Why?" as their response to everything you say. We laugh and think they are cute, but when an adult gets curious we often think it is annoying. I understand that. Our task as creative thinkers is to come up with a way to ask as many questions as we can and still get answers. Now there's proof of creativity!

Art always carries within it the artist's view of life. My first preference of subject is to paint moments---those moments that for some reason, remind us we are loved and that we love.

When we talk about waking up the artist within us, we are also speaking of recognizing ways to take better care of our souls. One of the first requirements is to acknowledge we even have a soul. You may not be surprised to know that modern thinking often excludes the soul. Thomas Moore (American writer and psychotherapist) in **Care of the Soul** said: *"Fulfilling work, rewarding relationships, personal power, and relief from symptoms are all gifts of the soul; They are particularly elusive in our time because we don't believe in the soul and therefore give it no place in our hierarchy of values."* Moore goes on in his wonderful book, to give ways of taking care of this precious part of us. He recognized the power of art in bringing health to this side of our selves. Joanne and I want to impart other examples where art and soul give us life, energy, emotional and physical health and a sense of adventure brought to us first through our imagination. This accompanies practicing an artistic approach to everything we do.

Today, skeptics devalue imagination. More often than not, it is considered an idle waste of time. In reality, imagination is the key to unlocking possibilities. The act of visualizing and making story a part of our everyday lives awakens our creative side. We begin to see all sorts of creative ways to make the things we imagine actually happen.

Waking our creative self is not a new idea. We hope to encourage you to move farther down the road toward being your finest art. One obstacle to advancing down this road is the current distaste for "religious thinking". When the soul is mentioned, people raise their defenses against the tyranny of dogma.

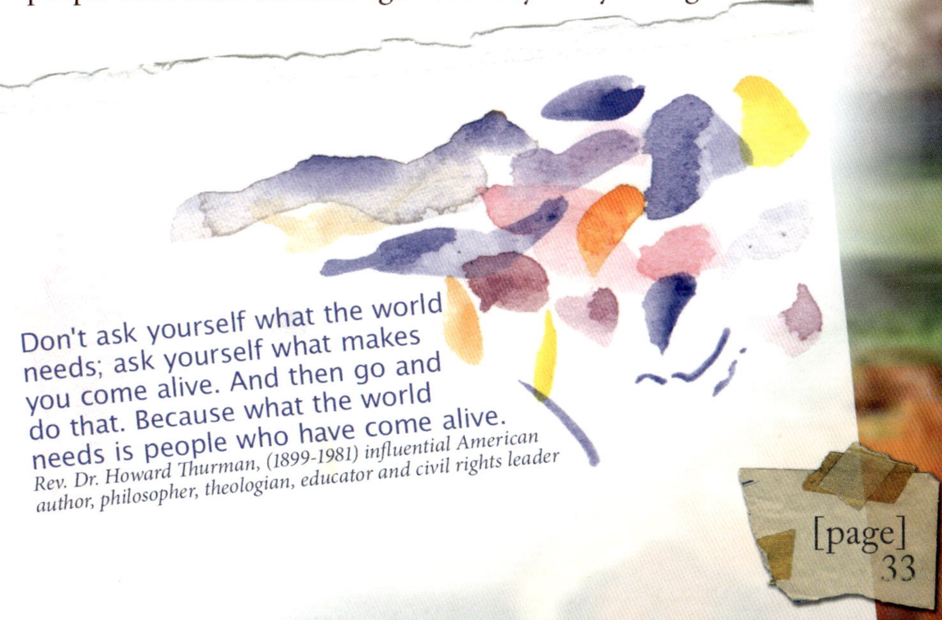

Don't ask yourself what the world needs; ask yourself what makes you come alive. And then go and do that. Because what the world needs is people who have come alive.

Rev. Dr. Howard Thurman, (1899-1981) influential American author, philosopher, theologian, educator and civil rights leader

I am one of those people. I **really** don't like religiosity. I was raised by a father who was a simple farmer who loved philosophy and conversation and Jesus. He did not preach anything to me or to anyone. He asked me questions. I found answers and then spent years trying to convert him. Finally one day after relentlessly trying to extract a commitment from him, he said: *"Dors, come in here and sit down."* I sat obediently at the end of his bed. He then said: *"Look up and see what I read every morning when I wake and every night when I go to sleep. This is what I believe."* In front of me was an embroidered cloth his mother had given him. It had these words on it: "Jesus loves me this I know, for the Bible tells me so". I was speechless. This, from a man who all my life had been a gentle example of kindness and respectful regard toward everyone who crossed his path, with the exception of those who used their religious ideas to hurt others or to place themselves on a higher level. I learn well. My dad did not have to repeat himself. I have grown, thankfully, farther away from "religious" thinking.

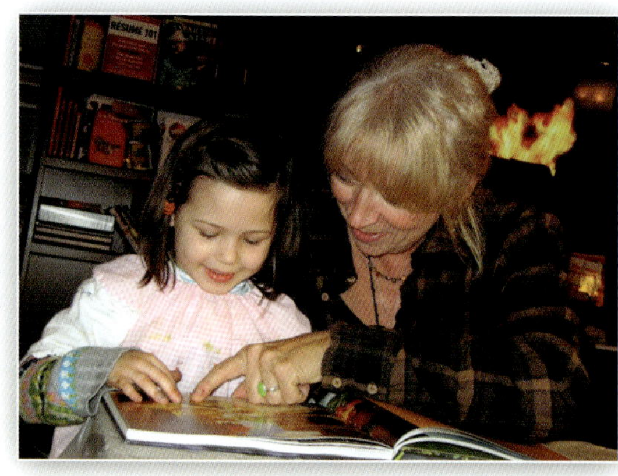

DORSEY'S FAVORITE STUDENT, Clara Isabel Logsdon (5), Joanne's granddaughter, who reminds us of the joy of creative play and who teaches us to stand back and tell ourselves (and everyone else) that our work is AWESOME!

Our Hope For You Is This

- That you will learn the value of tapping more into your right brain in order to live healthier and more intelligently.

- That you will learn your senses CAN be expanded in ways that reveal beauty we often miss, adding a greater element of joy and adventure to your daily life.

- That you learn how to reignite that sense of play and wonder you experienced as a child.

- That you will become more intentionally creative about your health, your home and your relationships, continually seeing new possibilities in the world around you.

- That you add CREATIVE to your list of credentials. As a NOUN. (It's ok. Really!)

We can say that care of the soul requires a special crafting of life itself, with an artist's sensitivity to the way things are done. Soul doesn't pour into life automatically. It requires our skill and attention.
Thomas Moore, American writer and psychotherapist

You are talented and you are original. Be sure of this.

Brenda Ueland (1891-1985) journalist, editor, writer and teacher, from her book, ***If You Want to Write: A Book About Art, Independence and Spirit*** *(1938)*

Awaken Your Senses

1. Reintroduce yourself to who you were as a child. How did you play?
2. What made you laugh? What brings you joy?
3. Do you ever long for that simplicity & connection to your imagination?
4. Is your own creative nature beginning to come into focus?

Put New Lenses in your Glasses

One day, while driving through the country after a rain storm, my husband abruptly stopped mid-sentence to point out the distant rainbow. I found it quickly and reflected on its beauty. We continued our catch-up discussion and while making a point, I took off my sun-glasses, gazing off in the direction of the rainbow. Weird...it had disappeared! I continued talking and put my sunglasses back on. Voila! The rainbow was as clear as it was before. Took my glasses off again and the rainbow disappeared. *Now that is weird!* And profound! How many times have I seen similar oddities from our tinted car windows or through a mist of water in a fountain?

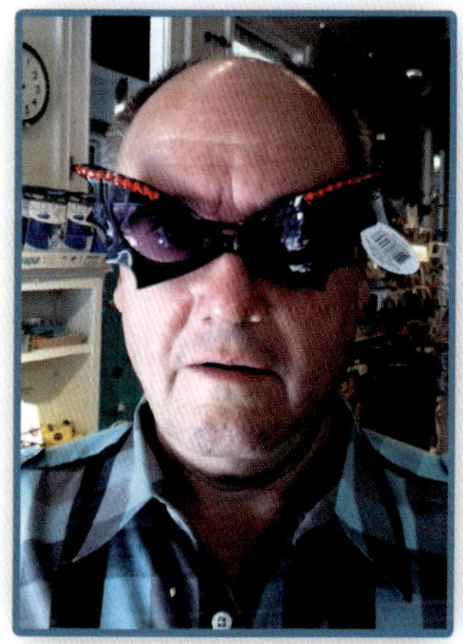

Daniel took off his sunglasses and found that for him, too, the rainbow disappeared. Well, you can imagine the conversation that ensued when we started comparing that incident to people who wear rose-colored glasses throughout their lives and those who refuse to put them on. And, of course we argued (kindly) over who would write about this parable of life. Obviously I won.

I know lots of people who scoff at living life with rose-colored glasses. It's impractical. It's living in denial. It's not being realistic. Because I believe that my life choices greatly influence

You see but you do not observe.
Oliver Wendell Holmes (1809-1894), ***A Scandal in Bohemia***

whether I see my days as living a great adventure or enduring this hell on earth, I choose to be impractical, in denial and unrealistic. I'm going to keep on my sunglasses! In fact, metaphorically speaking, I have had those sunglasses on for many years and I am quite comfortable with them.

In the same way having a positive attitude allows one to view things more favorably, tapping into the rich resources of your right brain helps make the world brighter, more vivid, more defined, more exciting! It is the ultimate in wearing rose-colored glasses! Being creative brings rainbows to my life daily. Metaphorically speaking, of course!

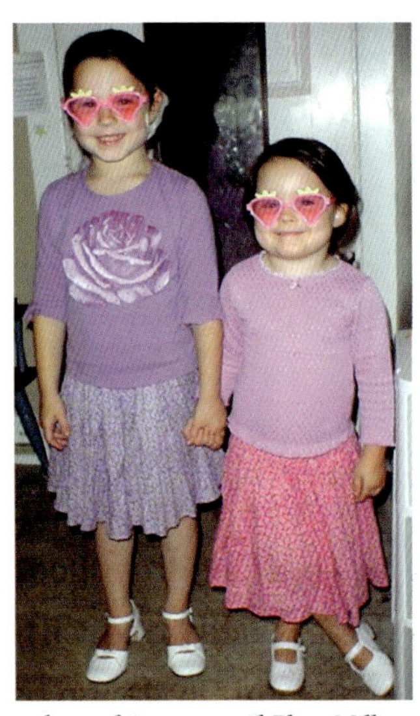

photo of Autumn and Eliza Miller

I remember when we took our daughter, Ashley, to the optometrist at age six because we were notified she might not be seeing things well at school. When I discovered she couldn't make out the big **E** on the first line of the eye chart, I was mortified it had taken me so long to notice she was greatly myopic. A few days later when Ashley walked into the daylight in her new thick-lenses I shed tears when I heard her exclaim, *"Wow! Look Momma! That tree has beautiful leaves! It's SO pretty!"* My mother's heart came undone as I watched her look with awe at a brand new world.

DID I LIVE ? DID I LOVE?
DID I EVEN MATTER?
Brendon Burchard, ***The Millionaire Messenger,***
Founder of Experts Academy

A child has no trouble believing the unbelievable, nor does the genius or the madman. It's only you and I, with our big brains and our tiny hearts, who doubt and over think and hesitate.
Steven Pressfield, author, ***Do the Work, The War of Art***

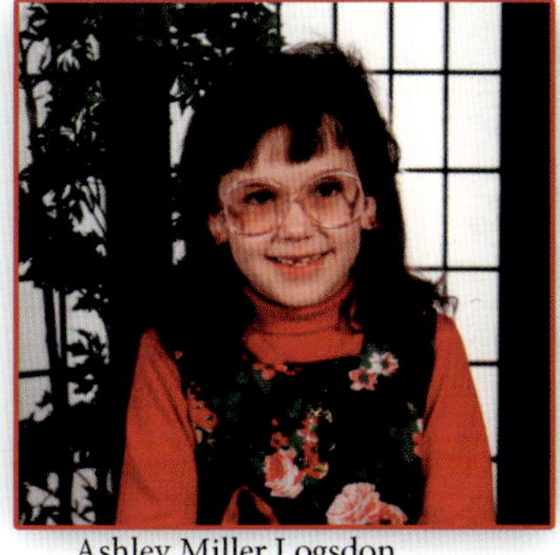
Ashley Miller Logsdon

Sometimes we need new lenses to see more clearly what is right before us. I don't buy the fact that some people are born looking at life optimistically and some are not. That's like saying some people are just destined to be failures and some are not. We all make choices. If we want something badly enough to do the work to get it or make it, plant it, paint it or write it, it can happen. From The Bible to Norman Vincent Peale we can find many writings to confirm positive thinking can be learned and cultivated if one so desires.

I'm a big Steven Pressfield fan. In his book, **Do the Work**, he says emphatically, *"The last thing we want is to remain as we are."* I know there are those who might argue this but I figure we only have this one chance to live Heaven on earth and I intend to do it with rose-colored glasses! I want to see rainbows that aren't there without them. I want to make a difference; a mark on the hearts and lives of others. I don't want to live an insignificant, average or mediocre life. I want to see the best in everything and everyone. And I'm willing to do what it takes to accomplish that goal. I will not remain passive, apathetic or indifferent.

Art Burbles

By Patsy Clairmont
Author, Artist and Founding Speaker for Women of Faith
www.patsyclairmont.com

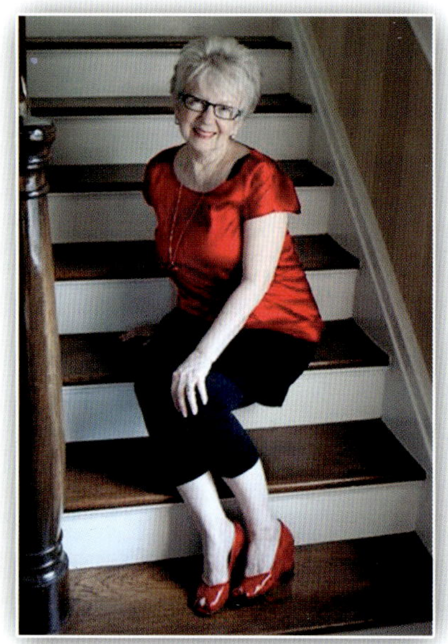

We were designed to be like our Creator. And we get an indication of what that means for the artist within us when we examine God's flair throughout creation. His pallet is limitless. We see God's passion for color and architectural design through a microscope and through the Hubbell telescope. We see an explosion of colors reflected in a dew drop, a puddle, and arched in the heavens proclaiming hope. We see it in the flash of a cardinal's wings, the iridescent flutter of humming-birds, and the pool of indigo on the buntings perched atop fence posts. God put the red in Georgia's soil, the blue in Kentucky's grass, the orange in Florida's orchards, and creative wonder inside each one of us.

For some, artistry has barely oozed out of us like too-thick paint, while for others it has gushed forth like an open fire hydrant. I'm thick paint. I've spent a lifetime trying to get the art out. Not always consciously, but as I look back I see more clearly my insecure splatters.

Recently I had a fresh revelation of who I am when I joined my friend Gail at an art class hosted by Joanne and taught by Dorsey. I had not anticipated what an eye-opening adventure it would be to uncap paint and pick up a palette knife. I had attended an art class, as an adult, years earlier, with a friend who was too shy to go alone. She did amazingly well, while I never quite 'got it'. So I gave up my fantasies of illustrating books, bulletin boards, and billboards throughout the universe, with my eclectic sketches that danced only in my imagination.

But art burbles.

Way deep inside of our "beginning" there is a bubbling-up that is ongoing. Art will seep out in some form. Mine came tumbling forth through my speaking career and my plethora of books. But somehow I didn't recognize then what I know now--that books were my canvas and words,my brush and palette of colors. I didn't know my need to create was coming out in my incessant reinventing of furniture layouts in my home. It also was evident in my passion for color, which was seen clearly in my splashy-sassy multi-dimensional way of dressing. I didn't equate my penning of poetic thoughts with art nor had I thought my attention to the details of design for our dinner table was a particularly creative offering. (I don't cook well, but I sure set a yummy-looking table. Too bad we can't eat the decor.)

Funny thing, I could see the art in others, but somehow missed it in myself. I saw it in the way my friend Luci packed a suitcase, inscribed a book, and selected gifts. I saw it in Stephanie's design work on her potter's wheel. And in Chris's way of charming strangers into friends with her warmth and mercy. I tasted art in Steve's cooking, Jenn's baking, and I took delight in Lauren's chalk board artistry.

But me, an artist?

Yep.

Little ol' me is finally taking ownership of my rightful heritage as a child of the Creator. I am an artist.

Wow! That was fun to write. The statement drips with freedom like an emancipation proclamation. It is who I am...an artist. And it is who you are. ***We have been created to color our world with the ochre of kindness, the crimson of generosity, and the titanium of praise.***

Expressions of creativity release the artist within. So arrange a bouquet of wild flowers, toss the confetti of a salad into a colorful bowl, teach with pizzazz, snap pictures with intentionality, and for heaven's sake join a paint class and experience the therapy of swirling color across a canvas, even if all you accomplish is one wing-ding of a swirl. It will loosen your tight places and somehow help you heal. I don't know how God does that, but He does.

Of that I'm certain.

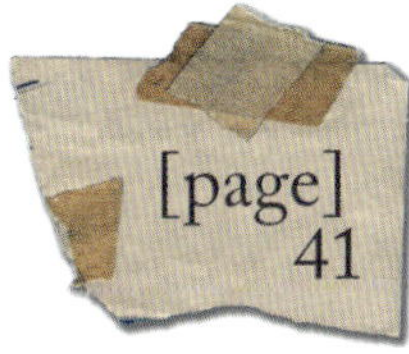

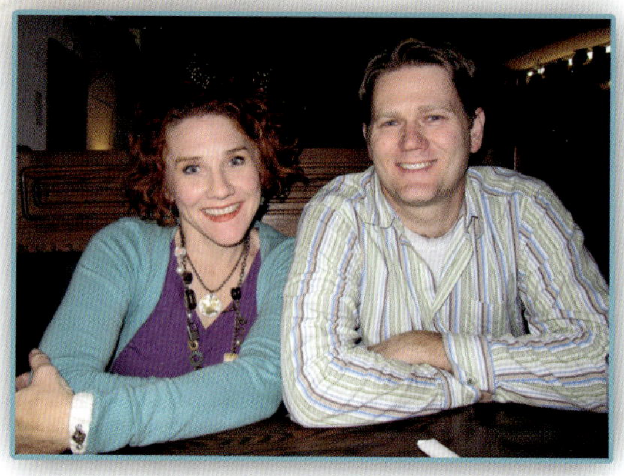

Creative? Not ME!

I had a conversation with Todd Hakanson who haltingly told me he wished he was more creative but felt neither his personality nor his job lent itself to using his right brain. I asked him what he did all day in his work. I already knew the answer but I wanted him to see this himself. He said he found ways to solve computer issues all day. People brought their complicated computer glitches to him and he explored ways to solve their problems.

"And you don't see that in solving these computer issues you are creating solutions to problems others can't see? You are being creative and you don't even know it. What else do you like to do?" I asked him.

Todd rather sheepishly told me he has a big white board on an antique door hung in his kitchen. He is the father of six kids from toddler to college age. He is the chef at home and each week he designs meals he posts on the white board. Early in the week his kids' friends often come over, check the board and tell him what meal they want to attend.

Not only does he cook, he designs menus, doesn't use packaged food, makes elaborate dishes and breads. Here's a guy who soaks oats in the whey he collects by putting yogurt into a sewed up baby onesie and lets it drip the whey into a bowl. Whaddya think? Is this creativity?

Todd says he over analyzes everything. He is in a well-paid job coming up with solutions to untangle computer glitches. However, like so many, he overlooks his own creativity. He told me of his research on healthy eating and discussed current misconceptions of dieting and lifestyle. I was fascinated by his inability to see his own creative value.

One clue telling me someone is creative is the amount of passion expressed. This guy can get excited talking about the health benefits of his creative cuisine and the fun he has organizing great menus! He has toyed with putting together a cookbook and has lots of great stories about healthy eating. His six kids and their friends love the healthy meals he makes, yet he feels he isn't creative when, in reality, the evidence is right before him.

> We can't solve problems by using the same kind of thinking we used when we created them.
> *Albert Einstein (1879-1955), physicist*

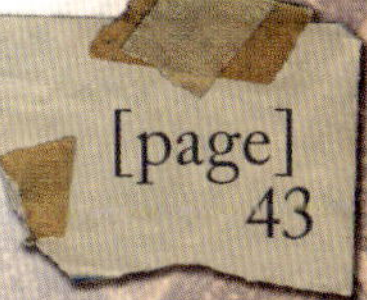

I told Todd how I had uncovered my own sense of creativity when I decided to take a drawing class. When he said I probably had the ability to draw before I took the class, I had to laugh. I didn't know how to draw. I ***seriously*** did not know how to draw. In fact, my long-time art teacher, Melanie Jackson, still uses me as an example of a frustrated student who wanted to throw her pencil at the teacher! It was hard work and would exhaust me. I had a difficult time sticking with it. But I kept telling myself I needed this discipline. I wanted to learn. And I knew if I was going to learn, I had to persevere. I think even back in those beginning years of unleashing my creative spirit, I instinctively knew this was going to be something big in my life. Little did I know.

> No matter what the tangible outcome is, you cannot help but become a better person when you follow a creative call. If you focus on the product, you get fleeting satisfaction from an end result. If you focus on the process you get a life, because life is a process.
>
> *Jill Badonsky,* ***The Muse Is In***

It might be important to this story about Todd (Mr. Uncreative) to note he is married to a very extroverted, artsy young woman with Titian red-hair, bright blue eyes and a very bubbly personality. Chanda makes incredible jewelry and her whole persona reeks of right brain. She told me, *"Creating is as important to me as the air I breathe".* She is passionate about creating and sees possibilities in everything around her. Even the way she dresses is a piece of art! Because she is so engaged in her right brain, her husband feels he needs to be like her. And therein lies the rub. Isn't the grass always greener on the other side? I talked to Todd about how I struggled to find my place in this world until I came to terms with who I am and how I am uniquely gifted. I read books and I began to see the world and my life differently through taking art classes. I now see with new eyes. That's what engaging your right brain does; you learn to see how the artist sees the world! The clearer you see and understand, the better you become at expressing yourself whether it is in words, actions or with a paintbrush, a food processor or a computer.

I encouraged this young man to take a **Drawing on the Right Side of the Brain** class. I told him he will learn how to see. And in doing so, he will begin to view his whole life differently. That book/course needs to be taught in every elementary school and yet, we live in an age when art, drama and music classes are often not taken seriously enough to budget into the educational curriculum.

I have witnessed the "drawing out" of those who felt "trapped" in left brain occupations who want to expand their options and see the world with different eyes. Some have been in my art classes. I am always in awe of the talent they possess. I think it surprises them as much as it does me, but I think that trek from one side of the brain to the other is a short one. One short hop to the other side.

Chanda's vintage jewelry: *www.StLouis.VintageMarketDays.com*

Be brave enough to live life creatively.
The creative is the place where no one else has ever been.
You have to leave the city of your comfort and go into the wildernes
of your intuition. You can't get there by bus, only by hard work and
risk and by not quite knowing what you are doing.
What you'll discover will be wonderful.
What you'll discover will be yourself.
Alan Alda, actor

Dorsey McHugh

When learning to swim you have to learn to relax. If you don't…if you fight it….you sink. If you relax, you breathe and move so you go somewhere. This is a good analogy for being creative. What you need more than anything else is to keep relaxing and enjoying the process rather than struggling. Struggling enhances fear. And fear becomes your focus. You forget what you are trying to accomplish.

I love how we are all created – with a natural 'bent' toward certain areas. We each possess different qualities and they all work together for a greater good. To me, that's the beauty of creativity and the mystery of the Creator. In working with Dorsey for the past decade, I've watched her artistry unfold and grow...and it's been a catalyst for the artist within me. She's been an encouragement in finding my own path, and resting in who I was created to be. My brain gravitates toward the administrative side of her art business and even in that spectrum, artistry finds its voice. There is a beautiful dance, a rhythm between the order of business and the creation of art. *Susan Macke Miller, actress and partner at Dorsey McHugh Fine Arts*

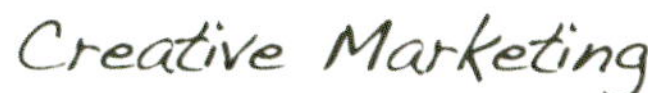

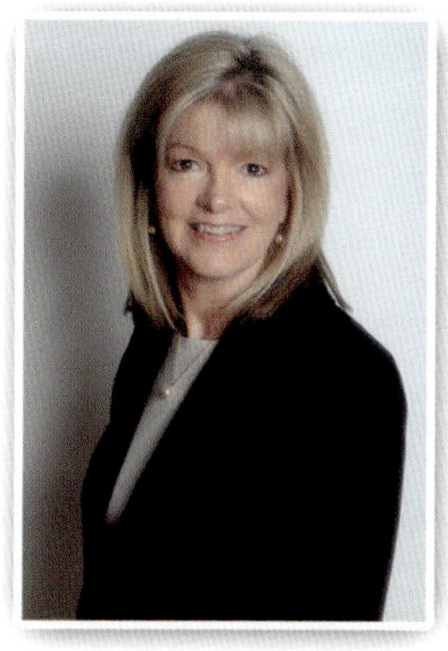

Dana Battaglia is in Nashville Real Estate. She is another great example of how one can embrace creativity in their occupation and create added value to clients. She says,

"I consider it a part of my job as a good realtor to help people 'see' a room. Levels of ability along that line vary widely among buyers. Some change the color in their head immediately and place their furniture. Others see the room only as a dining room because that is how the current owner uses it. My challenge is to creatively express to the potential buyer what the end result could be after transformation. Sometimes it also requires creativity to show someone how a small cottage or ranch can become a cozy nest. The goal is to help someone be content with less than what they think they want, but cannot afford. It takes creativity to market oneself to stand out in what is a very crowded profession!" www.cpcanashville.com

When I am in my favorite nail salon I usually watch the TV screen provided to occupy my head while they work on my hands. Typically they play a program where realtors take clients around and show them houses to buy. The goal is to pick out just the right house in a short time frame. I am always astonished when potential buyers walk into a house and reject it because it isn't painted the right colors. Seriously? How transformational a few gallons of paint and a little imagination in furniture placement can be.

FOOD FOR THOUGHT

By Todd Albertson, Culinary Chef
Dorsey's oldest son

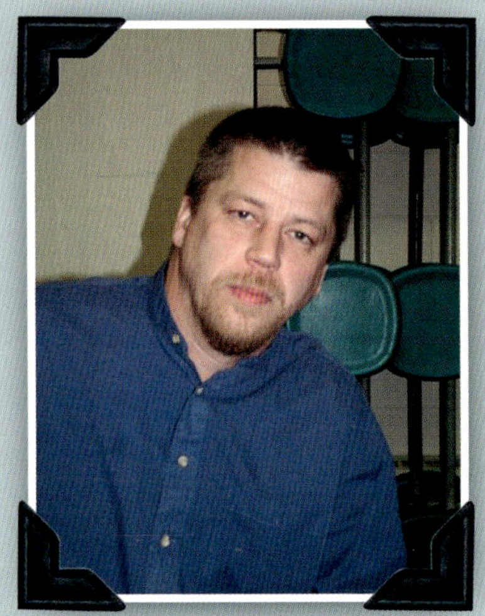

I've been working in kitchens for over 30 years.
I never saw the art in that...but, I think,
the lack of art is in the word work,
not in kitchens.
When I look back,
it was all art.
The pot scrubbing,
the carrot peeling,
the soul numbing hours.
The vast diversity
of the people I worked with along the way.
Like shadow and light,
like line.
I now see it all as a progression....
from learning form,
to expressionism,
to the abstract.
I thought work could not be art....maybe,
the idea that the more money it generated
the better the art....maybe,
The older I get, I seem to think,
only work is art......
That's what they all have been trying to do...
from the very first cave drawing
to everything that hangs in the
Metropolitan Museum of Art.......
"the search for truth in the essential."
There is nothing more essential to us,
all of us,
than food and drink.

Creativity is a fun way to problem solve. Take cooking for example. In my opinion, the recipe is merely a suggestion. Once I've done something, there is no fun in repeating it exactly as before. I want to do it slightly differently. That way I always learn something new. I value originality.

Nancy Bowron, artist, www.npbstudios.com

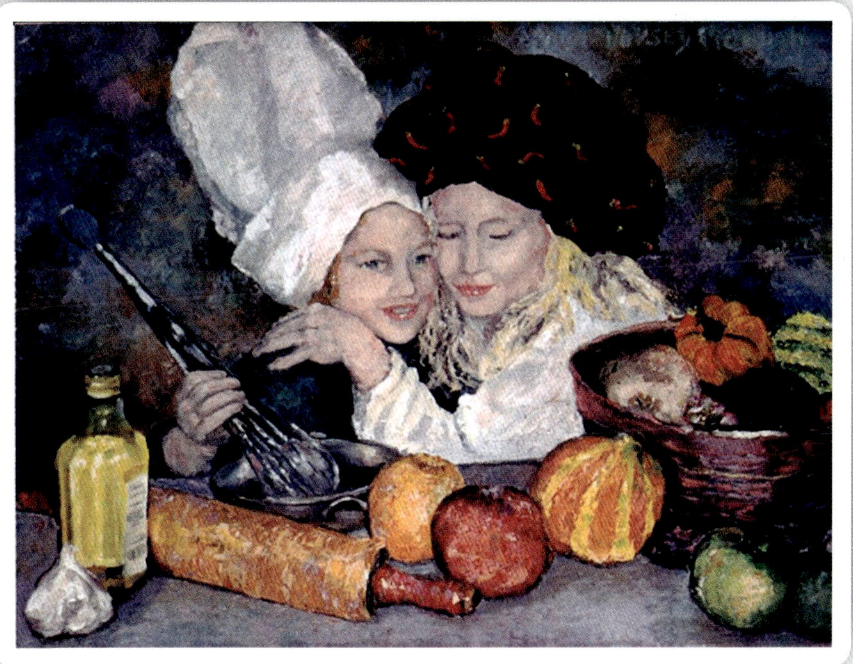

Oil on board, Tess and Ryan by Dorsey

A thing constructed can only be loved after it is constructed: But a thing created is loved before it exists.

Charles Dickens (1812-1870) English writer & social critic

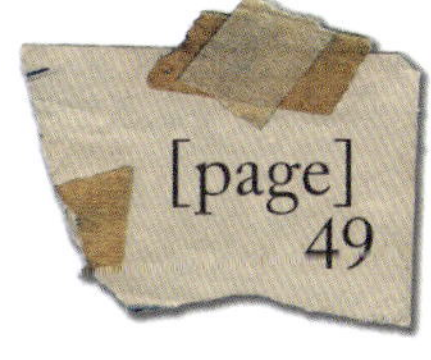

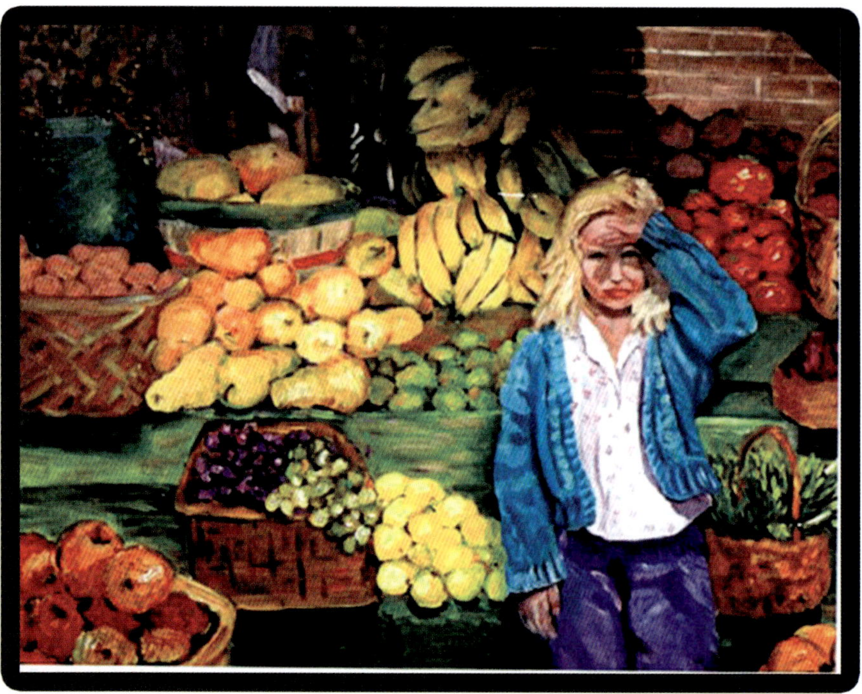

Oil on board, Fruit Stand by Dorsey

A Passion For Food

Susan Powers, of Enchanted Kitchen Catering, caters mostly to the many actors and musicians in the land of Country Music USA. However, she enjoys catering our events at the Sanctuary when her schedule allows. Her meals are always a creative expression of her love of tasty and nutritious food, mostly locally grown, organic and home-made. Visit her website at www.enchantedkitchencatering.com . She has an interesting story of turning a life-long passion for food into a lucrative business she loves.

A Love Affair With Food

"To say I was destined to be a career foodie is a serious understatement. As a child, I was surrounded by good cooks. In our home, food meant more than sustenance; it was a communication form. We were, and continue to be, a close family and I attribute the community of food as a basis of our core existence. My Grandparents on my Mother's side were an eclectic bunch. They loved to entertain and would often throw big bashes at their home for 50-100 or so. While they had kitchen help, they often dressed my older two sisters and me in matching aprons and had us serve their guests. The meals were outstanding. Everything was made from scratch.

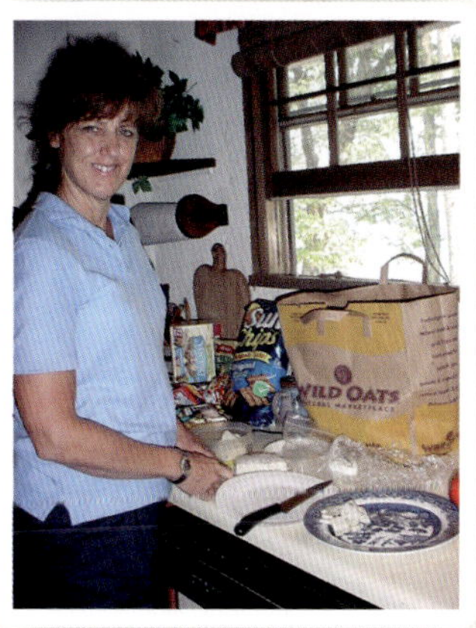

After college, I entered the world of advertising and was quickly entrenched in the business. It was fun, paid very well and enabled me to use my long-suppressed creative nature. That lasted 13 years during which I ate a huge amount of poorly executed catered meals. In 1995, I jumped off the corporate wagon and, with absolutely no prior research, started a catering company.

The catering business, while sometimes grueling, has been rewarding. The music video and commercial area of my business is continually challenging me with the vegan, macrobiotic, vegetarian, pescetarian and organic requests. It seems if you don't have a specific meal request you simply aren't cool. This provides many opportunities for creativity.

My latest creative foray is in commercial food styling. Making food look so appealing you can't resist eating it or making it. While, typically, there is a great amount of trickery involved, the food must be believable. I prefer the more **natural** styling food – minimal fluff. Food styling is tedious. Long hours in a studio to secure that one **special** shot. This has been a self-taught skill. Recently I spent two hours hand picking **beauty shot** beans from a case of baked beans – those were placed on a secondary mound of beans and spritzed with a mix of bean juice, water and oil to keep them glistening and moist under the camera eye. Another client wanted their chicken tenders to **pop** on camera so I deep fried them, glued additional coating on where it was needed and brushed them with a light coat of motor oil and a dusting of Cajun spice – sounds yummy, don't you think? This is my creative journey and love affair with food– thrilling, weird, bold, but most of all fun!"

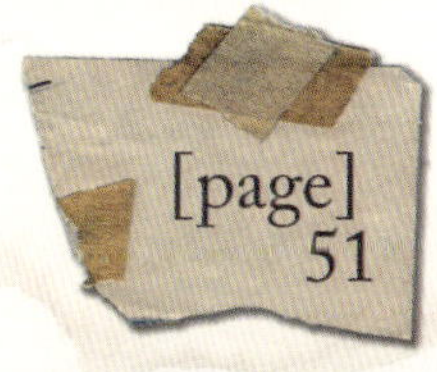

Work is love made visible.
And if you cannot work with love
but only with distaste, it is better
that you should leave your work
and sit at the gate of the temple and
take alms of those who work with joy.

For if you bake bread with indifference,
you bake a bitter bread that feeds but
half man's hunger.

And if you grudge the crushing of the grapes,
your grudge distils a poison in the wine.

And if you sing though as angels,
and love not the singing,
you muffle man's ears to the voices of
the day and the voices of the night.

Kalil Gibran (1883-1931), ***The Prophet****,*
Lebanese artist, poet and writer

Dorsey McHugh

No matter what someone does, they have to use their own artistry, their own creativity to accomplish it. Years ago, my older sister taught me the art of bread-making. Part of her advice to me was to get rid of negative thoughts before I began. She said *"a bitter woman bakes bitter bread."* I see this truth as deeper than I then perceived.

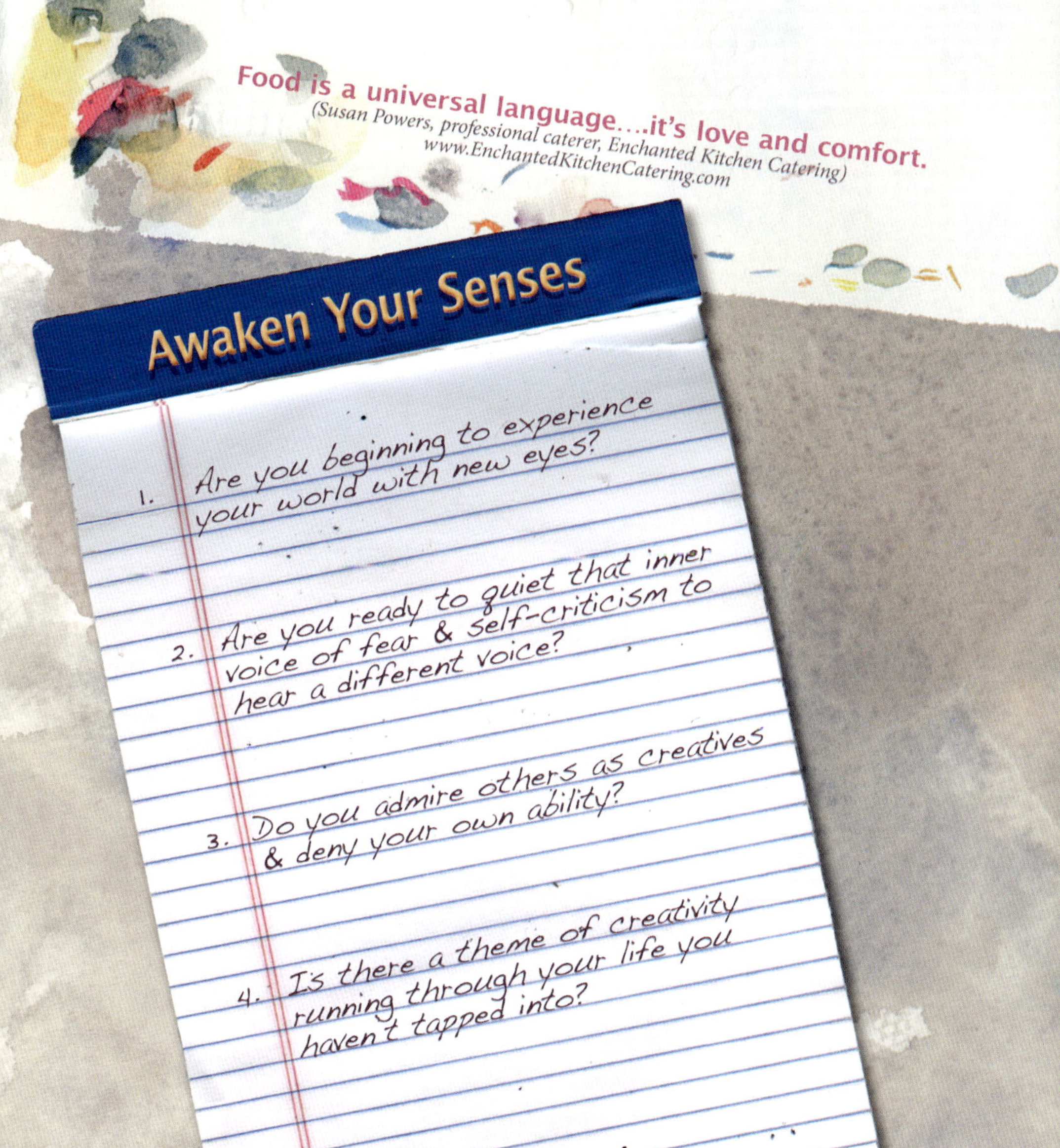
Food is a universal language....it's love and comfort.
(Susan Powers, professional caterer, Enchanted Kitchen Catering)
www.EnchantedKitchenCatering.com
Awaken Your Senses
1. Are you beginning to experience your world with new eyes?
2. Are you ready to quiet that inner voice of fear & self-criticism to hear a different voice?
3. Do you admire others as creatives & deny your own ability?
4. Is there a theme of creativity running through your life you haven't tapped into?

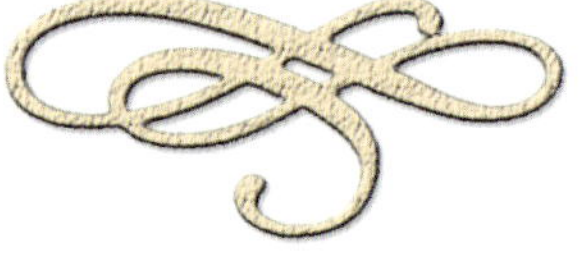

AWAKENING

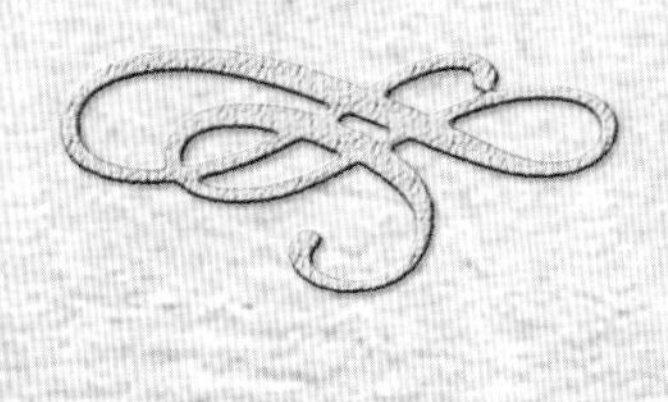

Dorsey McHugh

I was 40 years old before I even attempted to find art inside myself. When someone asked me if I drew or painted my reply was always, *"No, no, no! I can't even draw a stick person!"* Then several things happened at once. My philosopher Dad died. I quit working in a stressful restaurant job. I felt lost. It was probably pain that woke up my artist self. But when it happened, I was so thrilled with learning how to navigate in this new room, I carried a pencil and sketch pad everywhere I went. I drew my family members as we watched television. I drew the trees and buildings in front of me any time I found myself waiting for one of my children. I drew the stop light if it was red for any length of time. There was nothing I did not try to sketch quickly. At first, it embarrassed me to show anyone. After awhile, I gained confidence and began to drop my insecurities. The progression for me as an adult was much like a child learning to first crawl and then to walk. I moved from this to acquiring instruction for using brushes and paints. I was hungry to learn.

Someone told me years ago you can't learn anything you don't already know. That may sound like double talk to some. But I think it can be true. We are artists in our souls. If our creativity was repressed by comparisons, or by anything negative, we turned away from art. I sometimes imagine that the artist in me got bored and tired and depressed and went to sleep. But, he was awakened. Awaking does not necessarily mean you will paint a Mona Lisa. Although, you just might.

Awakening

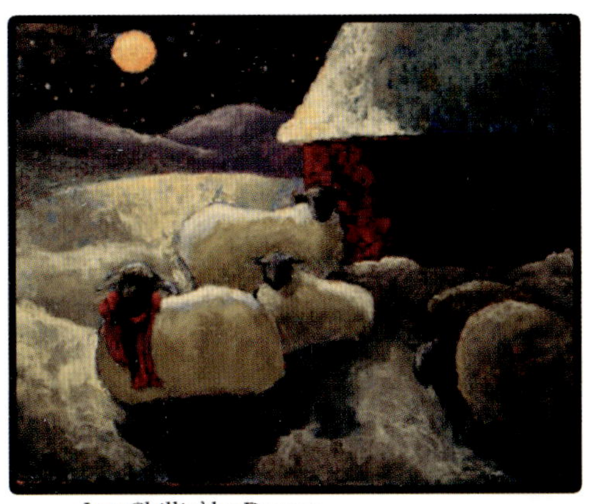
Just Chillin' by Dorsey

But, surely this awakening will make you feel better about yourself. It will help you in every area of your life. You will be a better thinker. You will be more innovative in your problem-solving. You will definitely have more fun!

Wake Up Those Senses

Years ago I read a book by Ken Gire titled, **Windows of the Soul**. It was the first of many I have read that have spurred me to look at the world differently. To see God in everything…not just from the church pew. Gire talks about how we long to have the assurance that God is with us in everything; that He is intimately involved in our lives. Our reality is often harsh, violent and myopic but with renewed ability to see with a broader paintbrush, our world becomes more beautiful and more generous. We have to learn to see with new lenses.

Yes, you've seen the bumper sticker. S--t happens! Life can be harsh. It can be cruel, painful and very messy. Hardship doesn't happen to only a few. We all experience pain, heartache and scars. But choosing and learning to live beyond your up-bringing, your legalism, your failures…and your present circumstances...

...and rekindle a desire to, as Thoreau said, "*suck the marrow out of life*" each day, can be transformational. *(Note that what Thoreau referred to did not embrace having wealth and many advantages. Instead, his desire was to escape the materialistic world and live simply in the woods of Walden. He had little respect for money and what could be done with it. Instead, he wanted to get back to the basics and live each day as fully alive as possible without the normal trappings of society. A great example of embracing what is right before us rather than waiting for our circumstances, financial stability and accumulations to be perfect.)*

Can we "suck the marrow" out of our lives without having everything perfect? In order? All our ducks in a row? Oh yeah! In fact, I know many people who have gone to third world countries, seen oppressed and poverty-stricken people who are so grateful for what they have they simply glow with gratitude. Usually having less makes one even more aware of beauty around them. They are not so burdened with the trappings of having so much stuff and continual activity in their lives.

I went to the woods because I wished to live deliberately, to front only the essential facts of life, and see if I could not learn what it had to teach, and not, when I came to die, discover that I had not lived. I did not wish to live what was not life, living is so dear; nor did I wish to practice resignation, unless it was quite necessary. I wanted to live deep and suck out all the marrow of life, to live so sturdily and Spartan-like as to put to rout all that was not life, to cut a broad swath and shave close, to drive life into a corner, and reduce it to its lowest terms."

*Henry David Thoreau, **Walden: Or, Life in the Woods**, essayist, poet, philosopher (1817-1862)*

Live With Gratitude

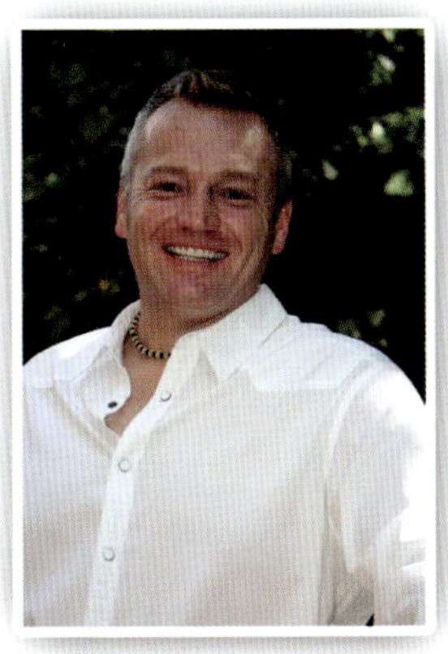

JM Sutton Parks has become part of the family. He has attended many workshops and live events we have had at our place and even joined us for Thanksgiving dinner. He always has a smile and a good word to say. He lives gratitude daily. But it wasn't that many years ago he lived out of his car. Through some poor decisions and an addiction to alcohol, he lost relationships and stuff. In 2011 he wrote his story in a book titled **You Can Sleep In Your Car, But You Can't Drive Your House to Work.** He shares an experience about house sitting for a friend who lived in a huge mansion with a swimming pool while he, himself, still lived in his car. He writes:

> *"The first night back in my car after living in this beautiful home I had yet another blessing. My seat was all the way back and I was trying to go to sleep. I looked up through my sunroof and watched the clouds pass over the fluorescent white, full moon. I thought...my friend in his million dollar home doesn't even have this incredible view from his bed that I have right now. Thank you, God! Finding gratitude is a beautiful thing."*

Sutton has taught us a lot about finding beauty and joy in what is right before us without having everything perfect. Yes, an attitude of gratitude is a beautiful thing. It can free us to put on new glasses, see beauty in the ordinary and live an intentional life of creative abundance. (Check out his website www.suttonparks.com and listen to his great music on iTunes)

Crumbs are those small things that the world would toss aside, seeing little value in them. However, to the one who lives under the eye of God, they are far from valueless... Spending your days in the fast lane of life impairs the quality of your seeing. If you want to see to the depths, you will need to slow down. ...Holiness comes wrapped in the ordinary.

Macrina Wiederkehr, author ***A Tree Full of Angels*** *(Seeing the Holy in the Ordinary), a member of St. Scholastica Monastery, Fort Smith, Arkansas*

Are You Listening? Really?

I was taking a walk down our lane with my walking buddy, Shaloma, when I stopped her in mid-sentence and whispered, *"LISTEN!"* Shaloma "gets me". She is used to me stopping to listen or to pick up something that catches my eye. She knows I am continually searching for…and finding….beauty in everything around me. So we stood for a moment under the trees and I heard water running….a beautiful trickling sound. Shaloma said, *"It sounds like cicadas."* But as we listened a bit longer, while searching for the source, we realized we were hearing the dry leaves in a nearby tree rustling together in the gentle spring breeze. No water, no bugs. But a beautiful rustling that was music to our ears. It was a moment of bliss taking in the sounds of nature God placed in our lives. Listening with ears "wide open".

Let us be silent, that we may hear the whisper of God.

Ralph Waldo Emerson (1803-1882), American essayist, lecturer and poet

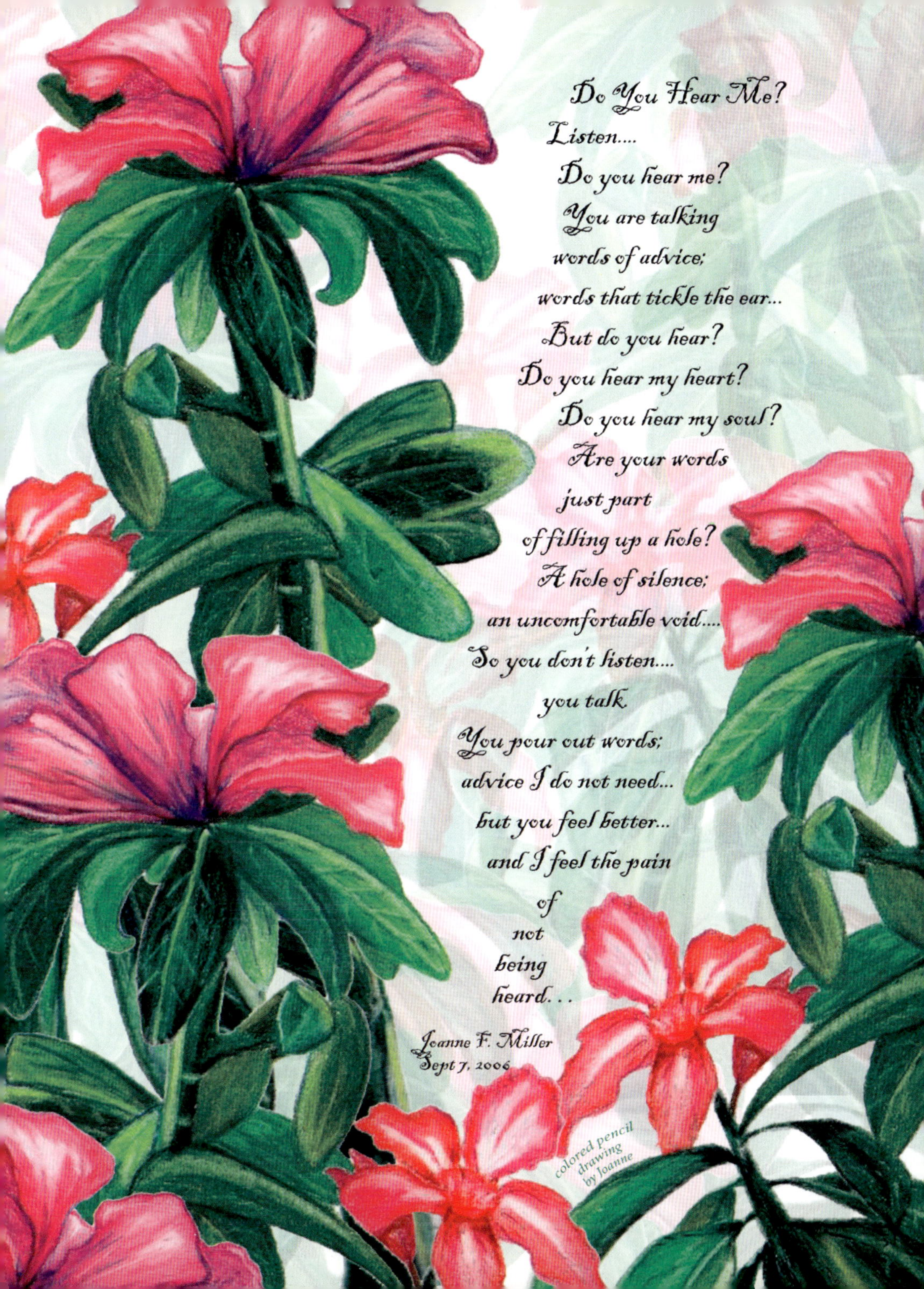
Do You Hear Me?
Listen....
Do you hear me?
You are talking
words of advice;
words that tickle the ear...
But do you hear?
Do you hear my heart?
Do you hear my soul?
Are your words
just part
of filling up a hole?
A hole of silence;
an uncomfortable void....
So you don't listen....
you talk.
You pour out words;
advice I do not need...
but you feel better...
and I feel the pain
of
not
being
heard. . .
Joanne F. Miller
Sept 7, 2006
colored pencil
drawing
by Joanne

We live in a world where noise abounds. Yet truly hearing requires practice to pick out the beauty hidden in the cacophony around us. I have never understood why people lug radios and boom boxes to the beach, out on a boat or into the woods. The chatter of bird song, leaves rustling, water trickling or crashing to shore, the chirp of grasshoppers, are beautiful sounds of nature that are often added to music CDs to evoke peace. We buy sound machines to lull us to sleep or create a peaceful ambience to our homes……yet we often fail to tune into those very sounds of nature when they are live and in surround-sound!

By awakening my senses to everything around me, I become a more interesting person. One who exudes joy and excitement, finds more in life to be passionate about and thus attracting others to follow. Interestingly, in expanding my right brain and delving more into my own creativity, I have found people have been attracted to what they see in a way that didn't happen as readily when I was in my more practical, get-the-job-done mode of thinking.

Listening has become a lost art and being heard is something we all long for. Listening deeply is something that has to be developed. I often take time to just sit, close my eyes and tune into all the sounds around me, identifying and savoring the richness of nature.

All nature seems to speak. As for me, I cannot understand why everybody does not see it or feel it; nature or God does it for everyone who has eyes and ears and a heart to understand.

Vincent van Gogh (1863-1890) Dutch post impressionist painter

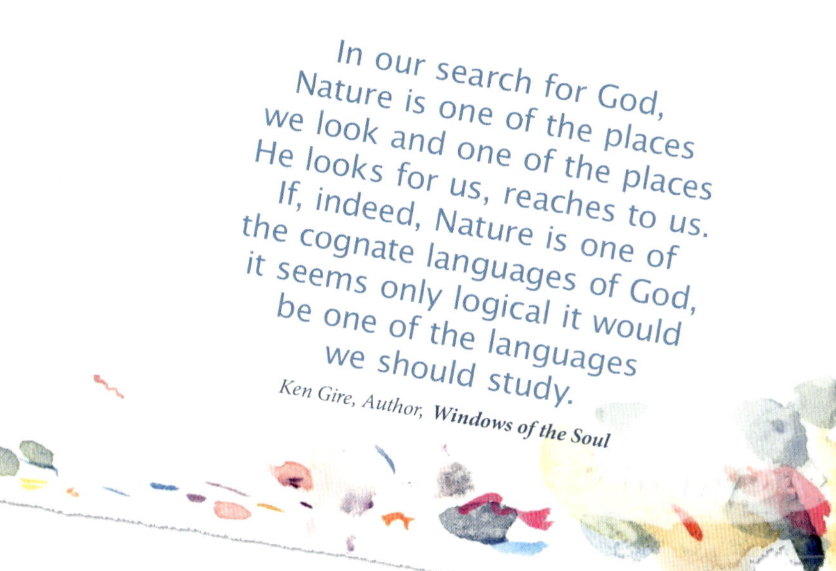

Word Pictures

Erica Bauermeister is a novelist and a favorite of mine. She has a way with words and descriptions that far exceeds most writers. Check out her inspiring website, www.ericabauermeister.com . I cherish her style. Her books make me want to give a sigh of delight, close the book, and hold it with both hands close to my chest, while digesting it much like a child holds a cherished blanket or teddy bear. Ms. Bauermeister transports me to a safe and comfortable place that lingers.

Reading her novels makes me want to be a better listener. They make me want to be more observant. They make me want to write in ways that ignite all the senses.

An Awareness Exercise

One morning I felt compelled to spend time just listening and observing. SEEING what was around me. HEARING the sounds filtering through my senses and not really heard for the chaos of my own mind and life. I gathered pencil and paper (I still prefer that to a computer), sat in a ray of sunlight from the kitchen window while sipping my tea...and wrote. What follows are my observations and musings during a dive into an amazing sensually creative journey.

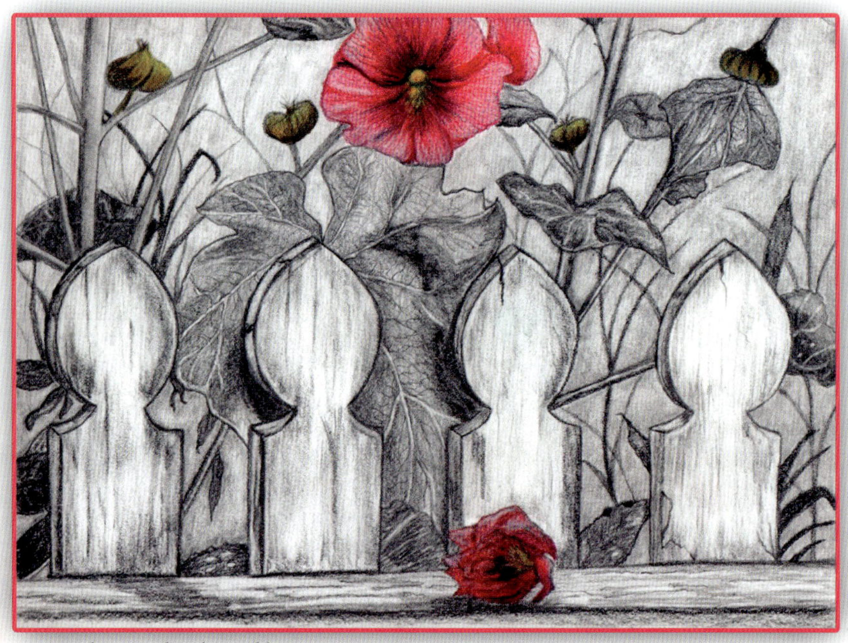

graphite & colored pencil by Joanne

Hearing and seeing can be cursory
or it can be all encompassing,
deep and reverent.
Joanne

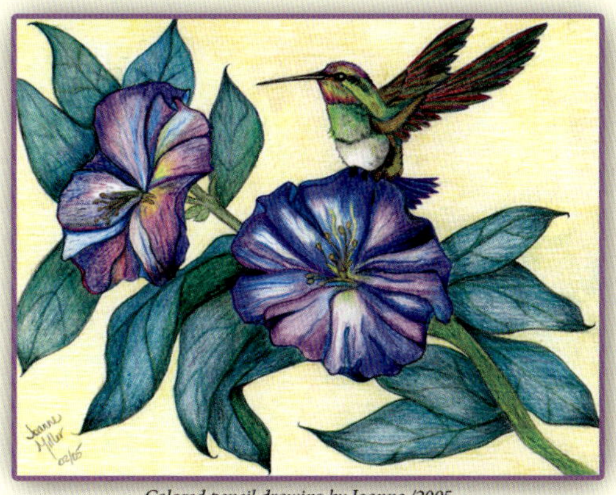

Colored pencil drawing by Joanne /2005

Joanne's Morning Musings

It is a cold and wintery entry into a new dawn.

As I listen this morning to the tea brewing, the water is coursing through the automatic coffee maker and drip, drip, dripping noisily into the carafe, sounding like a heavy spring rain hitting the bare tin roof on a country porch.

The refrigerator hums in the background like distant traffic miles from the door that one never really notices till you reach out with your ears.

The parakeet, Blue, awakens with little screeches that exclaim, "I'm here! Feed me!" as he dips down to the newspaper on the bottom of his cage--scratch, scratch, scratching for seeds and grain tossed from the feeder above.

The grass outside the kitchen window is brown as newly harvested wheat from a farmer's rich bounty. It will soon sprout new growth through the rain drops and sunshine and the world will be painted a verdant green for another season.

The dark barren trees are beginning to sprout tiny buds of life awaiting the warmth of sunshine and the caress of springtime breezes.

Tiny black dots of birds in flight zip like dotted lines through the white sky so fast I wonder if I only imagine them or if it is really just another annoying floater in my myopic line of vision.

A bird crashes into the picture window with sudden force awakening the adrenalin in my early morning lethargy as if an errant snowball was thrown and exploded on the glass.

The early morning chill invades my fingertips, toes, nose, midriff. It permeates the fabric of my clothing and envelopes me like a persona I wish to shake off.

Tiny snowflakes fall from the cloud-colored winter sky like flour through the sifter of Heaven; softly and miraculously changing the view from drab and overcast to a magical kingdom of soft edges and purity. Like fairy dust falling from Heaven and making the whole world magic.

Birds hop-scotch in the straw-grass; skipping over each other like kindergartners on a school play ground.

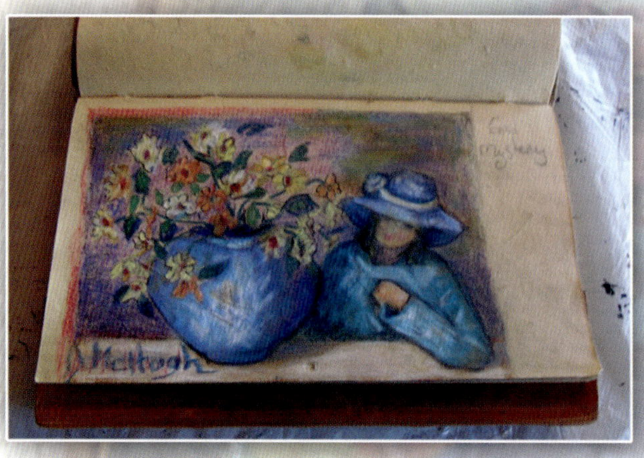

Dorsey's Musings In Colorado

Good morning Rocky mountains.... good morning joyful birds. Good morning dear friends. Good morning from Peace Ranch in Colorado. There is a lovely ridge of mountains surrounding me as I sit outside under the canopy of blue sky. My friend Shelly is drinking her second cup of espresso while staring sleepily out at the breathtaking view. I have just left the soft meandering conversation of two other friends drinking their morning tea in the little kitchen nook. We are in a valley filled with flowers, evergreens and aspens replete with trillions of leaves shaking in the breeze. The ridges in the distance are all green and rocky and red dirt. Whoever painted this for us to experience has left nothing out. We saw a bear, 2 elk, and a deer yesterday. I am expecting good things today. More than good, I am expecting to close the distance between myself and wisdom. Wisdom has gradually become the prize I want most. My path has held many turns. When I don't know how to continue, there has always been some kind of angel meeting me to give me the guidance I need for that moment. I am thankful. I am thankful for dear friends. I am thankful for the transparency we have developed with each other nourishing us all.

This air is filled with anticipation for a new day.
A growing day.
A day to love
and be loved.
A day for
listening.

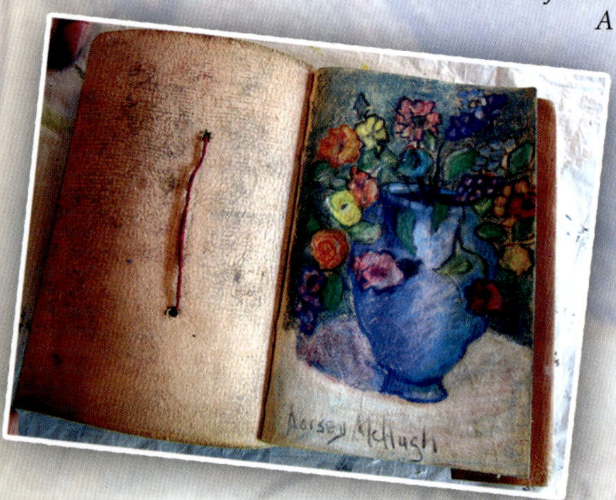

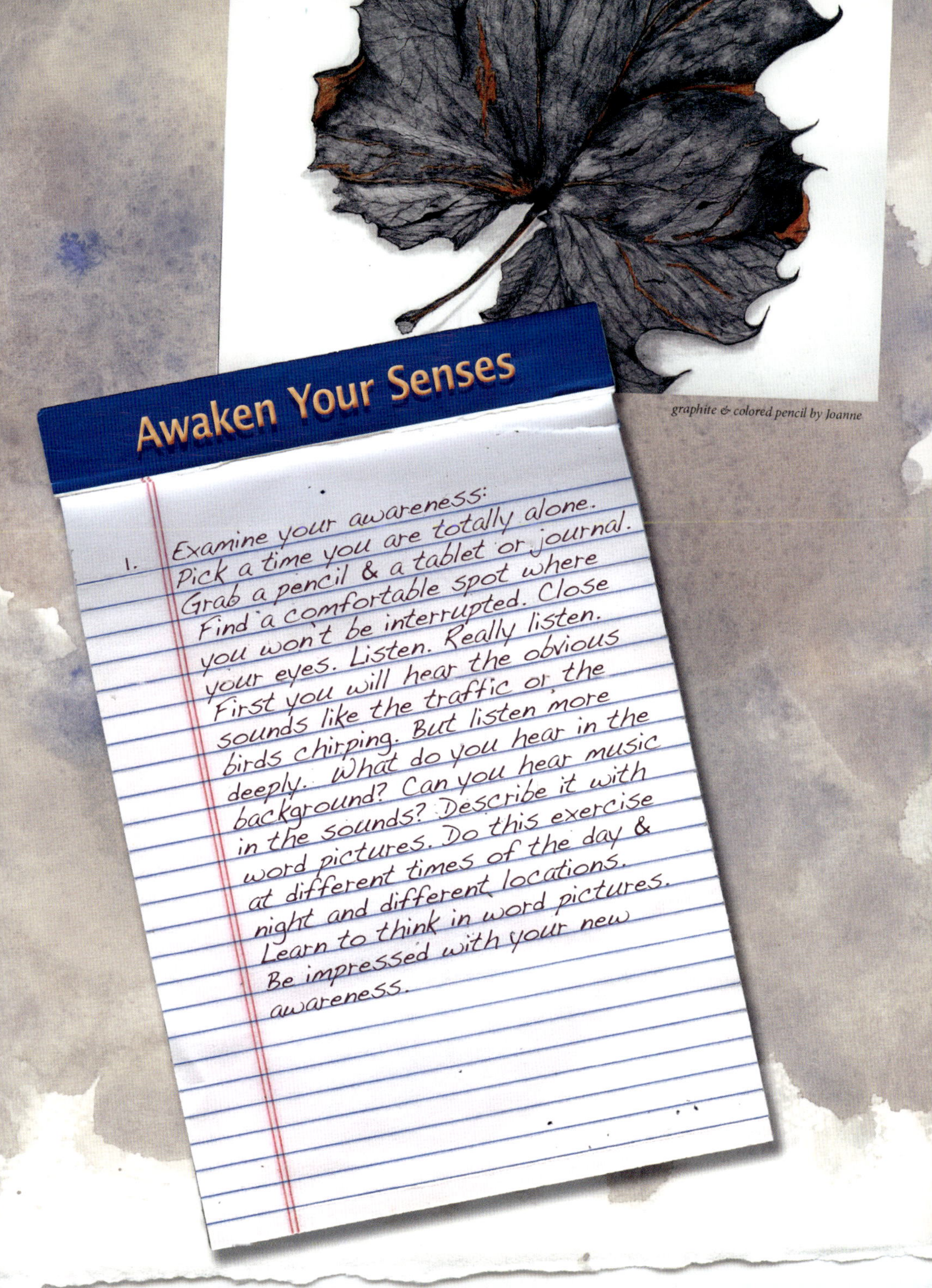

graphite & colored pencil by Joanne

The Music Is All Around Us

Awakening your senses opens windows of imagination, creativity and adventure you never knew existed before, bringing vibrancy and color into a sepia-toned world and life into the soul of our being. You open a curtain with a sense of awe that raises the hairs on your body and tickles the nerve endings. You never see the world in the same way again. You come alive in a way that changes who you are, what you say, and what you feel.

One becomes aware of another dimension far deeper than just a cursory glance. This new awakening draws one away from mediocrity and exports one into a world of action, joy and challenge. It excites the foundations of your very being and transcends normalcy, elevating one to a higher level in a close embrace with our Creator. Have we made our point clear enough? If you practice the AWARENESS exercise often you will find renewed passion for life.

Dorsey and I recommend a great movie on the power of listening. **August Rush** is about an 11-year-old boy who hears music in ordinary things everywhere…the rustle of the wheat blowing in the wind, the car horns, clattering of trash-can lids, the bustle of the city streets and the swish of a car racing by. In one memorable scene August asks his mentor, *"Can only some of us hear it?"* and he was told, *"Only some of us listen. The music is all around us. All you have to do is listen."*

Need a Listening Coach?

At a recent Coaching with Excellence (48Days.com/live events) event here at our Sanctuary, one of our attendees introduced himself as a Listening Coach. Huh? Say again? I was intrigued. I've heard a lot of coaching titles but this was a first for me. In 2003 Dallas and Nancy Demmitt *www.canyouhearmenow.org* of Gilbert, Arizona, wrote a book titled, **Can You Hear Me Now?** It was endorsed by Gary Smalley who said on the cover, *"Prepare to experience the power of listening."*

Dallas Demmitt is self-described as three quarters of a century plus two years old and is a licensed psychologist. He is not only a great listener but he can quickly help you see the importance of listening and how you can do it much better than you do, *even when you think you have it right!*

It wasn't long into a conversation with him I started to feel like he was cutting me down to size. I decided to take him on. We bantered back and forth as he helped me to see I needed to learn to summarize what the speaker is truly saying and, if I didn't understand, I needed to ask for clarification until I do understand, thus eliminating any breach of communication. Since I am always more comfortable speaking in written word rather than voice, I admit I was a bit intimidated at first. However, it wasn't long before the light bulbs started going off in my head and I understood what he was revealing to me and that he was enjoying the banter because he knew I was getting it!

Here is a quote from their book that Nancy Demmitt (a licensed Marriage and Family Counselor) sent to me:

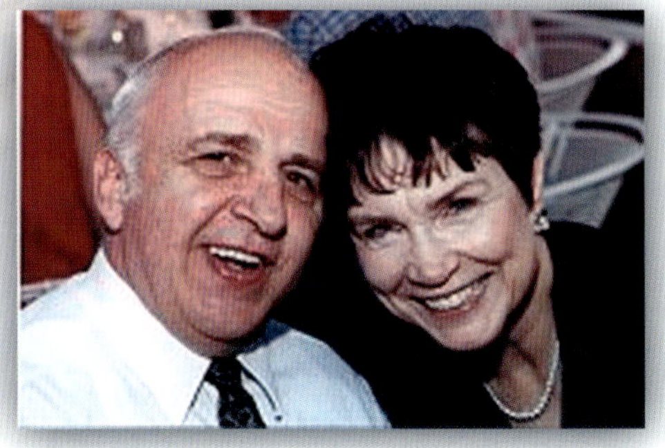

"I became a listening coach because I believe our world is in a listening crisis. People long to be heard, but few people know how to listen. Individuals don't know how to tune in to each other, or to their children, or even to their own hearts. We are in the information age—our lives are bombarded every day by media. The information superhighway whirls around us at dizzying speed. People reveal their souls to faceless strangers through anonymous and sometimes desperate dialogues that occur at breakneck speed. In cyberspace, people will take communication risks to try to ease the loneliness, while searching for answers. Despite these conveniences, our communication frenzy is still marked with an absence of caring, purposeful, loving listening."

That's a pretty powerful statement and one I believe to be true.

Dallas and Nancy's book has a lot of great principles for being a better listener, a better parent, friend and partner. Worth taking time to read and a great testimony to why they have been married 56-years!

A principle I learned quickly in talking with Dallas is to summarize what I heard. That is… "simply rephrasing what you hear into your own words without changing the meaning". **(Can You Hear Me Now?** Pg. 62)

Dorsey McHugh

Listening and love are the same thing. When we listen closely to what another is saying, we have an opportunity to give that person a gift. We affirm them as valuable. My dad thought I was funny. He laughed at my antics for as far back as I can remember. This always made me feel loved.

I recently had the opportunity to spend over a month in the enchanting country of Scotland. The people I met were as interesting and lovely as their country. The Scottish are good listeners.

Here, in America, we are overloaded with mental stimulation. We are constantly being interrupted with telephone, email, text messaging. In Scotland I had to walk a few miles to a hotel pub to get wi-fi. Lots of hotels don't have it. So if you are there for any length of time, you begin to calm down in a way our connection to the internet will never afford us.

It was easier to do the list of possibilities in order of importance in Scotland. When I got off the plane in Nashville, I was caught off guard. The peace I had been experiencing for the last month was bombarded with stimulation. I had to make choices again. I couldn't do everything, think about everything, and say yes to everyone. This is the constant state of most people I know. The chase for money and things is intense. The pressure of comparison is also intense. I know so many people who have

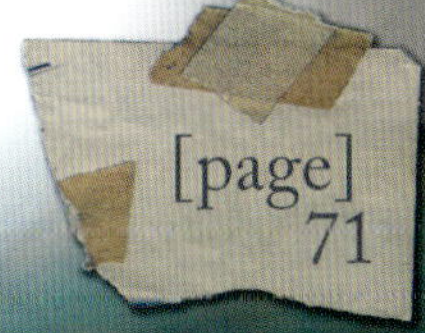

trouble sleeping because they can't turn off the noise in their own minds. So when, at a party, I was asked to tell someone about my journey, it didn't surprise me that into the third sentence of my answer, the friend saw someone who they remembered they wanted to talk to, and walked away from me, not realizing I was attempting to answer his question. This person was distracted by the buzz and had lost the ability to listen.

I am experimenting with listening. I want to listen with my heart as well. We need to stop the tickertape of melodramatic voices from taking over. It is a form of escape. We talk so we will be distracted from the discomfort of our lives.

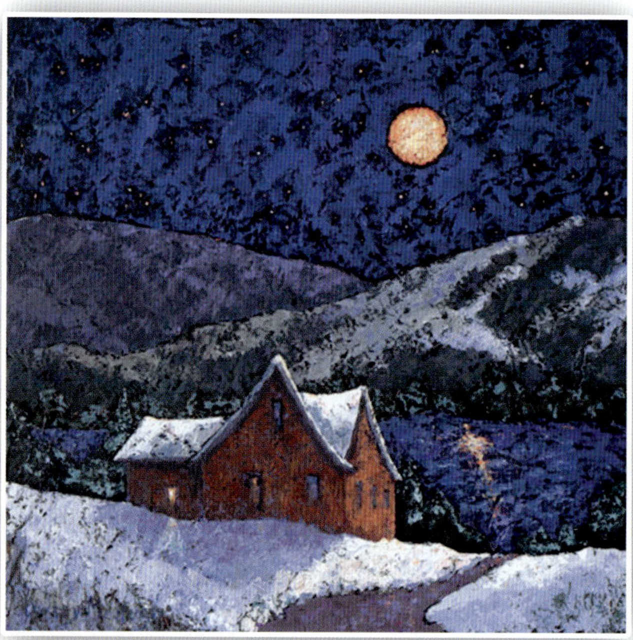

acrylic on board, Ancient Journey Home by Dorsey

He who answers before listening—
that is his folly and his shame.
Proverbs 18:13 NIV

A Deafening Silence

Once on a visit to see our grandkids in Woodland Park, Colorado, our son, Kevin asked us to come outside late at night and listen. Before he opened the door, he placed his finger in front of his lips and said, *"Shhhh….."* He ushered several of us into the chilly darkness under the late night sky at almost ten thousand feet altitude. We all stood quietly and listened. It was deafening. Deafening silence. If you ever experienced what

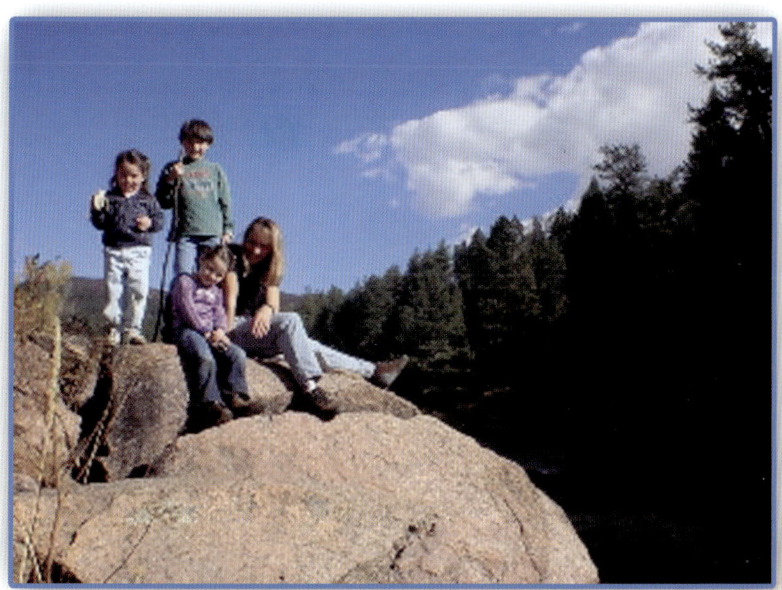

photo of Terissa Miller, Eliza, Caleb and Autumn Miller

we did that night you would understand that deafening silence is not an oxymoron. We are so used to hearing something that we simply can't adjust to hearing ABSOLUTELY NOTHING! It was astounding. There wasn't a bird, an animal, an insect, no wind blowing, no traffic (they live at the top of a mountain far from city lights and noise). It was the purest quiet we have ever experienced. You could only hear the blood rushing through your ears. Even on a deserted island you would hear birds, water slapping the sand and other sounds. But. This. Was. Total. Quiet. It was almost too much to fathom. In Tennessee no matter what season, you are going to hear coyotes, dogs, frogs, insects, birds, owls, trees blowing, skunks scurrying off into the woods. *Something! Lots of somethings!* But the Colorado mountain silence was deafening. And beautiful. And reverent. You won't believe it unless you go there!

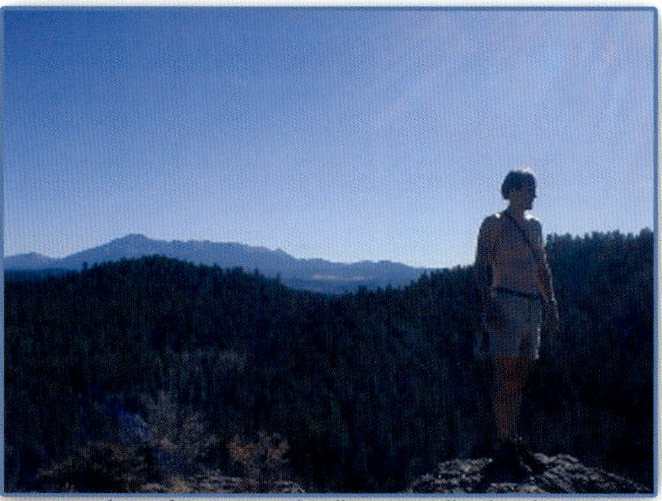

photo of Kevin Daniel Miller in Woodland Park, CO

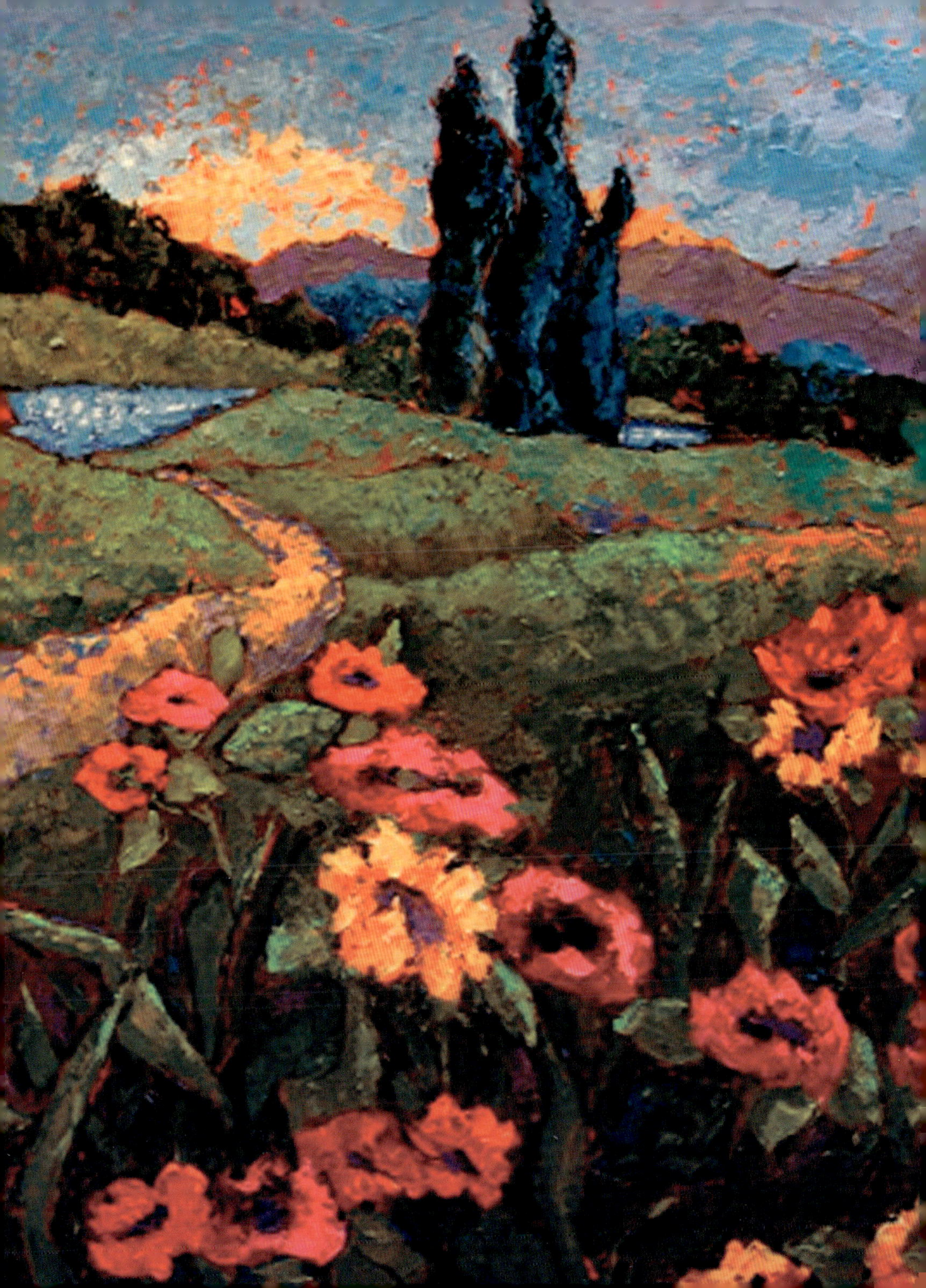

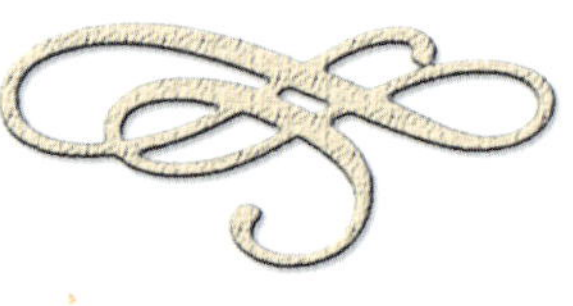

WHAT A WONDERFUL WORLD!

I love that God gave me eyes to see His beauty in everything and everyone, especially when it's the unexpected. But it's a decision, every day, to walk in that, and to keep my eyes open.
*Jared Miller Angaza, Author, **Wisdom Meets Passion**, Social Entrepreneur in Kenya and husband to Ilea, father to Saoirse and Francois.*

What A Wonderful World!

Anyone who receives a personal email from me will see Jared's quotation after my signature. I pray it helps to instill a desire to look at the day in a brighter and more optimistic slant. Our world needs that. In a big way. That statement packs a lot of maturity for a young guy who has had a lot of struggles in his life. Believe me, I know. Jared is our son and has learned the hard way how our attitude influences the choices we make and how we view life.

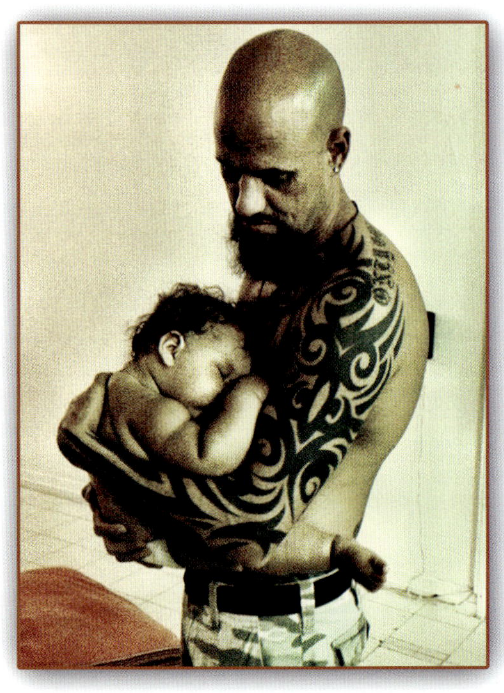

The highest form of ignorance is when you reject something you don't know anything about!
Wayne Dyer, psychologist, author and self-help speaker

I take seriously creating a haven of peace and joy in my home, my neighborhood, community and my centers of influence. I will do more good in helping the world I live in become a better place by filling my thoughts with beauty and positive input.

Recently I heard ole' Sachmo, Louis Armstrong, crooning words that made me smile. Words and thoughts we would all benefit by embracing. Not intended to be a hymn, yet, it brought blessings to my ears...

I see trees of green, red roses too
I see them bloom for me and you
And I think to myself what a wonderful world.

I see skies of blue and clouds of white
The bright blessed day, the dark sacred night
And I think to myself what a wonderful world.

The colors of the rainbow so pretty in the sky
Are also on the faces of people going by
I see friends shaking hands saying how do you do
They're really saying I love you.

I hear babies cry, I watch them grow
they'll learn much more than I'll never know
And I think to myself what a wonderful world
Yes I think to myself what a wonderful world.

So many people miss the beauty of our wonderful world because they are consumed with bad news that colors their total outlook on life. There is a lot to be said for choosing to see the world through rose colored glasses. We all make choices.

An anxious heart weighs a man down,
but a kind word cheers him up.
Proverbs 12:25

Al Siebert, PhD writes in his book, **The Resiliency Advantage** (Master Change, Thrive under Pressure, and Bounce Back from Setbacks) that *"psychologists have found that the least creative people think in judgmental ways.....people who are skilled at being creative have a perceptual, observing way of looking at the world. They notice many things happening without judging what they see as right or wrong, good or bad."* He goes on to say, *"People with a judgmental style of thinking give negative labels to others—labels such as perverts, weirdos, psychos, and such".* People who think critically toward others are often closed to learning new ideas or *fearful* that accepting someone else's differences might undermine their own belief system. Siebert says it well: *"Closed-minded thinking is incompatible with creativity. One cannot be creative if facts, details, and information have never been absorbed in the first place. Closed-minded certainty suppresses curiosity."*

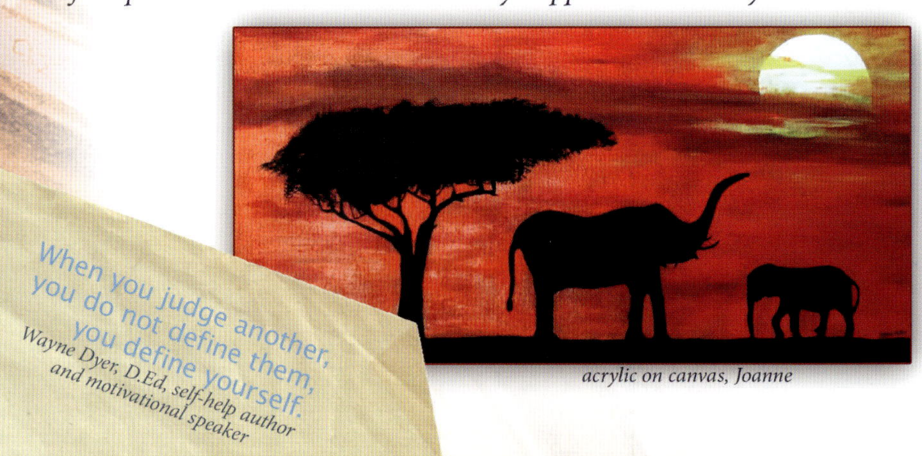

acrylic on canvas, Joanne

When you judge another,
you do not define them,
you define yourself.
Wayne Dyer, D.Ed, self-help author and motivational speaker

Dorsey McHugh

When people are critical, they are painting other people's shadows as ugly. In studying art it has become apparent to me that shadow is a companion of light. Light and shadow are not enemies. Shadows can also be seen as lovely, reminding me of one of my favorite quotes by Walt Whitman that is also an art principle…. *"Keep your face always toward the sunshine and shadows will fall behind you."*

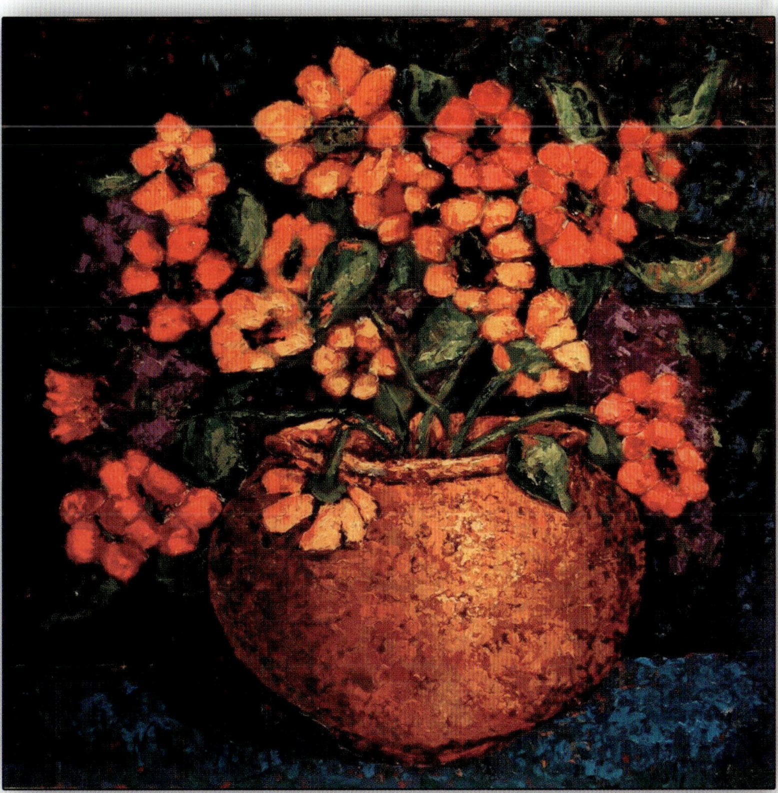

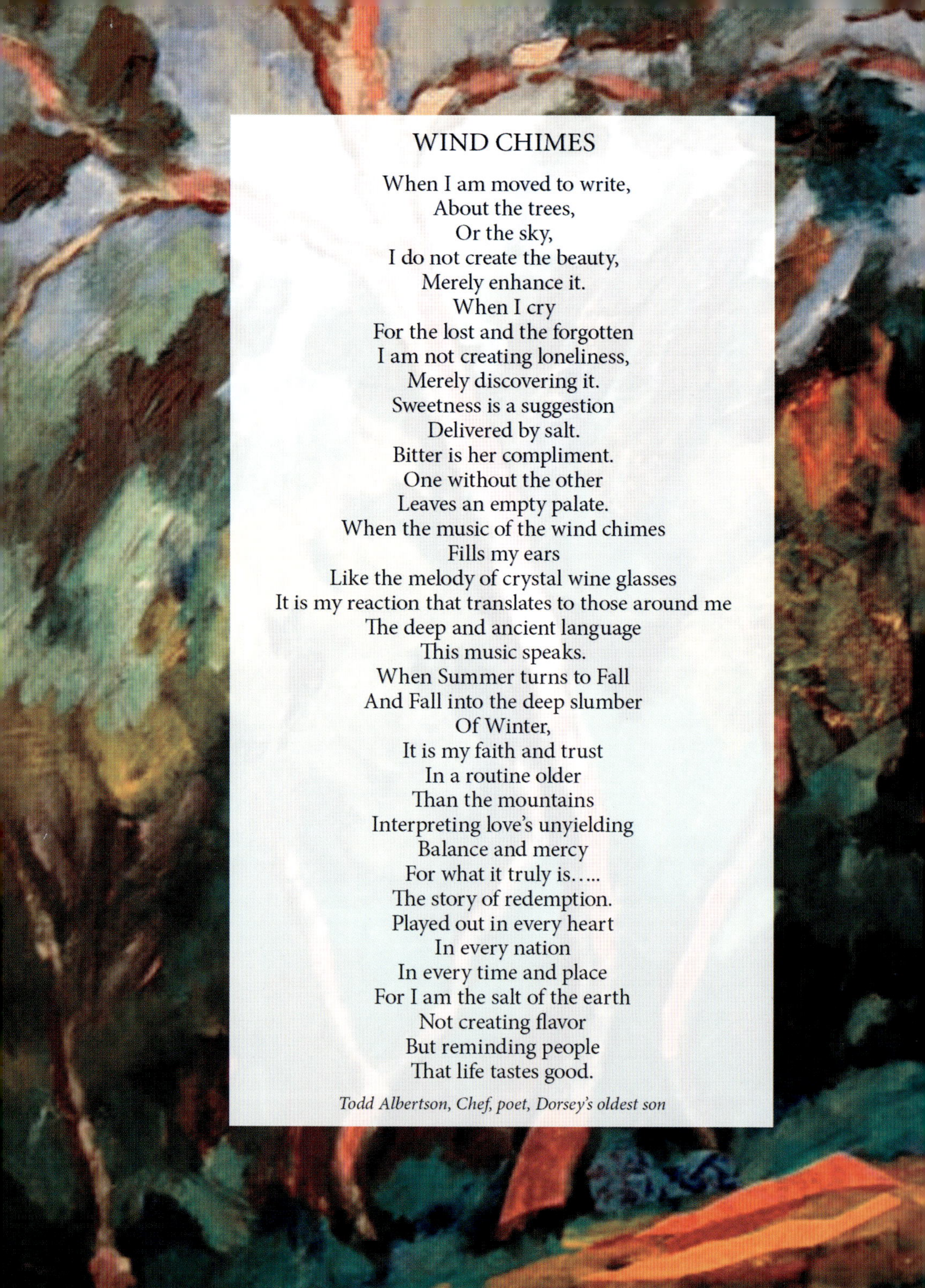

WIND CHIMES

When I am moved to write,
About the trees,
Or the sky,
I do not create the beauty,
Merely enhance it.
When I cry
For the lost and the forgotten
I am not creating loneliness,
Merely discovering it.
Sweetness is a suggestion
Delivered by salt.
Bitter is her compliment.
One without the other
Leaves an empty palate.
When the music of the wind chimes
Fills my ears
Like the melody of crystal wine glasses
It is my reaction that translates to those around me
The deep and ancient language
This music speaks.
When Summer turns to Fall
And Fall into the deep slumber
Of Winter,
It is my faith and trust
In a routine older
Than the mountains
Interpreting love's unyielding
Balance and mercy
For what it truly is…..
The story of redemption.
Played out in every heart
In every nation
In every time and place
For I am the salt of the earth
Not creating flavor
But reminding people
That life tastes good.

Todd Albertson, Chef, poet, Dorsey's oldest son

We have all had moments when we've experienced something we can't quite explain. Moments when God has touched our lives like a soft hand of morning sun reaching through our bedroom window, brushing over our eyes, and waking us to something eternal.
(Ken Gire, **Windows of the Soul,** *Zondervan, 1996)*

Thin Places

I had never heard the term thin places before I met Dorsey. It certainly sounded intriguing. People of faith often experience a strong presence of the Creator as a thin place. People experience thin places in many forms. Jared, our very right-brained son has more thin place experiences from movies than about anything else. He can find the most deeply spiritual insight that often flies right past me and makes me want to see the movie again from his point of view.

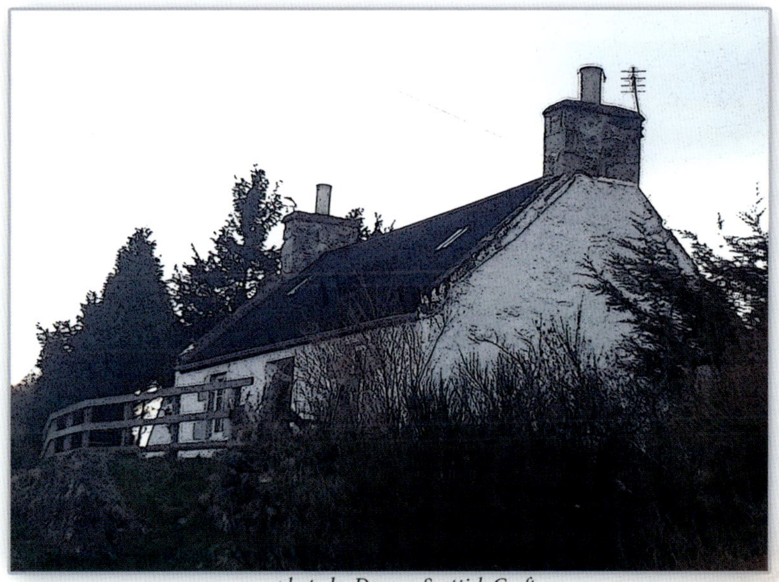

photo by Dorsey; Scottish Croft

Help me, O God,
Whenever I go to a movie, not to go just for entertainment, but also for enlightenment. Meet me there, I pray, and speak to me. Tell me something I need to know so I may live my life more graciously, more compassionately.
Give me moments of transcendence so I can leave the theater in some way changed, even if it is a very small way. Speak to me through a character, a scene, a line of dialogue, a musical score. Tell me something that will help me become a more understanding person, kinder and more compassionate. Thank You for those moments at the movies that have touched my heart. And for the fact that there is no place on earth that some echo of Your voice cannot be heard for the one who is listening.....

*(Ken Gire, **Windows of the Soul**, Zondervan, 1996)*

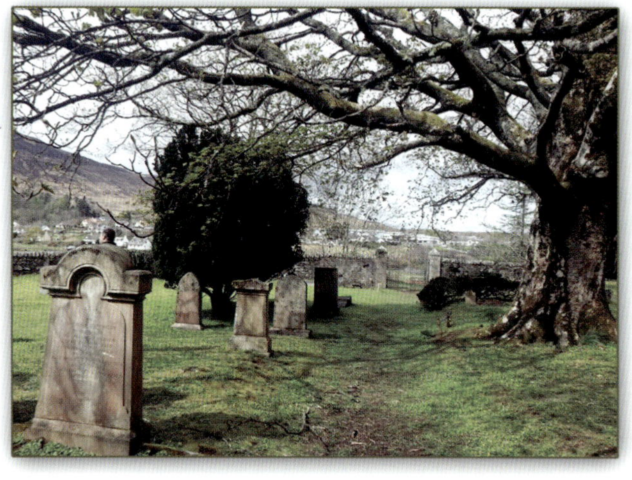

For many people transcendence to a thin place is through a book or through travel, through a church experience or something as simple as watching a sunset or listening to a baby's first cry.

Dorsey took a five week trip to Scotland in 2013.....in search of thin places. What follows are some of her blogs and thoughts on this wonderful experience:

What a wonderful world

Dorsey McHugh

April 5, 2013: According to Celtic lore, there are places where the distance between heaven and earth collapse and we are able to catch glimpses of the divine. These are called thin places. I find this intriguing. There is certainly no scientific proof that these places exist. But, I think we can agree there are places where one can see more clearly. Places so inspiring they give you the impression you are seeing some part of what is true. The same can be said about people. There are those who inspire us to be our finest self, people who show us a new way to look at things. People who we believe when they tell us we are loved. My goal is to develop an awareness of thin places. I want to paint and write about what I find...........

April 8, 2013: This morning, while wandering around the little town of Portree, I found a lovely (wee) path, which led into a stone, fenced churchyard. The yard itself was overgrown and run down. There was one enormous tree in the center of that quiet space that sang a melancholy, ancient song to all the graves, which randomly populated the grounds. I could hear the tree remembering a time when children and lovers climbed it to find a moment alone; remembering when there was laughter and picnics beneath its branches. After hundreds of years, the tree was now quietly guarding those graves and their chiseled, weatherworn stones. One grave told the story of a 59-year-old woman who had 3 children, and a young husband, all lost to war or disease.

Her husband, an infant, a 4 yr. old son, and an 11yr. old daughter all preceded her in death. I wondered about her life, about what strength she found to keep living. I shared briefly her sorrow, and wanted, irrationally, to find a way to comfort the dear, living tree, standing guard. Instead I found myself crying, anointing with tears that ground, those sorrows, which are now written in stone. More than that I wanted to comfort myself about the sure knowledge of our shared mystery.

We know only with eyes of hope and of faith what lies beyond these depths. In weeping, I felt myself comforted and knew a taste of her comfort, of her resolve to carry on, and of how strength flowed back into her in little bits. We keep going. We find joy in our journey. Our sorrows walk with us to remind us how important our joys are. This is yesterday's story for me, standing in a quiet graveyard on a hill in a tiny village on the Isle of Skye. From this place, I see more clearly. This moment is now a part of my own story, and a moment I will not forget.

April 15, 2013: As I sit here in front of my little Scottish cottage, I am watching the morning light win its battle against the low cloud cover trying to maintain its dominance over this day. Right now, I feel as if nothing can rob me of this precious light. It is alive inside me already today. I am thinking about my search for thin places. There is much scientific documentation trying to prove their existence and their value. Information I don't usually find easy to hold in my head. So, with what wisdom I have, I am staying open to the possibility of anything. Even fairies and leprechauns are in reserve as props for any stories coming out of this journey.

One serious observation I am having is my own distinct victory in the battle to relax. Being away from wi-fi for days at a time is a brilliant thing. So is spending several hours in silence, because of the relative isolation I have here in this magical place. Yes, I said magical. Don't expect any proof though. My planned resting is nearly over. I am ready to begin moving around again. Still looking for thin places, but, I will confess an emerging thought: Possibly the distance between Heaven and earth is bridged, in part, by the state of our own soul. Just a thought…

Do you think thin places could possibly be where there is so much historical energy that in our imaginations we get the rare gift of time slowing down or speeding up? We then gain insight to the past or the future?

Thin places originate in us, unique to our personalities.

James Brown, friend of Dorsey's, Nairn, Scotland

Kisses from Heaven

Ilea Angaza is my sweet daughter-in-love, married to our son, Jared. She emailed this to me from Nairobi, Kenya. She has a love and respect for butterflies as they tend to be a voice from the Divine she pays attention to.

"In my almost 8 years in East Africa I've experienced quite a few life altering thin place moments, where you know there is no real distinction between what we see and what we don't, where angels become real and the physical somehow loses its power. However, the longer I live here, what was once exotic becomes the familiar and thus, I have to look a little harder and pay attention a little more in order to notice when I suddenly and surprisingly find myself in the midst of that space where I can feel the spiritual.

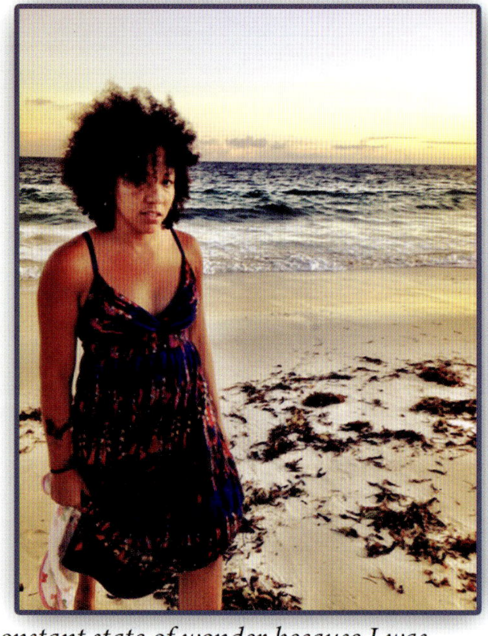

Over the last year, I've been in a constant state of wonder because I was pregnant and had our first baby. There is something so magically spiritual about being pregnant and, then, about meeting and getting to know your new little human. But there are plenty of hard days as well, as any parent knows. And sometimes you just need a little break. A couple months ago, during one of these much needed breaks I found myself alone for the first time since Saoirse had been born, wading into the perfect bliss of Mombasa's Indian Ocean sometime between high tide and low tide. That space in between tides is the best time to relax in the water because, though it is moving slowly outwards, it is somehow at its stillest.

It was morning, hardly a soul on the beach, and I had the ocean virtually all to myself. I walked until the water reached my thighs and then I decided to sit cross-legged in the water and be. I sat pondering our impending move away from our beloved sleepy beach town, Mombasa, and into Kenya's bustling capitol city, Nairobi. We had already made the decision to move, to take the promotion and resettle our little family, again. But it weighed heavily on my heart; fear of the unknown and sadness to leave the sea.

I sat in the water and breathed deeply, letting the salt and the sun soak deep into my bones, trying to implant the beauty as firmly in my mind as possible because this privilege of walking out our front door and into the ocean was soon to become a distant memory. I mourned the changing of seasons in our life, even as I welcomed it with open arms.

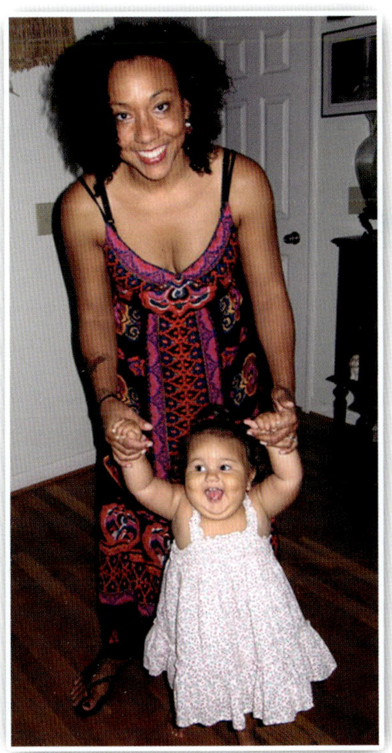

This lonely spot in the ocean was a thin place indeed, but I didn't yet know just how thin....until a lone orange butterfly fluttered in front of me. I wondered at the site of a butterfly over the ocean, like perhaps it was somehow lost. You expect to see butterflies while sitting in a grassy field or even perhaps in a forest. I did not expect to see one flutter over my head like a kiss from the heavens while I sat in the ocean 25 yards from the shore. And just then, at least a hundred more perfectly orange butterflies followed, fluttering their beautifully clumsy dance just beyond my arm's reach. I smiled and inhaled the beauty all around me, like I was in a dream.

And I knew that the Divine was in fact sending me hundreds of kisses, letting me know that the change would be beautiful, as it almost always is.

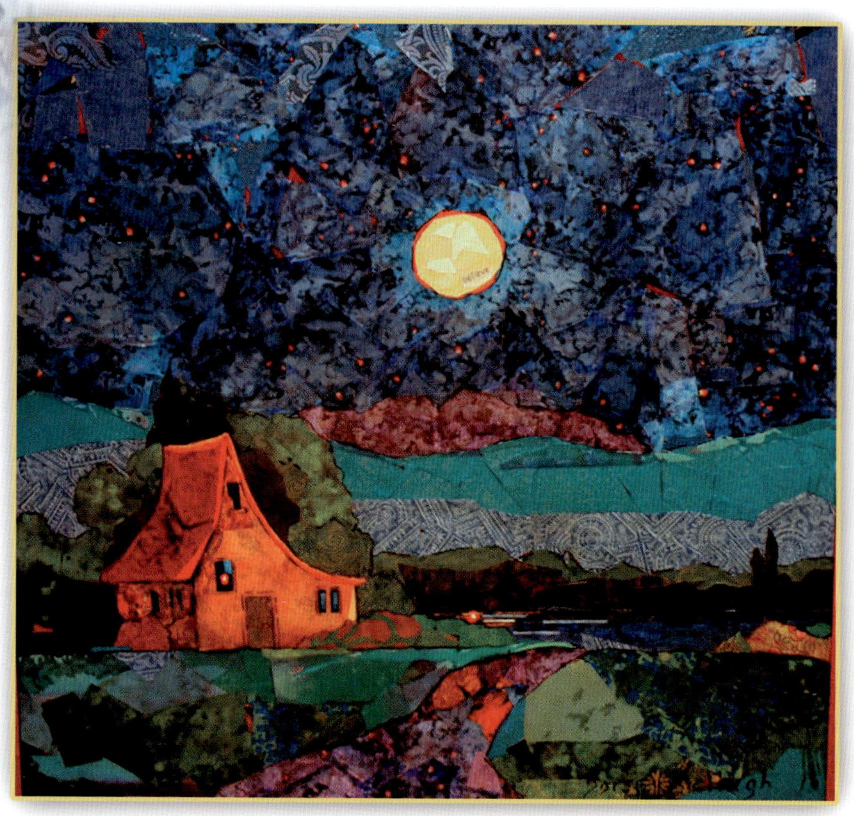

Secret Heart

Dorsey McHugh

When I look at this little landscape, I long to live softly, gently and with purpose. I want to love deeply, to know and to be known. I seek to love and to be loved. Let's celebrate the sacred gifts we have been given by sharing them with others. Let's find a starry, moonlit night and have a picnic. We can carry our blanket and basket to just the right spot, spread out our feast and listen to the sounds of the night while we count every blessing we have along with the stars.

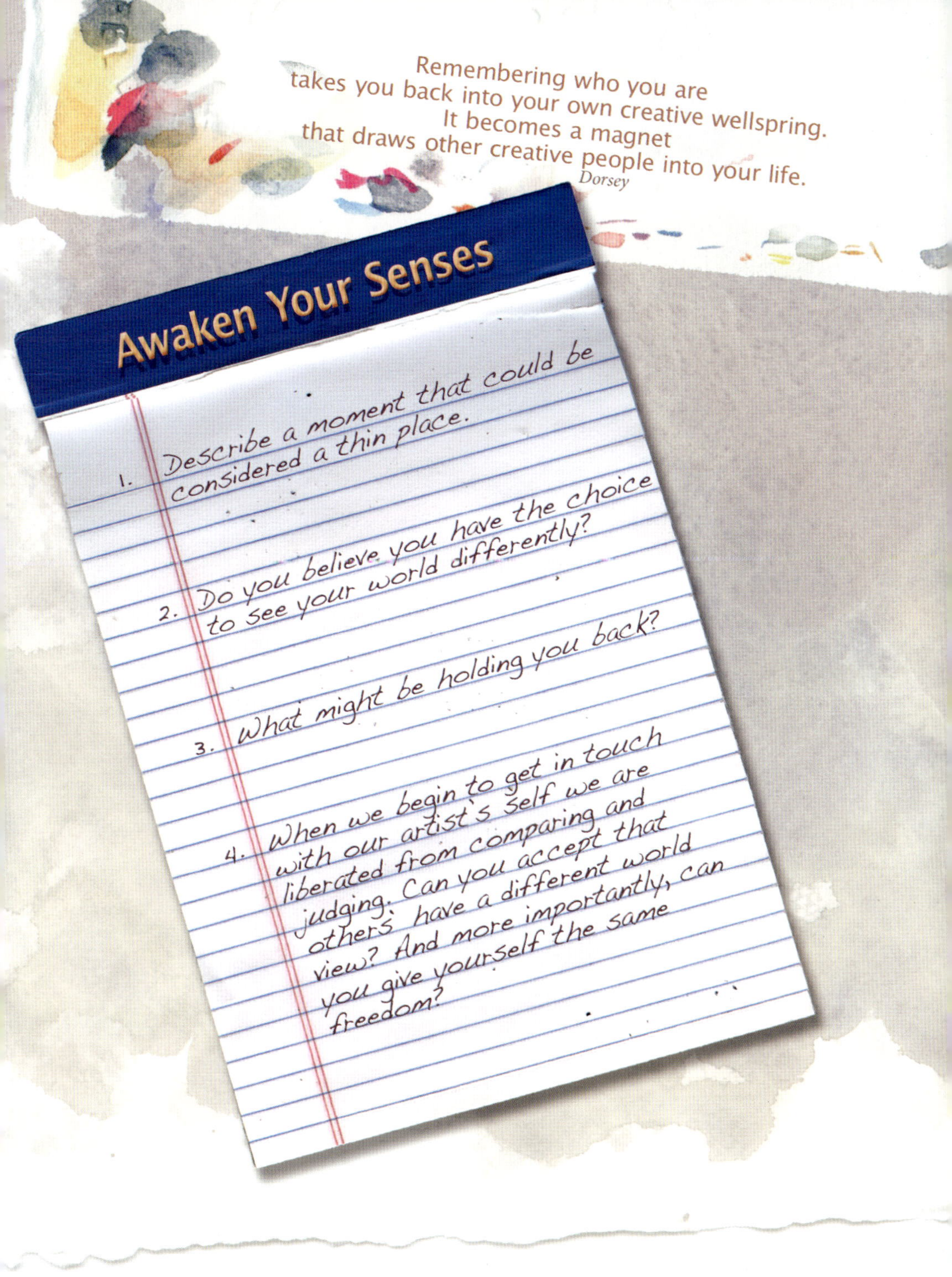
Remembering who you are
takes you back into your own creative wellspring.
It becomes a magnet
that draws other creative people into your life.
Dorsey
Awaken Your Senses
1. Describe a moment that could be considered a thin place.
2. Do you believe you have the choice to see your world differently?
3. What might be holding you back?
4. When we begin to get in touch with our artist's self we are liberated from comparing and judging. Can you accept that others have a different world view? And more importantly, can you give yourself the same freedom?

Birds Of A Feather

Relationships are important to success and happiness. The people with whom we spend time can influence us negatively or positively. Dorsey and I have talked at length about the importance of surrounding oneself with a positive, creative and open minded support group. People who are able to think outside the box. Our art class is a perfect example of surrounding ourselves with people who aren't clones of us but who bring enrichment, variety, challenge and enlightenment into our lives each week. Our goal is for each one of us to find our own voice. Not to copy someone else's style or even see in the same way, we are encouraged to express who and what we are and stand for. Sometimes, as in life, this takes a lot of experimentation, failed attempts and a certain amount of frustration!

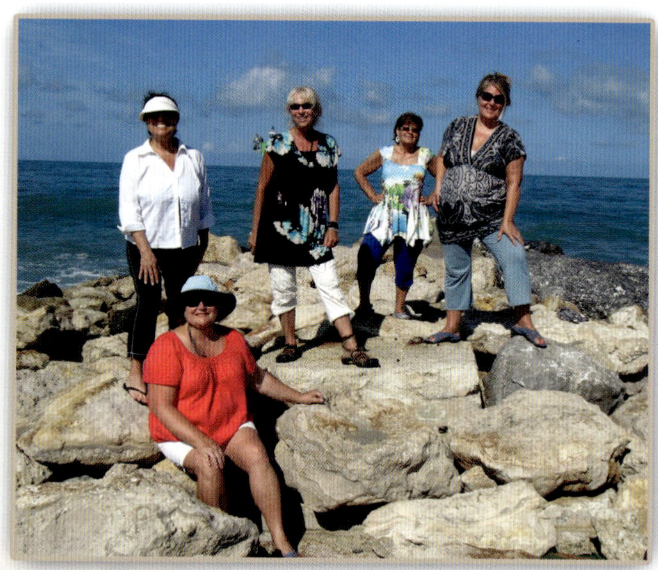

photo of Candy Richey (front) who introduced me to Dorsey. Left to right behind Candy are Catherine Carminati, Dorsey, Me, Deby Dearman some of our creative girlfriends on a trip to Florida!

Dorsey McHugh

Since childhood, I have known about my inner house. I have a vast landscape inside me. It has walls, a roof and furniture. Over the years, I have observed acquaintances cross over into real friendship. When this happens, I begin seeing them come into my inner landscape. True friends receive an invitation to know me. They get to see what my inner self looks like. The landscape inside me expands in knowing other people. We become a part of one another's stories.

Oh, the comfort—the inexpressible comfort
of feeling safe with a person,
Having neither to weigh thoughts,
nor measure words---
but pouring them all right out—
just as they are—
Chaff and grain together—
Certain that a faithful hand
will take and sift them—
Keep what is worth keeping—
and with a breath of kindness
blow the rest away.

Dinah Mulock Craik (1826-1887) English novelist and poet

JM

The poem above is in a book on friendship I gave to my husband in 1966. I can't count the number of times we have referred to those words and what it means to us as a couple. It is the true measure of friendship.

A few years ago I did my second thorough study of Julia Cameron's **The Artist's Way.** This book inspired in me the desire to find my own spring of creativity. I began reading, writing, journaling, listening to speakers, going to conferences and reaching out for anything and anyone who would nourish my soul. In the process I found my own voice.

One thing I can promise you is that when you are doing something that makes your heart sing, you will want to bring people into your choir who are as excited about life and growth as you are!

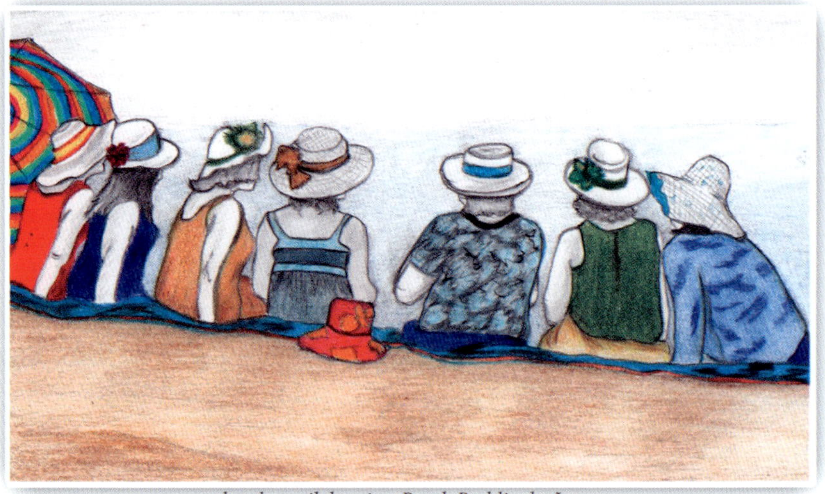

colored pencil drawing, Beach Buddies by Joanne

Don't you find it fascinating to note that so many of the great masters in art were not wealthy or even necessarily influential? But they were passionate and they were typically full of compassion….It fueled their creativity. It gave them fodder for their music, their paintings, their writing.

> The soul, though at all times hidden, is at all times revealed, expressing itself through everything we say and do. Through the ordinary brushstrokes of our everyday life, a portrait of our soul is being painted.
>
> *Ken Gire, **Windows of the Soul***

I dream of painting,
and then I paint my dream.
Vincent van Gogh

Vincent van Gogh worked as an evangelist in poor mining villages in Belgium but his religious fanaticism, asceticism, and his lack of charisma as a preacher marked him for failure, despite his humanitarian intentions and his sincere, even obsessive, devotion to the poor and the sick. By 1879, he had experienced a total spiritual crisis and had decided to become an artist, beginning by sketching the Belgian miners and workers with whom he lived.

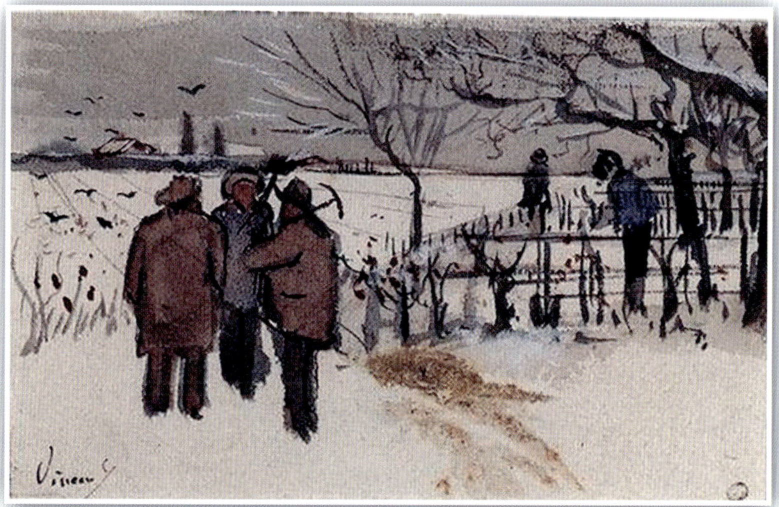

1849 Oil, Miners in the Snow by Vincent van Gogh

The key is to keep company only
with people who uplift you,
whose presence calls forth your best.
Epictetus, Greek philosopher (55 AD-135 AD)
who taught that suffering arises from trying to control what is uncontrollable.

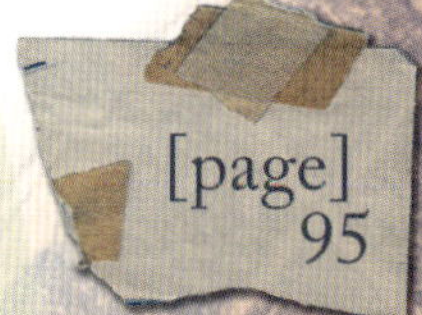

Dorsey McHugh

Van Gogh was one of many artists who were troubled by hard luck, poverty, mental illness, and addictions. Modigliani, and Edvard Munch are two others with similar stories. Sometimes I have thought they were only able to focus on their song. It was so important to sing this song, they dropped everything else. In order to keep working, they fueled themselves any way they could. I have had a taste of that passion. I think it is what has to happen if a person wants to be accomplished at anything. If you want to have excellence in any area, you have to make choices about what to drop. Art is a jealous lover. Once you enter its gates, you find it demands truth.

I care.
My commitment to caring results in my commitment to the extraordinary.
I believe the pinnacle of caring is passion.
Passion is simply a reflection of large amounts of care.
And you can't create extraordinary art (in the form of work or relationships) without passion.
Caring is at the core.
Caring wins.

Jared Miller Angaza,
(www.jaredangaza.com) The Caring Lens Blog

What a wonderful world

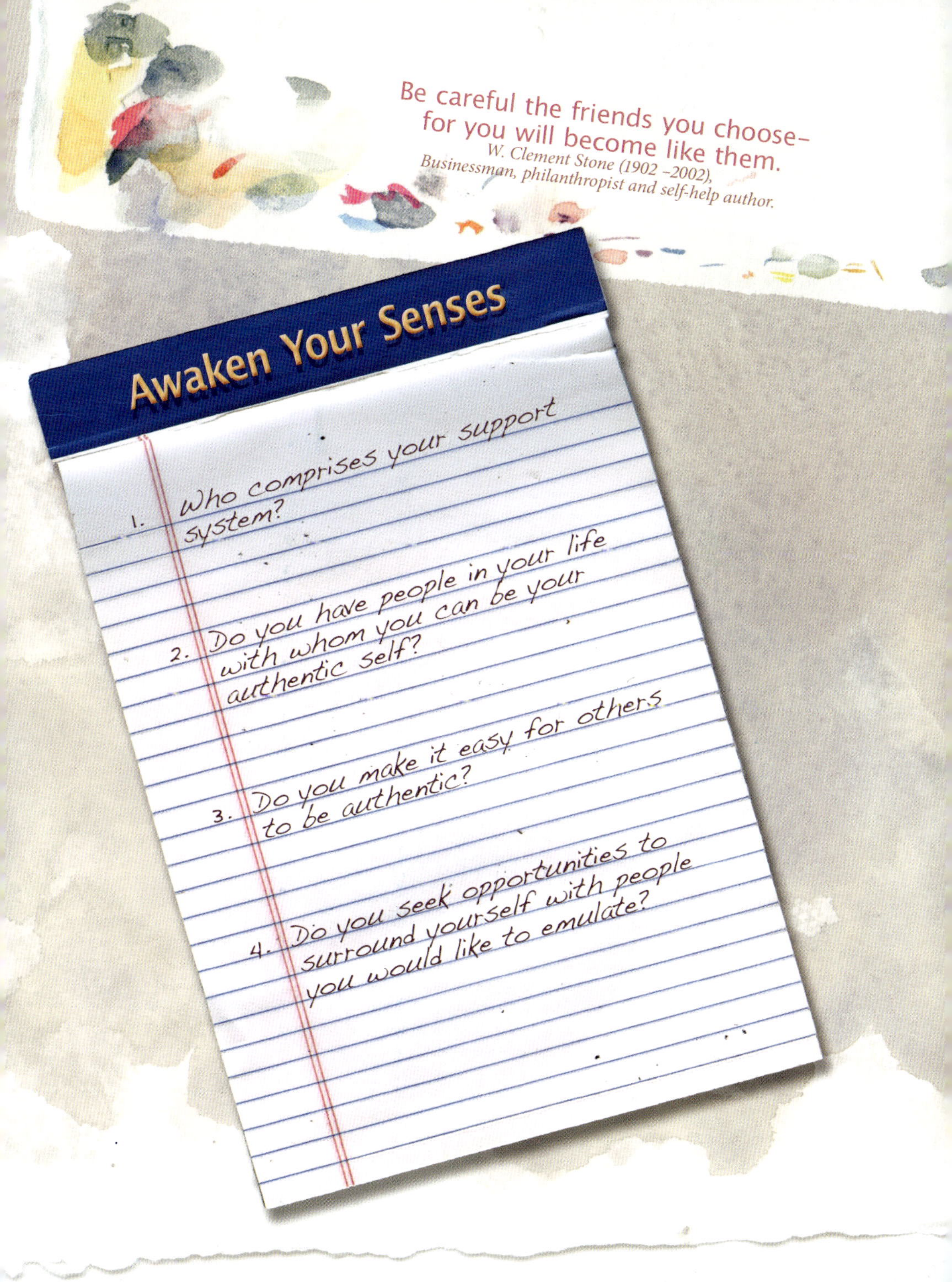

Be careful the friends you choose–
for you will become like them.
W. Clement Stone (1902 –2002),
Businessman, philanthropist and self-help author.
Awaken Your Senses
1. Who comprises your support system?
2. Do you have people in your life with whom you can be your authentic self?
3. Do you make it easy for others to be authentic?
4. Do you seek opportunities to surround yourself with people you would like to emulate?

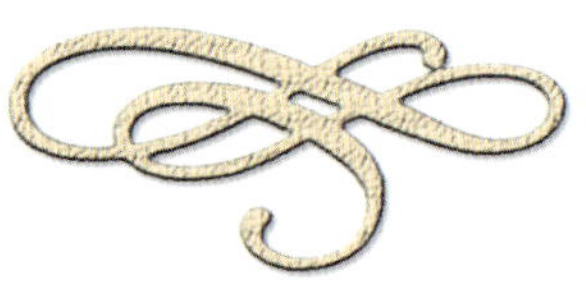

HOME
IS WHERE
YOUR
ART
IS

Opening New Doors

Dorsey McHugh

When I was a child, I was not encouraged to think of my own success. It was considered prideful to have ambition. But, since I did not know I was an artist until I was 40 years old, I had plenty of time to take myself more seriously. Before art came along, I thought little about color. Painting is primarily about light. We paint light and its relationship with objects.

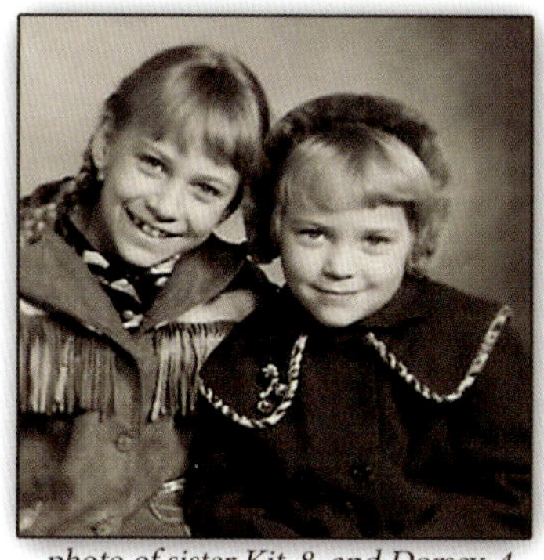

photo of sister Kit, 8 and Dorsey, 4

Early in my life, I began having a recurring dream of finding myself in a hallway located in the center of my inner house with ten or more closed doors before me. Each time, I found myself there, I tried to open every door unsuccessfully. They were always locked, until the last time I was there. One door opened and I was allowed into a whole new wing of my building. It was full of sunshine and color and secret drawers and a little garden for tea and conversations. This dream was pointing me in the direction of art. Once I began my art journey I no longer had this dream. Every moment with art has been full of meaning. Full of satisfaction. Full of adventure.

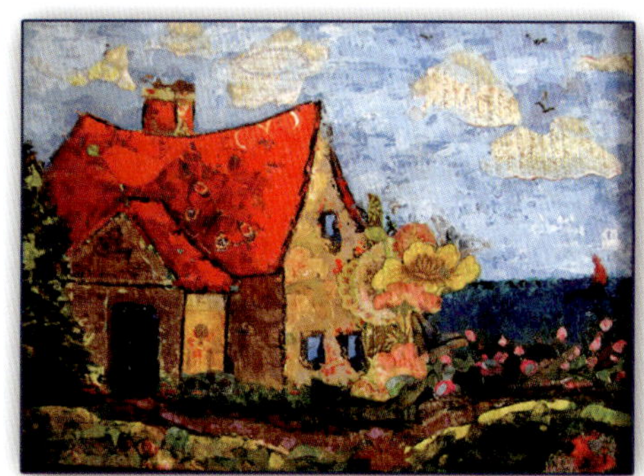

acrylic on board, FantaSea, Joanne

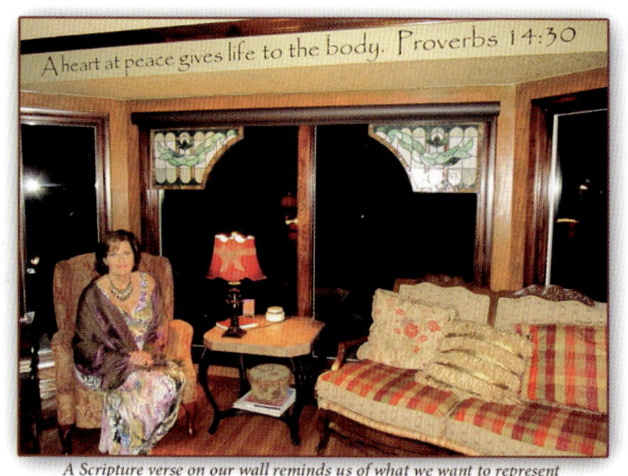

A Scripture verse on our wall reminds us of what we want to represent

In a March, 2013 issue of O Magazine, Oprah writes about her picture perfect home. She had a couple friends tell her the lavish mansion was beautiful but didn't authentically reflect Oprah and what she loves and feels. She talks about when she quit the daily Oprah show she no longer felt she was a visitor in her home. As she began to settle in full-time, she noticed little things... *"like the fact that my living room was not designed for living. There was no place to put your feet up and hang out."* She relates something her designer friend, Rose Tarlow told her, "This house has nothing to do with you." So she is on a quest to let her sense of self show through her lovely home. *(March 2013, O, The Oprah Magazine, pg 136)* Your home and office can reflect your personality, your memories, the important things and people in your life. A sense of who you are; what you love and what gives you peace.

Dorsey McHugh Our environment is important. It is where we hope to be most authentic. Our home is a mirror of who we are or want to be. As you begin your creative journey you will want to have your surroundings be a better reflection of who you are.

Create A Sense Of Peace

A heart at peace gives life to the body. Proverbs 14:30

Sight

De-clutter! Clutter gives the appearance of chaos and upheaval. Light the candles. They aren't just for company. Grace your table with fresh flowers. Grow them or buy them. Decorate with happy splashes of color and examples of what you want your life to SAY. Open the curtains and let the outside come in! CREATE LIGHT!

Sound

Play soft music or the sounds of nature CDs softly in the background. Lull your children to sleep with classical music softly playing in their CD player. Limit TV viewing to a minimum. Do NOT place a TV in the child's bedroom. Use indoor voices. No yelling allowed inside the home. No iPods or Radios when riding in the car. Encourage sharing verbally.

Touch

Have the home family-friendly, inviting interaction. Don't save the good china or the family silver just for guests. Use them often. Let your family & friends know they are important enough to use the BEST. Buy soft sheets, blankets and throws that invite snuggling and cozy spots. Use texture that invites and comforts.

Taste

Bake/cook with your family. Some of the best conversations and sharing is done by cooking together. The food can set the mood! Have tea parties often. A good time to teach manners and have an intimate moment.

Smell

The smells from a kitchen oven create amazing memories. Bake cookies or home-made bread just before the kids come in from school. They will associate that smell with HOME! Use scented candles and potpourri liberally. Bring in fresh flowers from your yard. Splash on your favorite perfume.

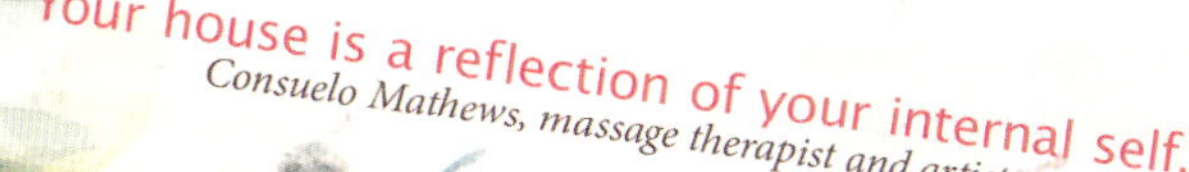

Your house is a reflection of your internal self.

Consuelo Mathews, massage therapist and artist

Awaken Your Senses

1. Have you had any recurring dreams that might be suggesting transformation?

2. Does your home reflect what you want it to? Is it a realistic representation of you?

3. Can you think of ways to make your environment more peaceful and stress-free?

Planting Rocks

When I was in fourth grade, my mother was a student in college. When she took geology, I would go with her on rock hunting trips and became an avid rock-hound. *(At one point in high school I belonged to a lithic and lapidary society. Look it up!)* We lived in a row of four very small square houses called the Steel Crafts. Looked like big steel boxes. They were drab grey. The ground around them was brown. Not much beauty in those Steel Crafts. And my soul craved beauty even then.

A neighbor moved in. Alma was into making rock gardens. She was serious about her rock gardens. *Real serious.* One day I went to visit her and she was baking poop. Yep, you heard that right. In her oven was some kind of animal poop....can't remember if it was cow, horse or chicken. She was baking it to sterilize it for her garden. I didn't want to ask what she might be baking next. But I was intrigued. I watched Alma turn her drab brown clump of back yard into a spot of beauty with her rocks, wild flowers and artistic touch. It fascinated me.

At nine years old I learned the beauty of "planting rocks". There was a neighboring wooded area not far from the Steel Crafts with a stand of trees sheltering a little "island" that seemed to me like a fairy island of moss and fern. A delight to a young child's imagination. I would often go there just to be alone and imagine fairies were lighting on the plants and spreading good cheer.
It was there I gathered wild plants, moss, fern and rocks to bring

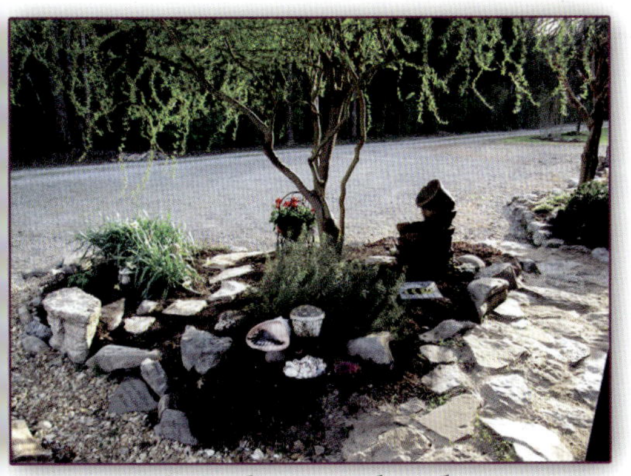

to our back yard and create an area of beauty. I found a love for rock gardens, rock walls and rock water features. God's beauty is so evident everywhere if you have eyes to see. Most people look at a big overlay of rock in their yard and want to cover it or dig it out. But consider how that rock could become a focus of beauty. This is a picture of my Faerie Garden with curly willow tree I grew from a twig, rocks Daniel picked up on our property for the pathway, little flower pot fountain, a conch shell we brought from Belize and little faeries and toadstools interspersed among the flowers.

The Rocks Speak

We probably have half-a-dozen or so rock-walled flower beds and rock gardens on our nine acres and a gorgeous rock water feature built by one of the most creative landscapers we have ever run into. Terry Wakefield *(Earth Adjustments, Goodlettsville, TN)* has built many of the habitats for the Nashville Zoo. When we first

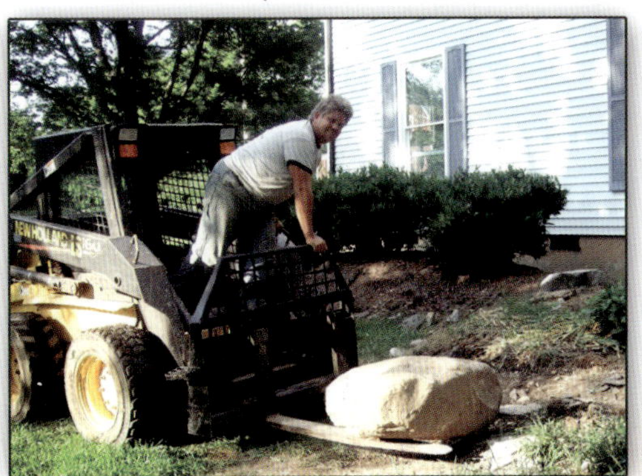

talked to him about building a water feature, he walked around and squinted up his pale blue eyes and talked about rocks like they had their own personality. He said he could do it and he handed Daniel a "contract" that simply said, *"I don't know what it will look like but it will be spectacular! The Millers will like it or they don't pay for it!"* We loved his style! We had talked to several other landscapers who drew up architectural, detailed renderings of what they could do but the lack of imagination bothered us. When Terry said he created as he brought in the rocks and they "spoke" to him we knew he understood our language. He and his helpers, Scooby and Angel *(don't you love their names?)*, created a miracle in our front yard. We loved watching them each day and when it was finished we all stood in awe as Terry turned on the pump and water started to pour perfectly over the top and flow exactly as he wanted without EVER having tried it in advance. I still marvel at his ability to see what the finished creation would do before he ever put water in. This guy isn't a landscaper. He is an artist. And he transformed an ordinary yard into a paradise that we enjoy every day of the year.

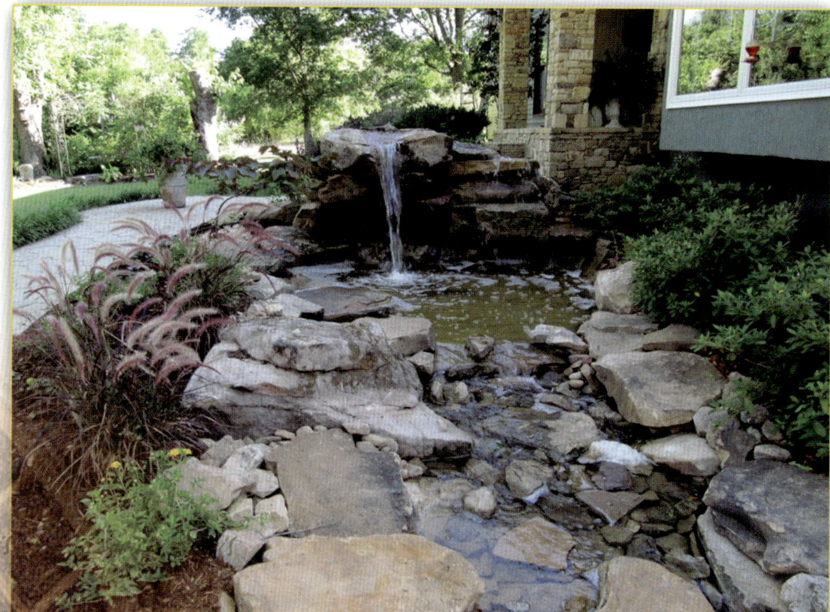

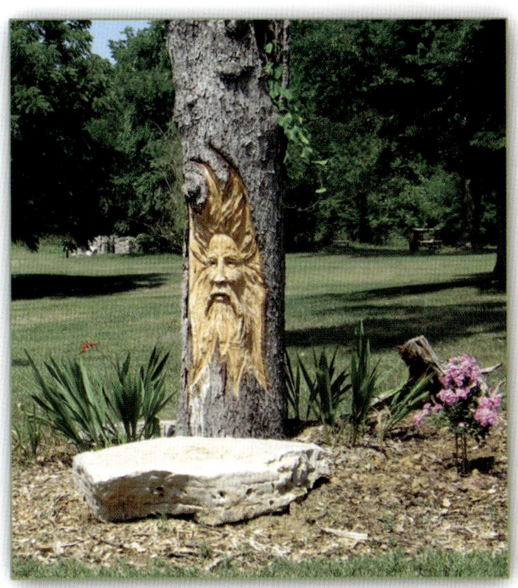

Carvings For Christ

We found another Terry who helped to make our Haven of Peace the beauti ful sanctuary we live in. We had a big old maple tree that died in our front yard. We hated to just cut it down and deal with an unsightly tree stump.

One day Daniel was in a shop to get his mower blade sharpened and got an idea. Why not carve something on that tree trunk that would make it a piece of art? He asked the shop owner if he knew of anyone who did tree carving. He was told of a wood carver but didn't know if she would carve a tree. Daniel got the number for Terry Brasher *(www.carvingsforchrist.com)* and called her. Terry came out and looked at the dead tree, walked around much as Terry Wakefield had and looked as if she was "hearing" the tree talk to her. Finally she told us she had done a lot of wood carving in her day but had never tackled a standing tree,

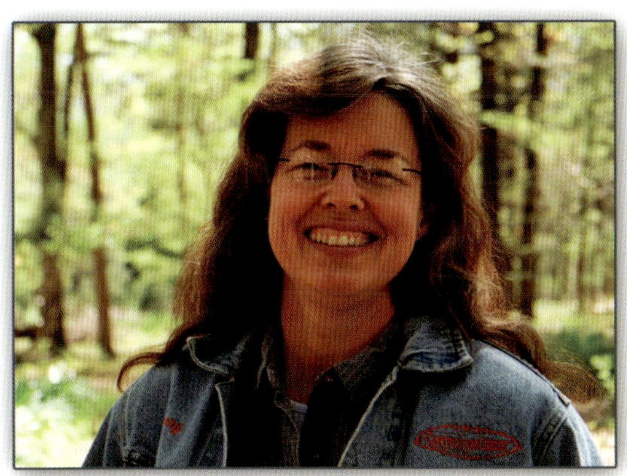

however, she was willing to try. We figured the only thing we had to lose was an already dead tree so we let her bring out her chain saw, her chisels and hammer and begin to carve what became Moses and Aaron in our Wisdom Garden. (there is another face on the back of the tree).

A few years later we had a beautiful stately cedar tree die next to the Sanctuary. We hated to chop it down. So Daniel called Terry again. He told her he thought maybe an eagle was waiting to be released in that old tree and she took the bait. She walked around that dead tree for probably thirty minutes just thinking, listening and seeing. Soon she looked at Dan with a gleam in her eye and said, *"I think you are right!"* Here is a photo of Terry working on Aristotle (as he was named). The wings are the first two branches of that beautiful old tree. The color of the eagle is a deep red that is the natural cedar coloring and no paint. It is a beautiful sculpture that graces the front of the Sanctuary you saw earlier in the book.

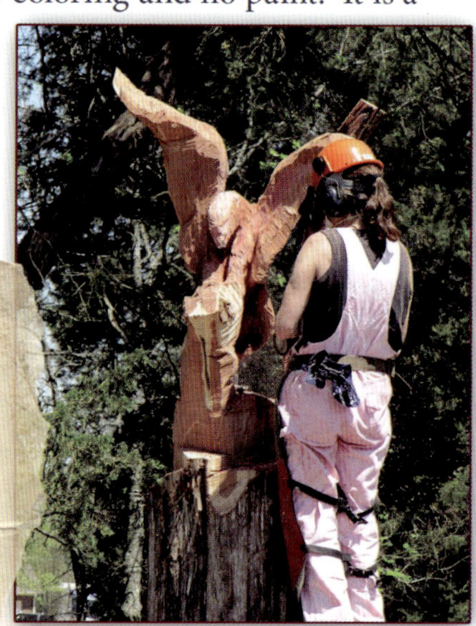

I believe that God blesses us with gifts and talents so that we might share them with others; not keep them to ourselves.
Terry Brasher, woodcarver

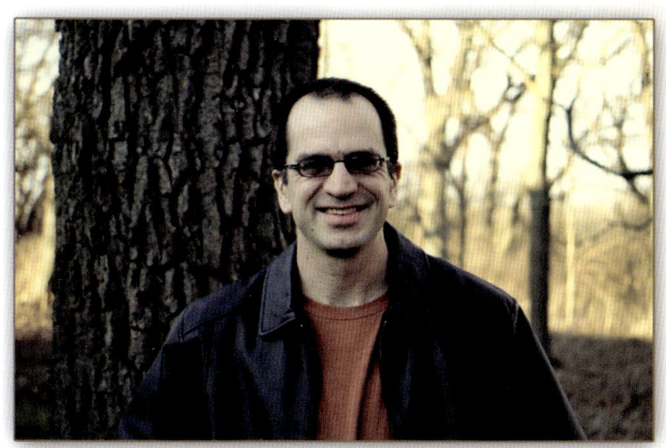

Creative Pruning

Jim Anderson is creative in his approach to landscaping. He challenged our thinking about how to incorporate beauty into our Haven of Peace. He calls himself an Aesthetic Pruner. Not a landscaper or a gardener. An Aesthetic Pruner. Wow! How creative is that? Jim walked with us around our property while "*interviewing*" us about what we wanted to convey with our landscaping. He showed us ways to create points of interest, stopping points and entrances and also helped to evaluate what needs to be pruned and removed in wooded areas to make them look more orderly and developed while remaining natural. He gave us a detailed evaluation with color photos of trees and plants he suggested were indigenous to our area of Tennessee. What a creative niche! We were thrilled with his input and have already started to implement some of his suggestions. Jim is a certified arborist from Illinois. Visit his website at *www.jimanderson.net*

Creative people do not simply think in words,
but use all of their senses, their entire bodies in the process.
They find sense cues that stimulate their thoughts on many levels—whether it be
the smell of something strong, or the tactile feel of a rubber ball...they are more
open to alternative ways of thinking, creating, and sensing the world.
...Stimulating your brain and senses from all directions will help unlock
your natural creativity and help revive your original mind.

*Robert Greene, **Mastery,** 2012 by Penguin Group, Vikin*

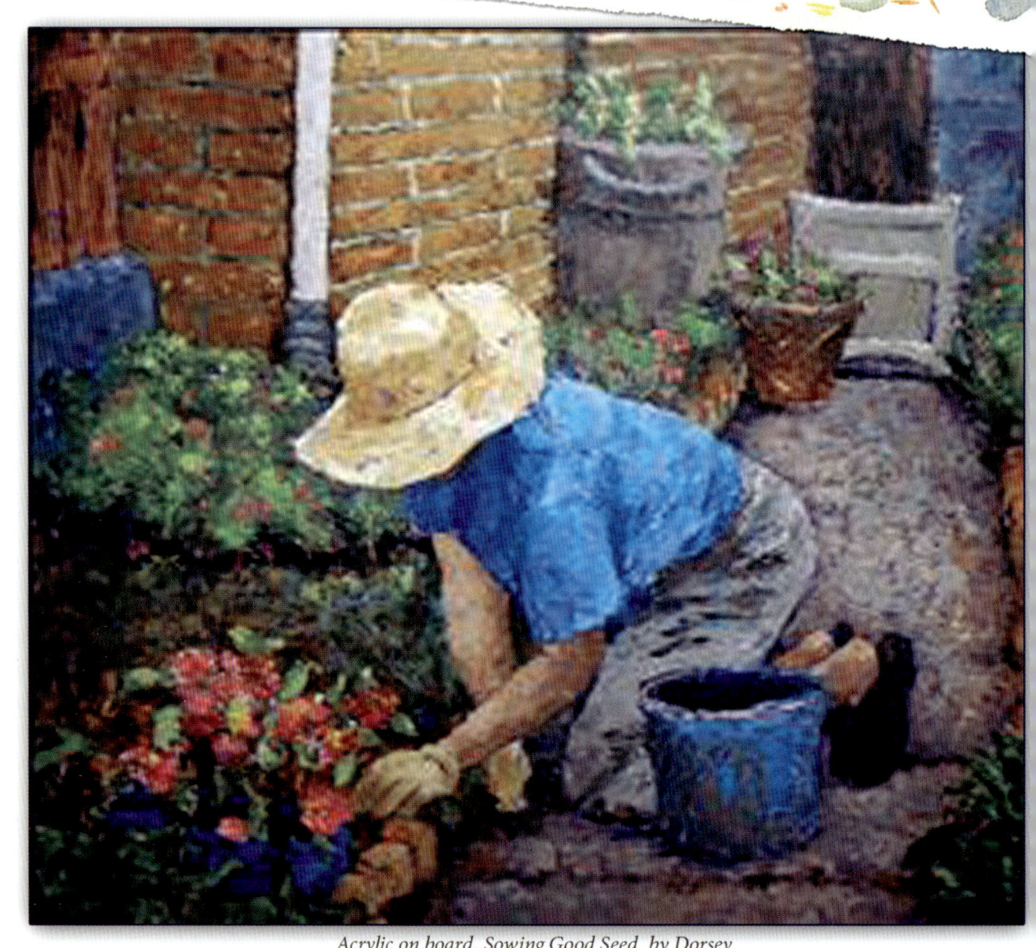

Acrylic on board, Sowing Good Seed by Dorsey
This painting is of a gardener I photographed in Anacostia, Washington DC.

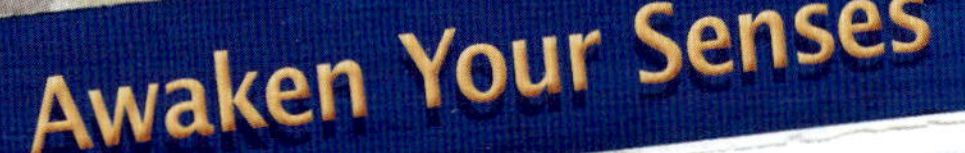

Awaken Your Senses

1. What do you see around your property you could turn into something of beauty & art?

2. Can you plant flowers or a garden? Can you put flowerboxes in your windows or pots on your balcony?

3. Can you find other ways to display art in & around the yard or deck? (Flags, sculptures, driftwood, string lights, candles, or water features)

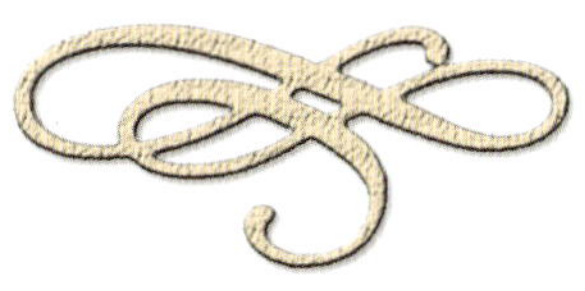

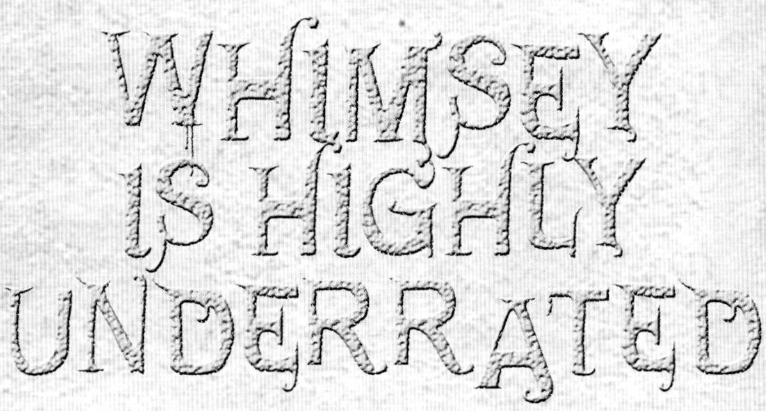

Ok, I can't take credit for this title. It came from my son, Jared Angaza's website on his "about" page. He says, and I quote....

"Whimsey is highly underrated and too rarely experienced. I intend to bring more of it into the world." Pretty good, huh?

He wrote me this: *'I'm always honored when you want to use my writing. I learned much of what I know from you".* Gotta love that kid!

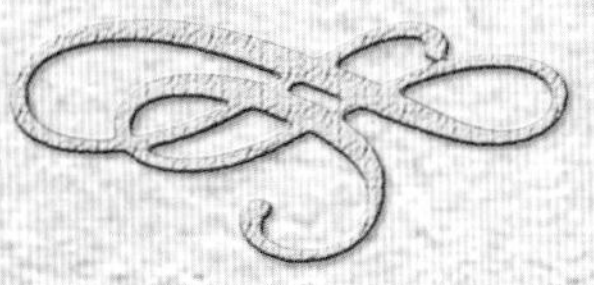

Faith, Love And Pixie Dust

While watching Disney's **Tinker Bell** movie with our grandkids, I got caught up in the quote, *"All you need is a little bit of faith, love and pixie dust."* Isn't that true, really? You understand our need for faith and love. When, along the road of life, did you hand over your imagination to the coat check and leave it behind? Did you even notice? Did you miss it? I hope you will get passionate about reviving that sense of excitement, wonder and mystery you had back in the days you first learned about Peter Pan, Tinker Bell and pixie dust!

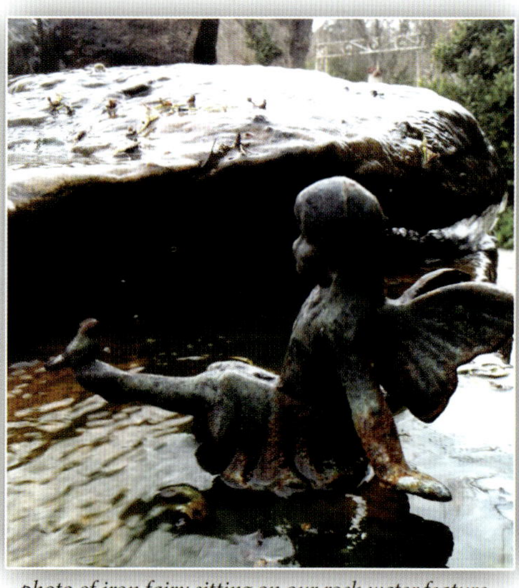

photo of iron fairy sitting on our rock water feature

If you talk to a roomful of 5-year olds they will all eagerly tell you they are creative…they can draw, they can paint, they can write, they can sing, they can build! Yet you ask those same children twenty or thirty years later if they are creative and only a handful will admit to it. Just the asking embarrasses them. Like it's a sin to admit you have a right brain! But we all do.

Tell me and I forget,
teach me and I may remember
involve me and I learn.
Benjamin Franklin (1709-1790)

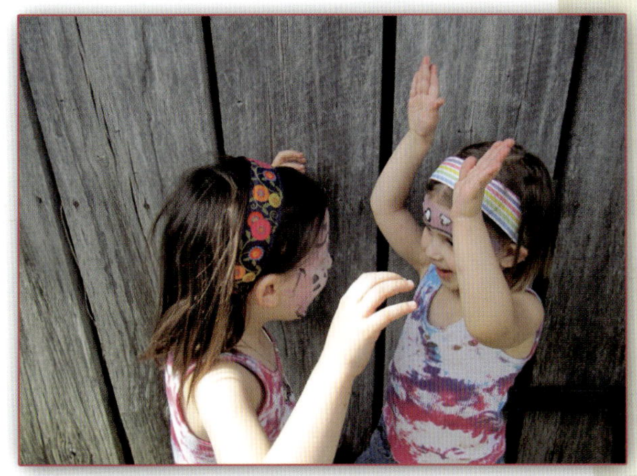

...when you are imagining, you might as well imagine something worthwhile.
L.M. Montgomery (1874-1942), author, ***Anne of Green Gables***

We can learn so much by watching a child. When she is engaged in play, work or learning, she is totally in the moment. She is not worrying about what she is going to do when she has to get ready for dinner or bedtime. She is not thinking about how she can be a better friend to her playmate. She is totally engaged in what she is doing and in her mind she is having a good time at it. She is able to tune out other sound and sight and truly listen and see what is going on right in front of her because she has not yet learned she must do for others, be for others, take care of others, control her environment, etc. A child instinctually has the capacity to concentrate in a way most adults have forgotten. It comes naturally and produces all kinds of benefit in imagination and learning capacity that *forced* concentration (as in school or sometimes a job) can squelch.

When you believe in fairies, angels and pixies it makes God bigger. It doesn't eliminate Him!
Melanie Jackson, artist

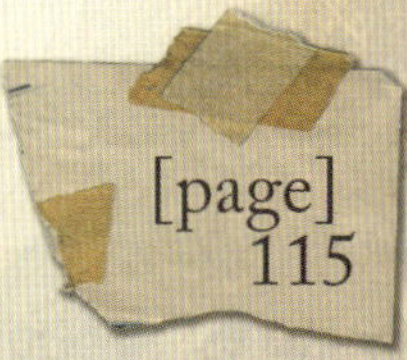

Being Creative Means

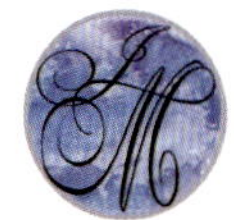

We Come Up:
~with more exciting ways to do things!
~to experience life!
~to be better problem solvers!

Being creative helps us make a lovelier home, create harmony in the workplace, solve crimes, romance a lover, put together a photo album, fix a gourmet meal. There are myriad ways in which we can be creative. We all have it in us and we can make our right brain stronger and more active. But it does require work and exploration…..and perhaps a bit of pixie dust!

Imagination is more important than knowledge.
For knowledge is limited to all we now know and understand,
while imagination embraces the entire world,
and all there ever will be to know and understand.
Albert Einstein, (1879-1955) German Physicist

If you Google "Is Everyone Creative?" you will find a zillion articles, speeches and books on the subject. Dorsey and I firmly believe we are all born creative. Yes, some are more right brained, more gifted in their creative expression, but their share doesn't deplete the pot. Being creative doesn't just mean we paint, sculpt, draw or write. It means we use our imaginations to come up with more exciting ways to DO things.

We do not need magic to change the world;
we carry all the power we need inside ourselves already:
we have the power to imagine better.
J.K. Rowling, author, ***Harry Potter*** *series*

Why is tapping into your right brain important? Many people are content to just *be*. They don't feel the need to take an art class or read a book or journal or exercise that part of the brain they have left dormant through the years. We hope your desire to see your world differently is so strong you will go searching for rainbows with your sunglasses on. You are sure to find them.

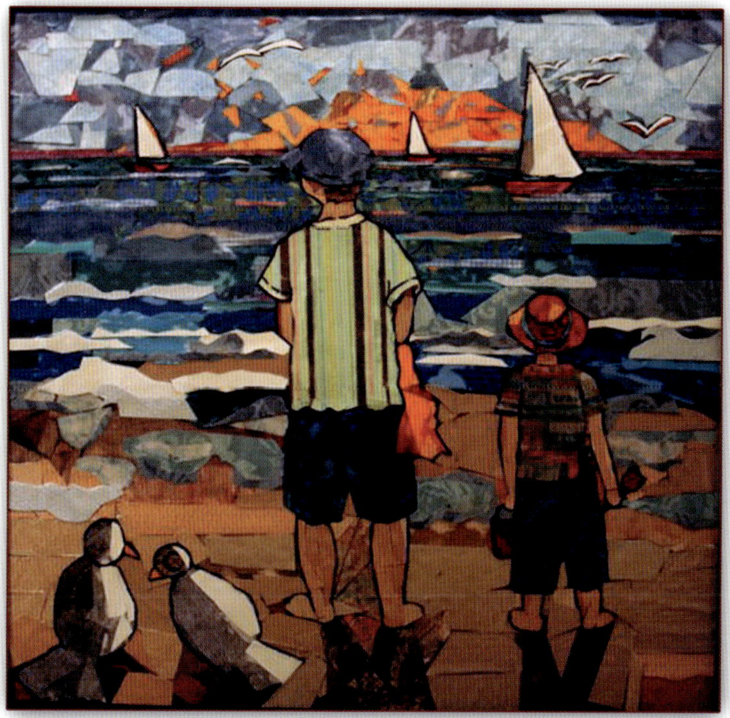

Paper on board, "Where I Want To Be" by Dorsey

Adding imagination to our learning can put wings on our possibilities.

Dan Miller, speaker and author,

Wisdom Meets Passion, 48 Days To the Work You Love

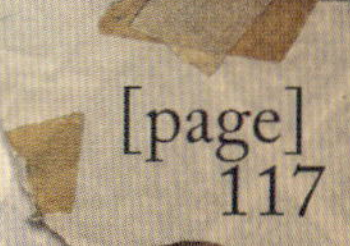

Don't Be A Half-Brain

You may wonder what the right brain does. One idea is that it assesses the world without logic. Hard for a lot of people to do. Now, logically most of us don't really think there are fairies, unicorns, mermaids, Santa Claus, The Easter Bunny and The Tooth Fairy. Yet we love to read stories to our children about these concepts and spark their imaginations. Including these concepts in their lives brings them a sense of awe, mystery and adventure.

> It's delightful when your imaginations come true, isn't it?
> *L.M. Montgomery,* ***Anne of Green Gables***

Daniel and I had some pretty interesting discussions about whether or not we would allow Santa Claus to infiltrate our Christian home our first Christmas together. Having grown up in a strict conservative Mennonite home, Daniel never experienced the wonder of Santa gifts, bright decorations and other "worldly" aspects of my more pagan upbringing. I argued that I never saw a conflict in engaging my imagination and I wanted to weave things of mystery, myth and fantasy into the tapestry of our children's lives. Those parts of my life were always a bonus. It added richness beyond just fact and reality.

> Everything you can imagine is real.
> *Pablo Picasso (1881-1973), Spanish painter, sculptor*

Today, my grandchildren and I walk through a woods and see fairy moss. Sometimes we bring it home and place it in my Faerie Garden. It helps me go into their world and it makes my own world richer. When do we lose that desire? And, more importantly, why?

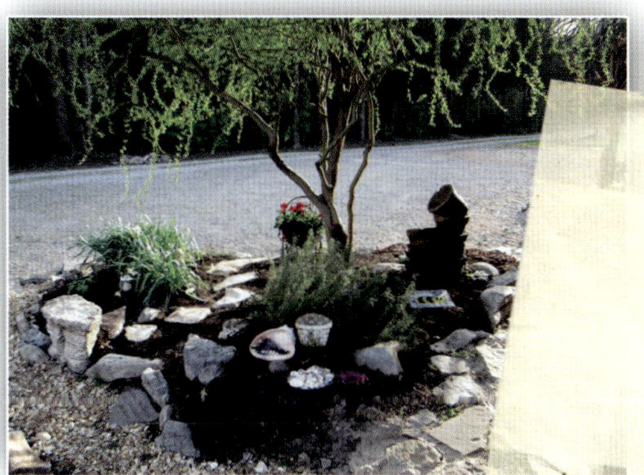

photo of Joanne's Faerie Garden

We've all forgotten how to PLAY! We grow up so fast and we forget to nourish our inner child. We need to cheer up that little person.

Dorsey

Recently a remark I made prompted a discussion with a friend about my perspective on fairies. She was obviously questioning my sanity and just rolled her eyes at me. Because she loves and respects me, I'm sure she figures I'll come to my senses at some point. I hope I don't. I hope I never grow up in some areas. And I suspect my friend, a very intelligent and well educated wife and mother, will embrace fairies when she has grandchildren who take her for walks through fairy moss.

When the first baby laughed for the first time, his laugh broke into a million pieces, and they all went skipping about. That was the beginning of fairies.

J. M. Barrie (1860-1937), From the 1902 novel, ***The Little White Bird****, author of Peter Pan*

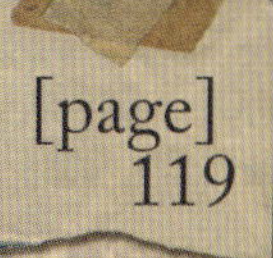

I adore **Anne of Green Gables** by Lucy Maud Montgomery. If you haven't watched the series or read the books, you have missed out on a wonderful tale. Buy them for your children or grandchildren and sit with them and watch or read it together. There are so many amazing quotations and perspectives on life. Anne eloquently articulates her world with such passion and awe you can't help but love her. Below is one of my favorite lines from this story, and one I adhere to:

"....Isn't it splendid to think of all the things there are
to find out about? It just makes me feel glad to be alive
—it's such an interesting world.
It wouldn't be half so interesting if
we knew all about everything , would it?
There'd be no scope for the imagination, then, would there?"

Those areas that encompass my imagination, my love of fantasy and mystery in life encompass the same part of me that embraces faith in a Creator I can't see or feel or smell or hear except through the very creations placed before me in my life every single day. I want to have a chance to better define, better enhance my ability to experience my Creator in a way that shouts, *"WOW! LOOK AT THAT AMAZING RAINBOW!"*

When I watch my granddaughters revealing their dreams
with paint and canvas, dressing in magical dresses,
talking to the goats, or catching tiny frogs in our pond,
I know they are discovering personal passions
that will lead to an exciting and purposeful future.

Dan Miller, ***Wisdom Meets Passion***

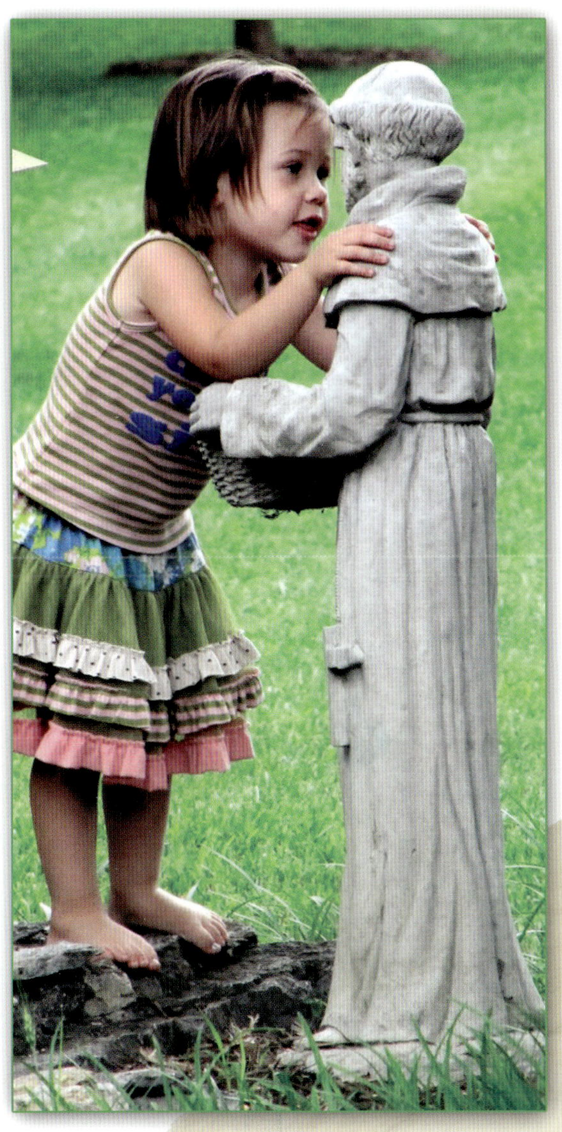

When my granddaughter, Clara, was three years old, she would go up to any statue and talk quietly, embrace and kiss it. She always said she was talking to Jesus.

Didn't matter if it was a cowboy statue or a monk (as in this photo), to her it was Jesus. Who were we to tell her differently? To her it was very real and very serious stuff. That unabashed certainty and faith is enviable.

Arguably,
no artist grows up:
If he sheds the perceptions
of childhood, he ceases being
an artist.
Ned Rorem, Pulitzer prize-winning American composer and author

Dorsey McHugh

Have you ever had a really serious discussion with a child? Like you expect them to carry on an adult conversation and answer with unusual maturity? When my oldest granddaughter, Tess, was four years old she asked, *"Where was I before I was born?"* Surprised by her question, I answered, *"Wow! That's deep stuff, Tess."* To which she replied, *"Ohhhh.....I was in the deep stuff!"* Perfect!

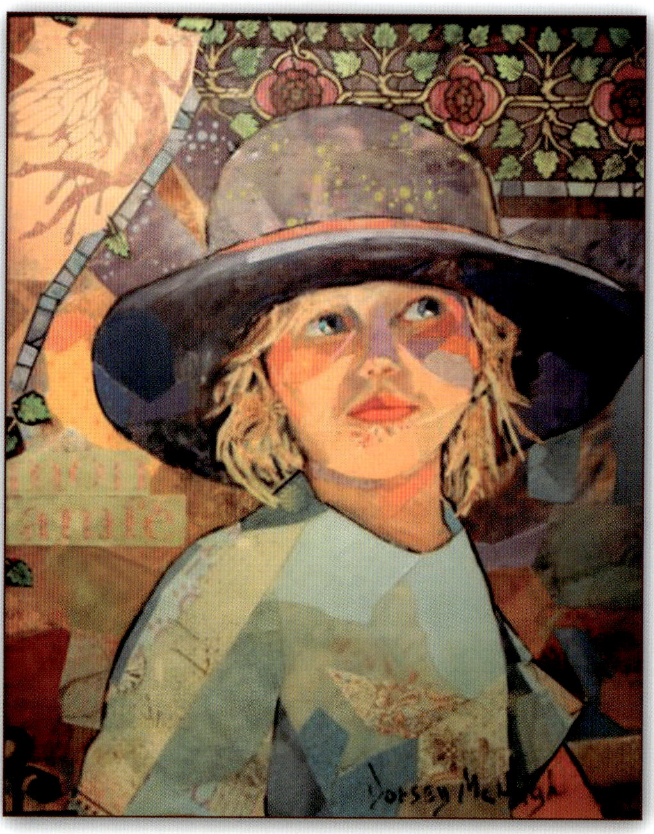

Just because you can't see something doesn't mean it's not there.
A line from Disney's ***Epic*** *movie (2013)*

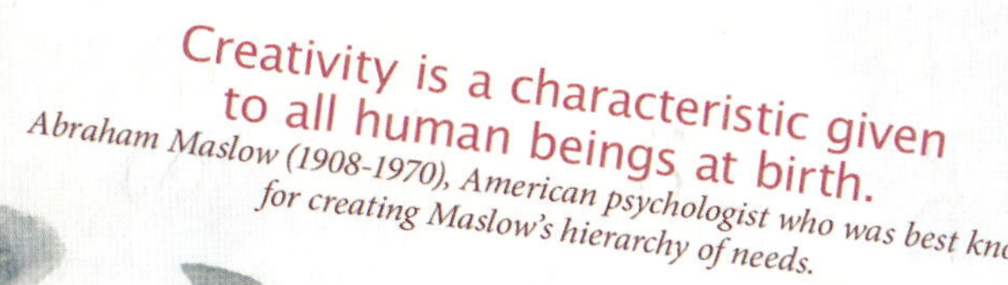

Creativity is a characteristic given to all human beings at birth.

Abraham Maslow (1908-1970), American psychologist who was best known for creating Maslow's hierarchy of needs.

Awaken Your Senses

1. How difficult is it for you to engage your imagination? Were you allowed to use your imagination as a child?

2. Can you take time to watch a child or group of children & learn from their spontaneity & creative play?

3. Can you be intentional about being in the moment when life is crowding in on you?

A Comparison Of Left-Brain And Right-Brain Characteristics*

Left-Brain

Using words and/or numbers to describe and define
Over-dependence on logic
Likes to read directions, follow step-by-step
Likes structure…thinks in an orderly sequence
Likes to make decisions based on fact and logic
Can rarely be hypnotized
Thinks in sequencing fashion
Good at math/algebra/spelling
Often needs quiet to read or study
Usually rational thinking and action
Prefers to read and write non-fiction
Loves the details of a story or project
Likes to finish a task before starting another
Likes an agenda...less flexible
More orderly and neat in appearance and in living/office quarters
Often doesn't trust feelings, gut reactions
Sees fewer options in solving problems
Likes to gather information
Relies more on the IQ
Leans towards functional and practical

Right-Brain

Likes variety in most things
Is more aware of his/her surroundings
More visual and tactile
Uses gestures more than words
Often doesn't like time constrictions/schedules
Has more difficulty with structure and discipline
Reads directions as a last resort
Seeing the whole picture without benefit of all the details is preferred modus operandi
Usually very flexible. Plans can change quickly and often
Loves color, light and texture so attire may be more creative and less "put together"
Relies more on gut feelings
Often more intuitive
Better at problem solving because he/she engages more than just the facts
Looks at less obvious options available
Better understands metaphors and nonverbal expression
Often understands humor better because he/she is not looking for logic behind the joke
Relies a lot on emotional cues (EQ); facial expression, intonation, body language
Leans towards flowery, flashy
Dressing is art

**Remember there are extremes in anything and a lot of variance in between. We think working towards more balance of the two hemispheres makes for increased ability to see things in better perspective, clarity and excitement! It gives you more brain-power!*

Dorsey describes below a beautiful word picture of her encounter with God in a day dream she had before she ever began to explore her creative self.

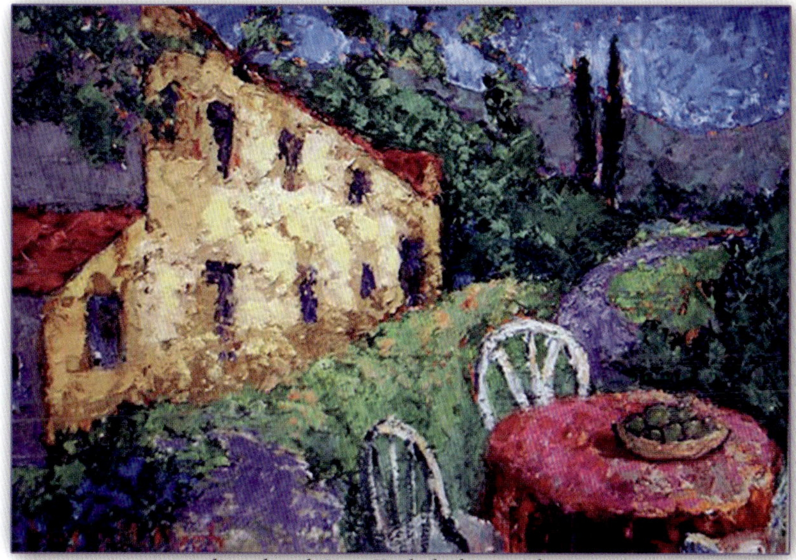

acrylic on board, Some Kind of Adventure, by Dorsey

God's Sun Room

Dorsey McHugh

Before I began to paint…before I even imagined I would paint, I worked as a waitress to help with our family income. During that time, I attended a little Bible study of a few women. As we began our weekly meeting with prayer I think I fell asleep because, much like **Alice in Wonderland**, I found myself in another place.

I was walking barefoot in a sunny garden. I could hear bees buzzing in the air; it was warm and peaceful, like an afternoon nap in a hammock would be. I approached a screened-in sun porch and strained my eyes to see inside. I could make out a person standing at an easel who motioned for me to enter. It was cool in the sunroom.

My eyes were still adjusting to the contrast of light, but my feet could feel the comforting pleasant coolness of the stone floor. I thought at the time that the stones felt as if they were alive. They were definitely rejoicing; sending their lovely song through the bottoms of my feet. As I began to see the Artist, I noticed that He was painting with sticks of color which were leaning upright in a basket beside His easel. The paint sticks and the canvas He was painting on were also alive. The paint and the canvas became one as they danced. The Painter's face was in shadow, being contrasted by the sun outside, and I could not see what He was painting, but I heard His voice inside me.

Then He spoke at length but I have never been able to bring into my conscious mind what He said. I listened closely and loved our conversation. I loved being in His sunroom with Him. Our moments together had a timeless quality. They were only this moment. Just being there was pleasure in its purest sense.

At some point, I felt myself being pulled back into my body. I did not want to come back. I wanted to stay there with Him. My heart was longing to stay in this world with Him. I wanted His reality to be my reality. He answered me in return with laughter and love in His voice as he spoke, ***"My reality IS your reality."***

Whimsey is highly underrated

I opened my eyes to what seemed only seconds later. My life had been altered. It was literally only a few weeks later a houseguest gifted me with a book by Betty Edwards, **Drawing on the Artist Within**. Another gate had been opened for me into this world of Creativity. It was the beginning of a whole new adventure.

"The Narnia books are a part of my inner furniture."
Dorsey

As I am typing Dorsey's story on the computer, I am listening to a piece from the soundtrack of **Narnia: The Lion, The Witch and the Wardrobe** and it is uncanny how reading Dorsey's story is enhanced by the music that just happens to be playing in the background. It makes the dream come to life and my mind's eye can see the Master Creator in a way that brings chills as Dorsey must have felt relating this dream in words. A beautiful symphony of words that reflects how God can speak to us in ways that demonstrates His role as the Creator of all.

Grug: "The rules. They kept us alive."
Eep: "That wasn't living. That was just not dying."
Line from Dreamworks movie, ***The Croods*** *(2013)*
Grug is the caveman father and Eep is the teen daughter.

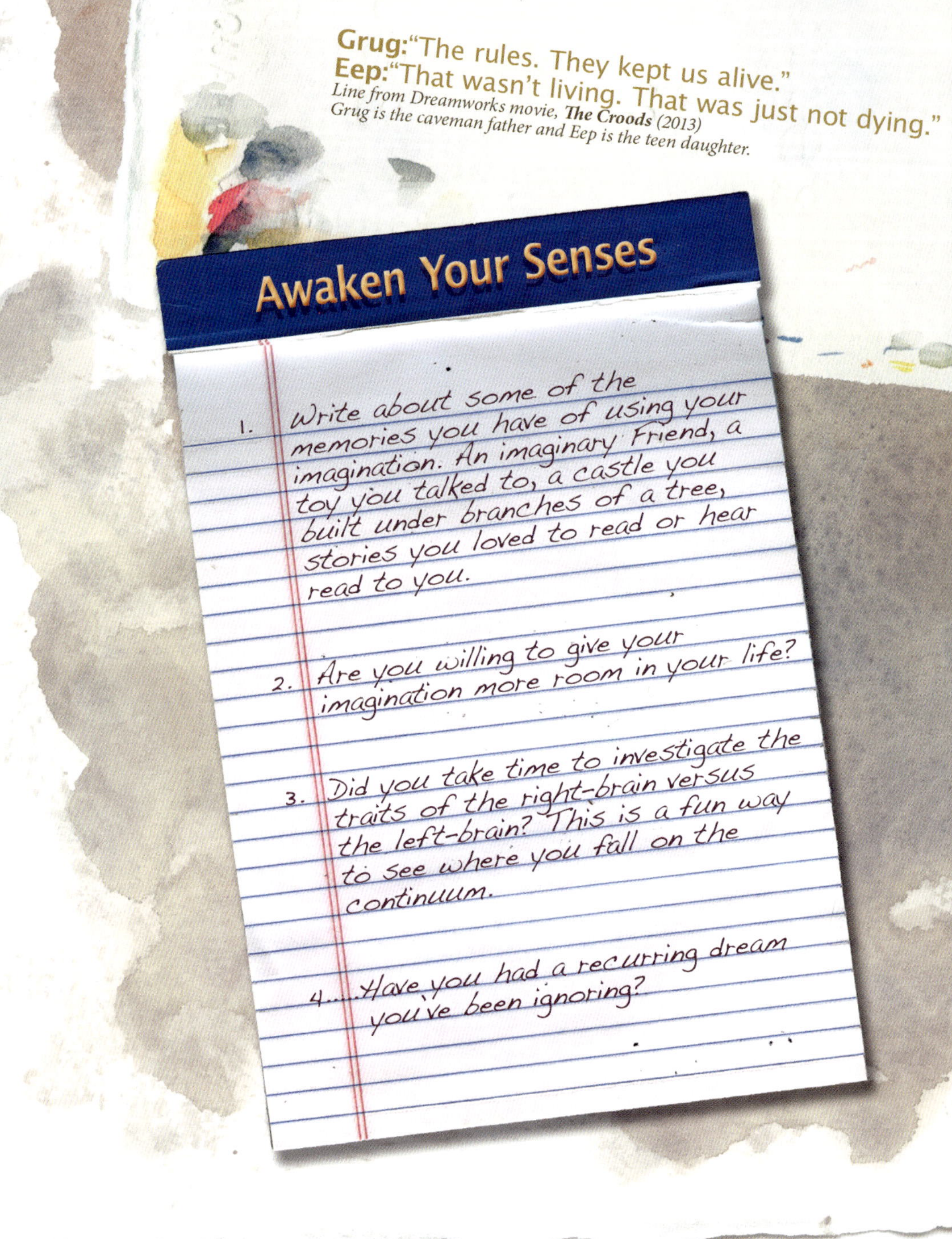

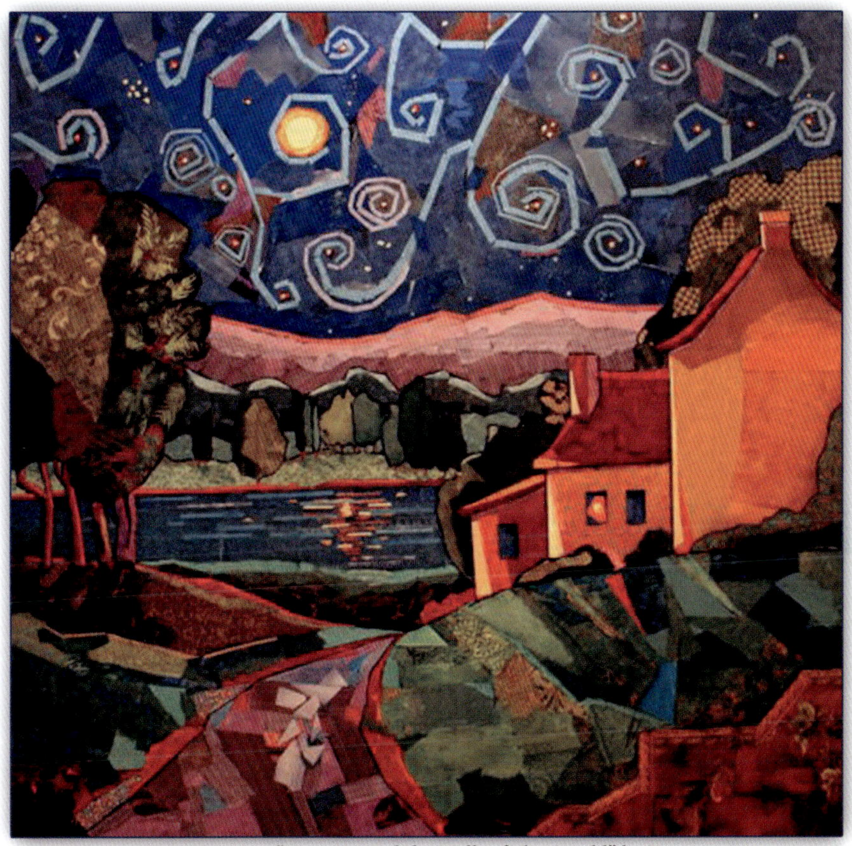

Paper Painting "Hope Beyond the Walls of This World" by Dorsey

Why Am I Not In My Right Brain?

Interestingly, often we are in our right-brain and don't even recognize it. But realistically, most of the time we are so busy figuring things out, taking care of business, lost in the details of our lives...

To engage the right brain is
to assess the world without logic.

Isn't that an amazing concept? *Not having to make everything logical, practical, productive and by the rules?* I took my grandkids to the theatre to see **The Croods**, an animated film about a family of cave people whose father told them daily, *"Never leave the cave. New is always bad. Never NOT be afraid!"* One day a free-spirited boy takes the family on a journey to great adventures in a quest to follow the light. His credo was far different from the others. He said, *"Change the rules so you can live."* By the end of the movie Grug, the father, regained his family's respect and admiration because he began to see the merit in changing his thinking; gaining new insight into what it means to *really live.*

Eep: "The Croods will make it because we changed all the rules. The rules that kept us in the dark. And because my Dad, who taught us anyone can change……From now on, we'll stay out here where we can follow the light."

Line from the Dreamworks movie, ***The Croods*** *(2013) Eep is the teen daughter.*

Dorsey McHugh

Usually, I tell my students to take the time and make the effort to find out what are the general rules of composition, color and technique, before they decide to break those rules. The rules of art are diving boards designed to assist in our jumping. There is no right or wrong in art. Even knowing the rules enables one to break them successfully. That is how we discover new things and it is how we will grow ... in art as in life.

Rules are temporary guidelines for people who have yet to gain the wisdom to make the right decision, without the need for rules.

Caleb Daniel Miller, Joanne's grandson, age 18, graphic artist, Woodland Park, CO

Kids have little difficulty in assessing the world without logic. They do it all the time. That's why they can make forts out of a copse of trees and shrub or wear their Halloween costume for everyday attire.....all year long! Think how fun it would be to find a career that would embrace your creative nature.

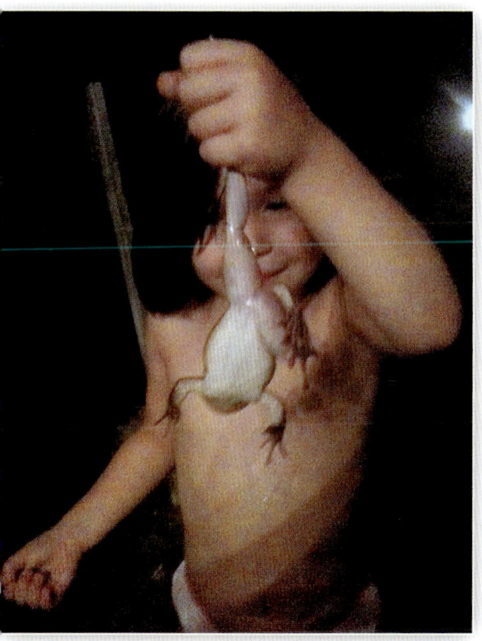

Clara, age 5, pulling frogs from the water to examine them

Our daughter, Ashley has no problem going into the magical world of imagination and fantasy with her little girls:

"In conversing with my 5-year-old, we got on the subject of God, and exactly what 'our Creator' means. With her love of animals and fascination with evolution, she had a hard time grasping that not everyone believes we are all interconnected. When I asked her how God made us, she said, 'God painted a beautiful picture full of color and all the things in the whole universe. Then the fairies *(they are real, Mommy - I've seen them!)* ***took God's painting and made it come to life!'"***
Don't you wish you had such faith and imagination?

Some things you see with your eyes;
others you see with your heart.

A line from the movie, ***Land Before Time****, Disney*

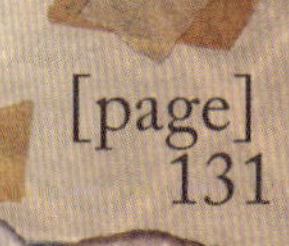

Cathy

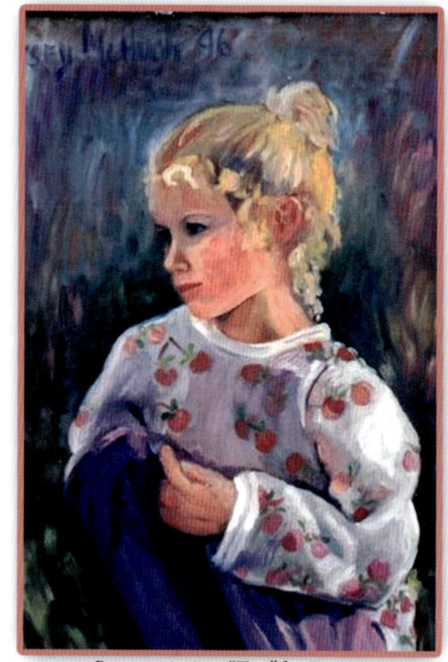

Paper painting, "Tess" by Dorsey

Jared, our middle child, must have been about four years old when he started talking about his imaginary friend, Cathy, and including her in his games and activities. She was very real for Jared. He usually had me set a place at the table for Cathy and, on occasion, even for her parents. I can remember times when Jared would tell me he was sad because Cathy was ill. I would dutifully check with him now and then to ask if she was feeling better.

Interestingly, the neighborhood children, many of them older than Jared, readily accepted Cathy in their games and never made fun of him for being fanciful. They would knock on the door and ask if Jared and Cathy could come out to play. I think everyone loved Jared's imagination and some, perhaps, envied his ability to create such fun escapes from reality. In fact the neighbor girls crocheted earrings and necklaces, bracelets and belts that Jared proudly wore to school, but that's another story. To say Jared was (is) very creative is probably a gross understatement. He set up permanent residence in his right brain.

Whimsey is highly underrated

So one day, when Jared was about four years old, we got a call from a nearby food mart. Not sure how they knew to get hold of us but the clerk told us that Jared was there by himself. As any good parent would do, we panicked and raced over to rescue him. Jared had gone down a long path through the adjoining cornfield and across a very busy highway to get to this store. He had gone there before with his older brother but was told NEVER to go by himself. We weren't sure whether to be elated that he was safe or to tear into him for being disobedient. As I recall, we did a little of both. But here was the problem. When we discussed that he had been told explicitly not to go there alone he looked at us in all seriousness and said, *"But I WASN'T alone! Cathy was with me the whole time!"* Oh, boy! Where do you go with that? Things like this are not covered in parenting manuals.

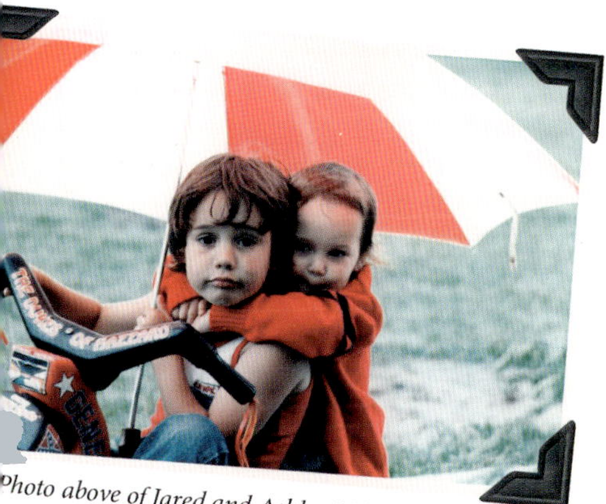

Photo above of Jared and Ashley Miller as kids

Cathy got Jared into trouble on other occasions. One vividly stands out in our family memories. We had been saving our money for a trip to Opryland in Nashville, about an hour away from where we lived in Kentucky. We had hyped up this big event with all three children and, in truth, Daniel and I were just as excited as they were. We had worked hard to find the time and money to take a day off just for fun.

It was a beautiful day and we were all piled into the van waiting for Daniel to come out and hop in the driver's seat. We waited and waited. Finally I went inside to find him searching frantically for the money he had in a bundle...about $400 as I recall...on the dresser. He said he looked all over and couldn't locate it. I helped him search pockets and behind the dresser, under the bed.....all the usual places. No money.

We were dumbfounded. We went out to the car and asked the kids if they had seen it. No one had. All of them said no. So Daniel and I scratched our heads and tried to imagine how we were going to come up with another $400 to take us to the long-awaited trip to Opryland.

As we pondered beside the van, I had a rise in my blood pressure as I popped my head in and asked our child, *"Jared, does Cathy know where the money is?"*
"Oh, yeah, Mommy. Cathy knows where it is. She hid it in a safe place."

"Really?" I said, gritting my teeth and trying hard not to strangle him, *"Can you show me where Cathy hid it?"* So Jared obligingly took us into the house, into his bedroom, into his closet and picked up a brown cowboy boot where he proceeded to pull out $400 in cash!

Whimsey is highly underrated

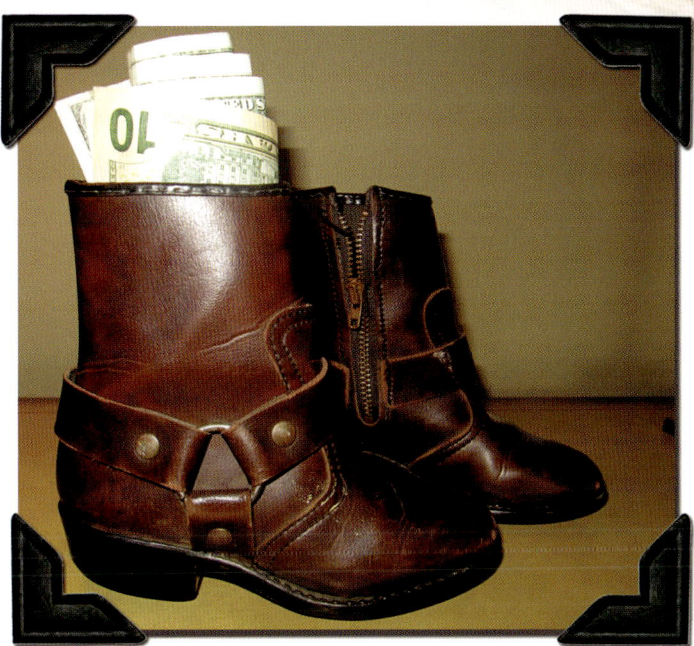

photo of those very boots!

Ok, obviously Jared is still alive which is testament to the loving parents we were to embrace such a vivid imagination. Trust me on this one. We weren't always feeling very magnanimous! Perhaps this is one example of an imagination gone wild!

I live in a world full of dreams,
faith and whimsy,
where anything is possible
if you believe.
Jared Miller Angaza, ***Wisdom Meets Passion***

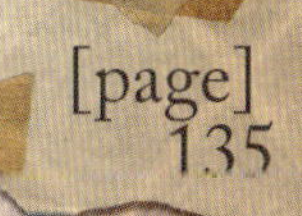

In Jared's words:

"I remember Cathy from the beginning....like you and Dad. She was always with me. I remember talking with her late at night. I never slept well...I struggled with my dreams. Cathy walked me through a lot of stuff...or at least consoled me during the process. When I was awake, she would talk with me so I would forget to be scared from my dreams. She would put her hand on my forehead while I closed my eyes, to comfort me and help me sleep. Sometimes I would awaken to find that it was you.

She was my guardian angel and my best friend. She looked after me. She encouraged me to explore and gave me courage. She taught me to appreciate the beauty of gray in a black and white world...to explore the mysterious and the unknown. You saw this play out in my long walks (for my age) to the food store and the battles with alligators and my belief that perhaps I could fly off the roof if only my cape were designed properly. (yes, I did make him a cape)

Cathy was older than I ...maybe in her 20s or early 30s. Interestingly, I don't remember her voice or even remember her speaking, but communication was there, stronger than words. I remember her showing me things, like a new cave, or a cool room in an abandoned house I was exploring or a new trail through the corn fields. I remember seeing that alligator too. Just as real as the ones I see here in Africa. I remember walking with her, holding her hand as we walked down the street. I felt very secure with her.

I don't remember when or how she drifted from the forefront of my mind to the back. She's never really stopped being a part of my life. I believe she morphed into my memories of SaraLisa and I still talk to her, only now it is SaraLisa who is pictured in my mind. There were times, especially during my difficult years where I was not in tune with her, but she's always been there in some form and still lives through my conversations with SaraLisa.

And I thank you and Dad for allowing me to have her in my life. She's part of who I am somehow and influences how I respond to life."

Note: Jared is now in his mid-thirties and living with his family in Kenya, Africa. He changed his last name legally in 2012 to Angaza, a Swahili word meaning instrument of light. Life has to have meaning for Jared and so did his name. He asked our blessing before making this change and Daniel said, *"I hope I have a more important legacy to leave behind than my name. Go for it!"*

SaraLisa Rae Miller (1974-2000) is Jared's first cousin and dear to his heart. Her death at age 26 was a devastating blow to Jared and the whole Miller family. It is not at all surprising Jared still has conversations with her. This can be a healthy healing process.

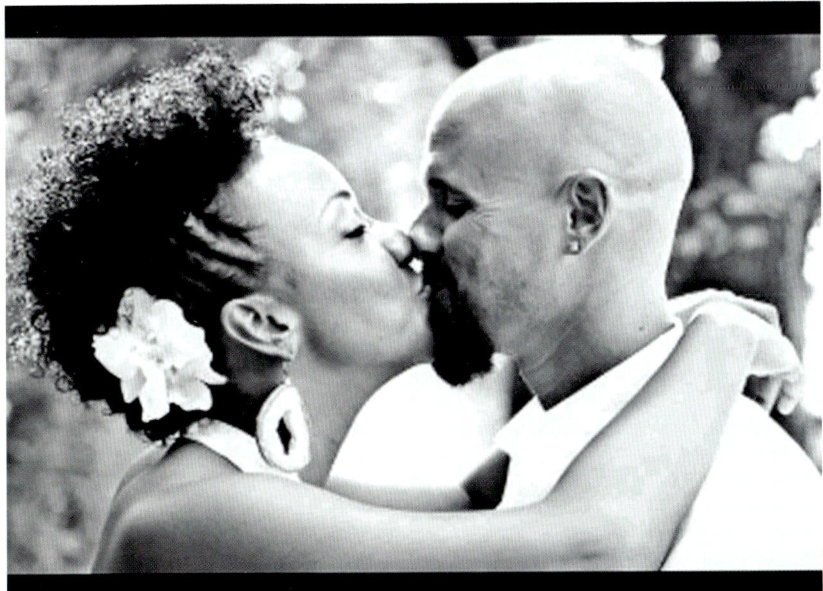

photo of Jared and Ilea Angaza on their wedding day May 8, 2010

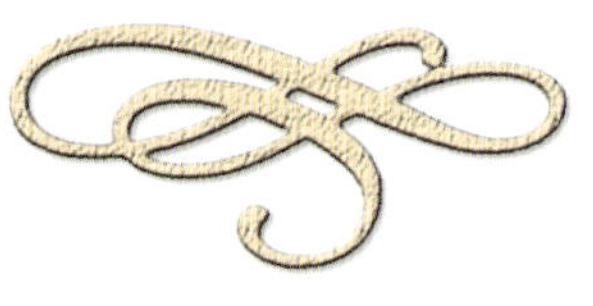

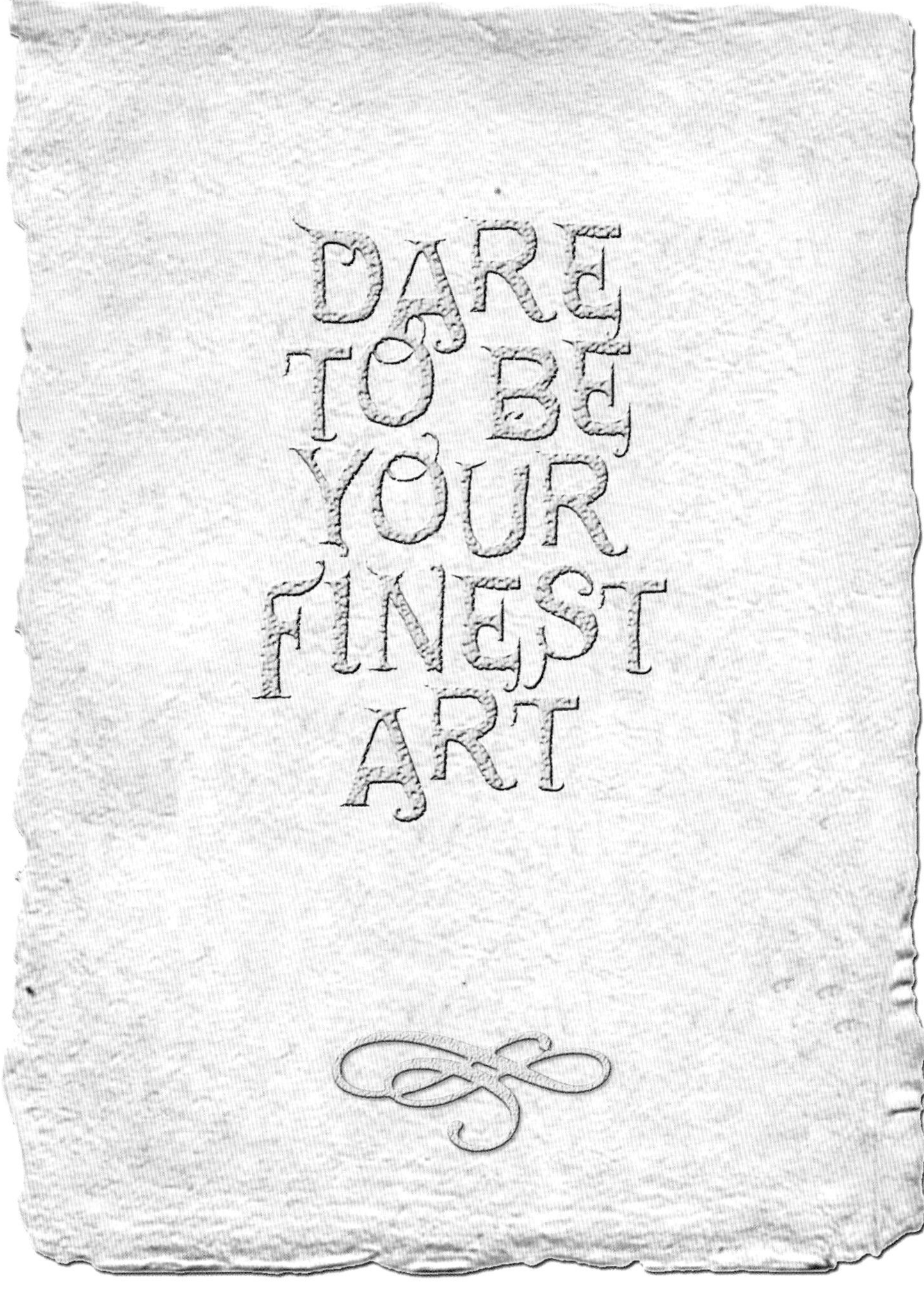
DARE
TO BE
YOUR
FINEST
ART

Who Are You, Really?

Probably the greatest life principle Dorsey and I have gleaned from our creative journeys is that the more authentic you are, the more fulfilled and excited you will be about life. This is a process that, hopefully, will continue as long as we live. As you become more authentic and real to yourself and to others, the more exciting you will be to be around; your passion, gratitude, and energy will make you shine.

WEBSTER'S DICTIONARY:
Authenticity: Real, genuine.

Unfortunately, we live in a culture where it is more prevalent to be what we think people expect of us than it is to be who we are. In early childhood we see true authenticity. Kids are just who they are. No pretenses, no affectations, no facades. As we watch those same carefree children grow up, we find they often become much like the people they hang with as well as what they think others expect or demand of them.

Photo of Eliza Joy Miller

Art is our expression of God's uniqueness in each of us.
An expression of our inner self.
Dorsey

Dare to be your finest art

By the time a child reaches teenage status, he/she is at the peak of wanting to "fit in" and will go to great lengths to change personal behavior, appearance and attitude in order to gain the admiration and respect of their peers.

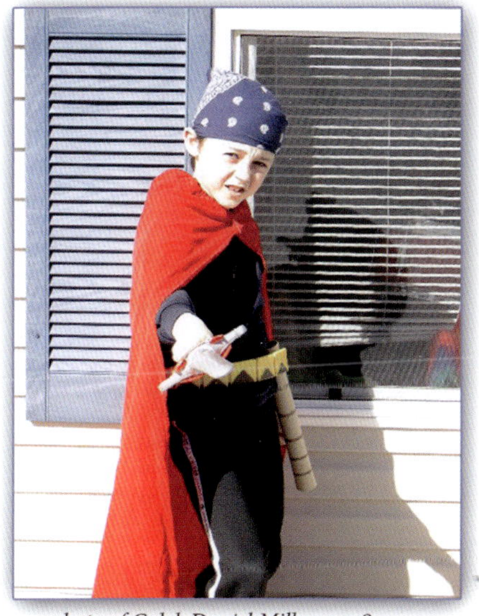

photo of Caleb Daniel Miller, age 9

To know what you prefer instead of humbly saying Amen to what the world tells you you ought to prefer, is to have kept your soul alive.
Robert Louis Stevenson, (1850-1894) Scottish novelist, poet, essayist

An amazing benefit of getting older is that one often begins to shed pretenses and expectations. In the quest to rediscover their fullest potential, often absorbed in fulfilling the roles of mother/mate/daughter/son/employee, one might find his/her "inner child" needs time to play. Some adults never had sufficient opportunity to play as children. Entering into a season where one can recapture that child-like quality of discovery, curiosity and mystery is often provided through getting back in touch with the creative self long buried.

We all have a social self we present to the public. It is always an incomplete picture.
Dorsey

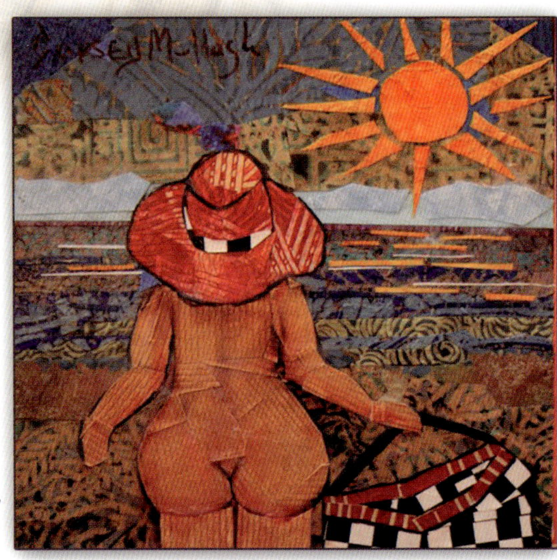

Paper on board,
Little Miss Sunshine,
by Dorsey

We talk a lot about authenticity in our class sessions. After all, how can one find his/her true voice if being guided by false pretenses, facades and wrong expectations? We have a saying in class that always brings a chuckle, *"Don't let anyone 'should' on you!"* No one can be you but you!

Dorsey McHugh While driving to my Wednesday class one day, I was thinking of the word "authentic". How it is so attractive in individuals, in relationships. I am convinced it is the spark of life in truly great art. Art without authenticity is only a picture. Real art is more. It is alive.

Joanne and I began this day by talking about what the word authentic means. What the essence of it is. We asked each student to write, without discussing the answer with each other, what is the essence of authenticity and how is it reflected in your art? Here are some of the replies:

"Authenticity is revealing my true self without any reservations or preconceived ideas of what others expect. Revealing my authenticity in art means I'm innocently creating and allowing genuine ideas to flow through me. To create authentically is to create without considering what it should look like and to allow each piece to develop and grow, almost maturing as it becomes its own genuine self."

Susan Kirby, artist, realtor, mom and grandmother

"Authentic is what is true and real to me. This concept shows up in the colors I use, but most especially in the subjects I choose to paint."

Cheryl Brunet, artist, amazing Cajun cook and educator

"My art is very affected by my authenticity. I could paint or draw what others want me to – within the lines or something exact. Yet where I see the true artistic form take shape on my canvas is when I paint from within, regardless of what other people think. People appreciate authenticity – they admire that which is genuine. True art is most often personal – an outward expression of the creativity brewing within – that's what people are really seeing and appreciating."

Ashley Miller Logsdon, Joanne's daughter, artist, Chief Inspiration Officer for 48Days LLC, wife to Nathan and mother of Clara, Ellie and Juliet.

"I plan to listen more to my own inner voice, my intuition, which is there to guide me. I would have saved myself a lot of grief if I had done more of this. I plan to embrace those things that capture my imagination; the things that make me feel alive. I would like to say I started this journey because I wanted to make myself a better person but the truth is I got so tired of the phoniness around me and equally tired of pretending I was part of a world I really didn't enjoy. It's a slow progression from a world that has been telling me who I am and what I like but it is so liberating to realize that it's okay to be the me that God created me to be. Oh, and it turns out I prefer a glass of sweet tea over a glass of red wine. There, that's better!"

Vickie Riley, photographer, www.vickierileyphotography.com

Dorsey McHugh

You are here, all around me……my Creator, my muse. I go to all our secret places, just to get a hint of this passion you infuse in my life……….. I felt it even before I knew who You were, and every time I think it could not possibly get any stronger, it does. You are incredibly faithful. I love that word. Faithful. It partners with trust, and with authenticity.

When I am frustrated because I haven't been in my studio or able to do visual art and I return to the canvas, I find I have grown because the art of living has taught me something.

Authentic……...Life. Let's be alive. Let's live every moment authentically. How can we infuse this authentic life into everything we do; into our conversations, our days, and our art? Our goal is to turn our backs on the fear of making a mistake or of feeling rejected. In that moment we have the opportunity to give up our concern for what someone else may think. We need to jump into these deep waters, with our whole heart.

> While we have the gift of life, it seems to me the only tragedy is to allow part of us to die, whether it is our spirit, our creativity or our glorious uniqueness.
>
> *Gilda Radner, (1946-1989) comedian, actress*

Remember Who You Are!

How do we get introduced to ourselves? How do we identify the gifts in us that make us who we really are? We try very hard to stuff ourselves into places where there is no fit. Often we do this to make someone else happy.

In John Bunyan's book, **Pilgrim's Progress**, the traveler leaves his path, is locked in a prison, nearly loses all hope, and gives up to be a prisoner forever until he remembers a key was placed in his pocket at the beginning of his journey. He tries the key, opens the door and is released, rejoining his path. *He had forgotten the means for unlocking his prison was in his pocket the whole time.*

What have we forgotten? What valuable gifts do we carry within us? How can we find them and use them? These are good questions to ask ourselves. I am convinced we all have keys in forgotten places. How do we find them? I don't have a formulaic answer for this question, but I know some things about my own journey. Art has been a key for me. It has been the entry for new spaces into my inner landscape. The meditative discipline of painting or writing has shaped me in very real ways.

Several years ago, I worked in a restaurant to help with family finances. If you have ever done that kind of work, you will understand how stressful it can be. I didn't mind working, but being away from my children during the day was depressing. At one point, as I turned onto the road towards work, I asked, *"Is this all there is?"* The answer was immediate. I looked down at my chest and envisioned a huge many faceted diamond inside me. It was so bright I could only glance. It was there! An inaudible voice said inside me, *"Isn't this enough?"*

A few months later, I began the art journey. I wonder if one of life's most important quests is to *remember who we are.*

The Soul of an Actor

Nan Gurley is a professional actor, singer and writer who has become our dear friend and fellow art student. We have rarely met anyone so thoroughly authentic as Nan. She does everything with gusto and with honesty. We love her enthusiasm and amazing creativity. We asked her to share with us how she knew she was born to create:

"Some of my earliest memories are ironing the shirts of my father and three brothers while listening to the sound tracks of the songs from the latest Broadway shows. I memorized the songs and sang them at the top of my voice. It made the ironing chore bearable and began my lifelong love affair with music and drama.

My parents were actors and singers and encouraged me to love the theater. I remember playing Helen Keller in **The Miracle Worker** *in a college production when I was 8 years old. The thrill of knowing the audience was watching my every move made me relish the privilege of their attention while I told them Helen's story.*

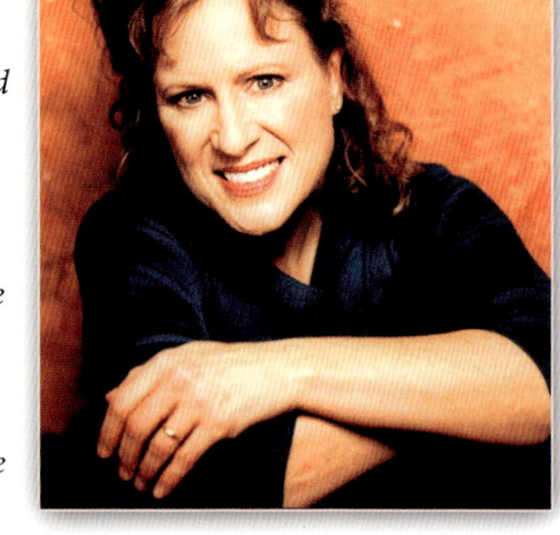

My parents also instilled in me the truth of God's love and His kind intention for my life. My father was a minister of music in our church for decades and as I sang the old hymns every week, the truth of the love of Jesus sank deep into my heart. I felt an overwhelming joy begin to grow inside me and I wanted to express my love for Him in some way. I would dance around the house while my Dad sang and played the piano. When asked what I wanted to be when I grew up I'd say, 'I want to be a missionary ballerina!' Even then, I wanted to combine

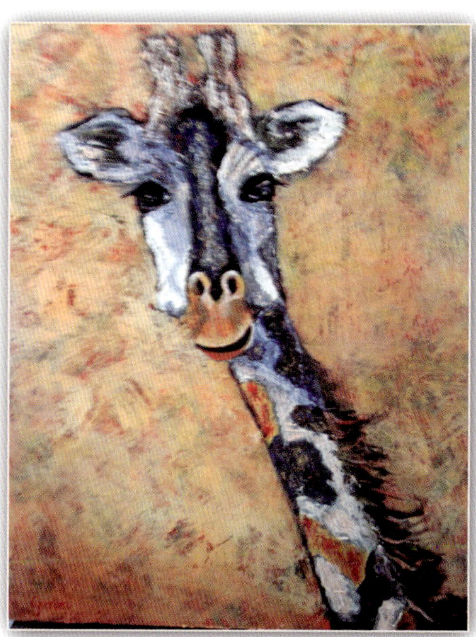
Acrylic on canvas, "GiGi" by Nan Gurley

my love for Jesus with the arts!

My life has been a combination of writing, singing, acting and now painting. In each endeavor, my overriding impulse is joy and the desire to express it through my craft. I feel an urgency to excel in each so the story I tell is one that attracts others to the Truth.

I remember an acting teacher who told me something that has stayed with me for a long time. This teacher liked to end each class with what he called check out. This was a time for anyone to share something they were experiencing in the moment.

I shared that in public gatherings I was often told, 'Hey, I knew you were here. I could hear your laugh!' This was said in a way that made me feel self conscious and a little worried that my laugh was annoying. The teacher said, 'The next time someone says that to you, tell them you are making it your goal to be as vivid as possible!' I decided these were good words to live by. Yes, I would be vivid! I would not apologize for laughing, or being who God made me to be, and sometimes that includes being loud. I also apply it to my art. I want it to be vivid. I want it to tell a story. I want it to make someone stop and listen, think and wonder at the Source of all JOY."

Visit Nan Gurley's website to read about the musical she wrote with Bonnie Keen,
Women Who Dare To Believe.
www.womenwhodaretobelieve.com
It is outstanding!

I believe I am called to use music to carry a message to the world that imparts peace and mercy and rest to troubled people.
Melanie Riekena, artist, musician, song writer

Self-love or self-esteem...has come to mean a healthy appreciation and regard for oneself that does not preclude the ability to love others.
Karyl McBride, Ph.D., ***Will I Ever Be Good Enough?***

Dorsey McHugh Because my friend Susan Miller is an actor, I have pondered acting as an art form. The actor uses her body, voice, expression, and movement as her brush and palette. She paints a character's portrait with the medium of her soul. Her voice and her movements become the colors of her art.

Loving You!

JM We are taught from a young age to respect and love others and often fail to learn to respect and love ourselves. We do a great injustice to ourselves in not taking care of us.

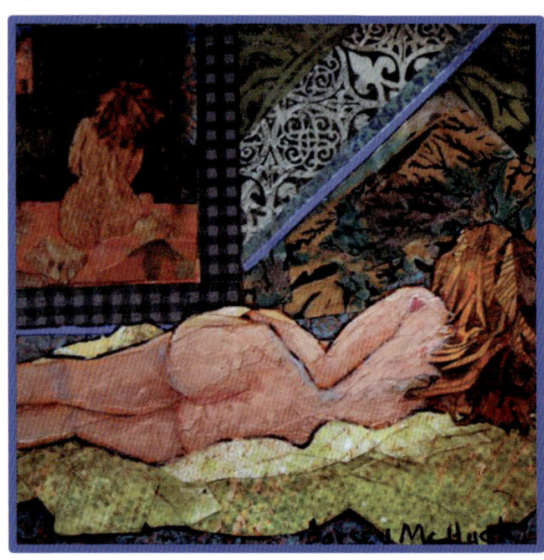

paper on board

"Be Mine"

by Dorsey

Each of us possesses a creative self. Claiming that is a transformational art. When you begin to act on your creativity, what you find inside may be more valuable than what you produce for the external world. The ultimate creative act is to express what is most authentic and individual about you.
Eileen M. Clegg, author and visual journalist

Unfortunately some of us have been in religious or cultural circles where being confident and loving oneself would be seen as prideful *(Heaven forbid!)* and ultimately sinful. My Bible tells me I am a child of God (Romans 8:17, Galatians 3:26, 2 Corinthians 5:17) and *that* assurance tells me I am a glorious creature made in *His image.* If I believe that, then I have the freedom to spend my life being the very best I can be. I don't know how that is possible if I don't first learn to love who God made me to be. Now I may travel a circuitous route finding my authentic self but I believe it to be a task worth carrying out. It truly is a journey and takes patience and a lot of work.

The push for conformity in society
and in the church is great.
Too often, it creates codependency
and people-pleasing behavior.
It teaches us to be uncomfortable with individuality.

Dr. David Hawkins, The Relationship Doctor,
When Pleasing Others Is Hurting You

My friend, Joel Boggess *(www.FindingYourVoiceRadio.com)* wrote an eBook on **7 Days of Self Care** with many great suggestions on how to take better care of YOU on a daily basis. It's a good, quick read. Be intentional about taking time to grow, gain better mental and physical health and to PLAY!

When a child walks up to a playground, her eyes are full of possibilities and opportunities. She is not judging, criticizing, or thinking about the end result. She is focused on the experience. To keep yourself from getting stuck, throw out the rule book, detach yourself from the outcome and do something simply for the fun of it.

an excerpt from ***7 Days of Self Care*** *by Joel Boggess*

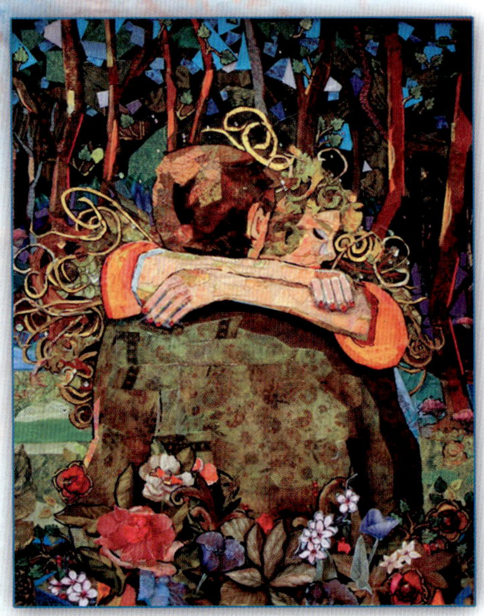

"Hold Tight" by Dorsey

A Living Tapestry

Dorsey McHugh

It is morning.
The sun is up.
The birds outside my window are having a party. It is going to be a lovely day. My routine is to get up, go down the stairs and drink a cup of coffee on the little patio outside. It's a soft place to land while contemplating the day.
It is a good moment to be thankful.

Thankful for the air we breathe, for the space we get to take up on this planet. There is plenty of time to record some thoughts. It's a way to ease into thinking about the class I'll be teaching in a few hours. It takes only a small amount of time and no anxiety. I like trusting the words to come at the appropriate moment.

There is a lot to say about art and life. The way they flow together. It is my intention to have an artistic life. To let art weave its way into my thoughts and my vocabulary. Life is filled with so much possibility that there really is no excuse not to make each second a deliberate piece of the larger sculpture, which is our own individual artistic expression.

It is satisfying to make clothing and jewelry and makeup and hair part of the colors and the textures that give my day a little more interest and fun and art. Every day is a new part of a living tapestry. Words become the vehicles that transport me. They are a means of flying. Just as in this moment, words are gliding through the inner sanctuary of my own imagination.

This is something worth sharing. Relationships have art in them as well. I like the art in our relationships. Of course life gets jumbled up and there is always a mixture. It is one of the flaws that have been woven like a weed into our reality. It can be minimized, but not eliminated. We can build our relationships with as few weeds as possible. Love is the best art of all. Love is really the only way to create something. Let's have our own party! We can be creative today! We can learn how to fly! Let's give ourselves over to Love!!!

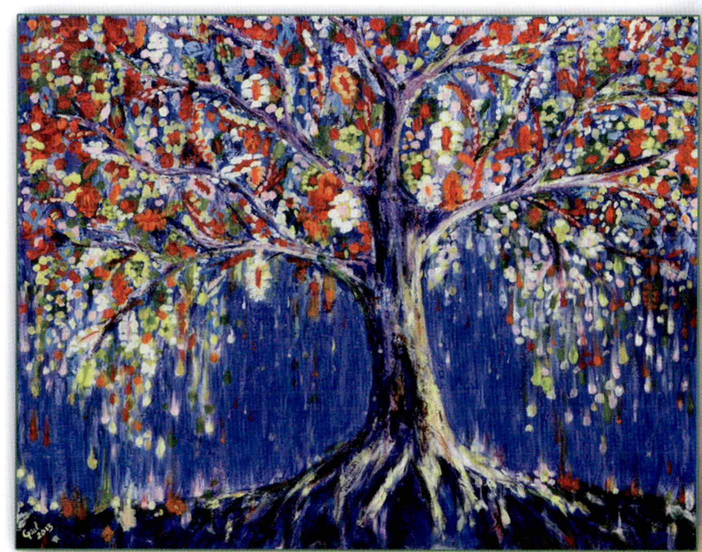

Acrylic on canvas, "Abundance" by Gail Hyatt

In living artistically (creatively), we have to see through our own hearts. This takes knowing ourselves. More importantly it takes accepting and liking ourselves.

-Dorsey

Awaken Your Senses

1. Do you feel you are living your most authentic life?

2. Make a list of things you would like to give yourself permission to do.

3. What is holding you back? Explore your feelings through journaling, painting, drawing, or simply walking & thinking.

I am not a teacher, but an awakener.

Robert Frost (1874-1963), American poet

What's Important To You?

If I had to list my top three loves it would be writing, mentoring and relationships. I approach each of those areas seriously and lovingly. I can't imagine a life of happiness and peace without including the people who love me and whom I love. I work hard to nurture relationships to keep them alive and healthy and that often embraces creativity.

Dorsey McHugh

Let me interject my observation of Joanne here. Like an actress, she uses her whole self to creatively maintain her relationships. She is very creative in showing regard for other people.

I am thinking about what is important to me and a line from Dr. Zhivago comes to mind: Dr. Zhivago is a dreamer, a peaceful man who is being destroyed by the war around him. He says to Lara at one point: *"I just want to live."* This desire has joined the important group on my list. It is in company with: love well, listen well, tell the truth, and make a difference wherever I can. I don't mean I want to cling to breathing for as long as I can. (though I do). It means I want to pay attention to now, to this moment. I want to be all I can be, hear all I can hear, and say only what needs to be said. This is my artistic platform.

JM Daniel and I take mentoring Seriously...with a capital S! When we got married back in the '60s, we had not experienced home lives we wanted to emulate in our own family together. We knew we had to get creative about reshaping our family tree. That was our goal. We would put a new branch on our family tree that didn't include broken relationships, broken homes, and broken lives. We were young. We hadn't had good marriage or parenting skills as examples, so what to do? We decided we needed to find good mentors. Some of those mentors were through books we read, classes we took, workshops we attended. But many of the mentors we sought out were people who crossed our paths and who, through our eyes, possessed the skills in relationship we wanted to cultivate. We took on this search with vigor. I remember distinctly when I came to the realization that we were not going to find the perfect person who excelled in all the areas we wanted to grow and learn. So we sought mentors for specific areas such as spiritual guidance, parenting, marriage, sex, work, play. We wanted to learn. And we wanted to be the best we could be in each area.

We were fortunate *(which means we worked HARD).* We have found many great mentors throughout our lives which have guided us towards success in many areas. Yes, we have had failures, heartbreaks and perhaps a few regrets along the way. However, we place an incredible value on what we have learned from others and we continue to seek mentors in any area we wish

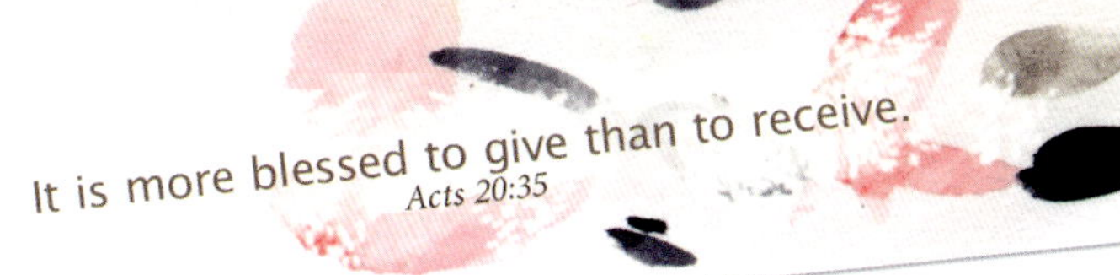

to grow and learn. Getting creative about learning, growing and thriving is essential to success in any area.

Now in our sixth decade of our lives, Daniel and I find ourselves frequently being asked to mentor others who have entered our lives in various capacities. First we find it ironic. Most of these people probably have no idea what value we have placed on finding good mentors and how hard we worked at this. But secondly, we take the role very seriously. If we don't feel we have good advice or input on something we are asked to do, we refer to other sources who might be better equipped. No one but God has the ability to be great at everything.

The more you have invested in something,
the less likely you are to let it fail.
Rory Vaden, motivational speaker and author of ***Take the Stairs***

Inspiring others to do better is what good mentoring requires. It isn't about knowing everything or being the very best. But it is about inspiring others to be better.

Give and it shall be given unto you, pressed down, shaken together, running over, shall men give unto your bosom.
Luke 6:38

Dorsey McHugh

I have always been more comfortable with the giving side of this thought. In the last few years, the circumstances of my life have demanded of me wisdom which I did not think I possessed. At every important leg of my journey, there has been someone waiting to give me the wisdom required for the next stretch of the road. I hope to be that for others. It is a noble profession. If I am excited about anything, I talk with everyone about it.

Mentoring and being mentored is a thread running through my whole life's tapestry. We pass on to others what we have been given. You can always find help and guidance when you open yourself to it.

The mediocre teacher tells.
The good teacher explains.
The superior teacher demonstrates.
The great teacher inspires.
William Arthur Ward
(1921-1994) Inspirational writer,
author of ***Fountains of Faith***

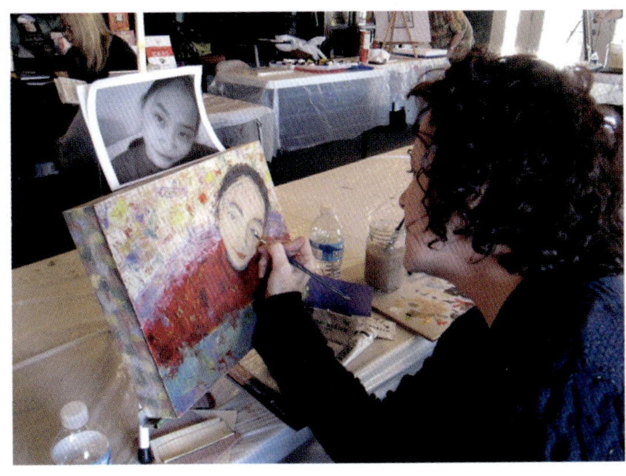

photo of actress, artist and author, Nan Gurley, in Dorsey's class

A Lost Art, Found!

I mentioned that one of my top three loves is writing. Guess that is obvious by now but here is a creative twist on both aspects of mentoring and writing that came into my life recently.

A few months ago Daniel and I were asked to write a foreword in Claudia and Michael Good's book on marriage (***Compass**, An Innovative Life Directions System for Couples, www.rise365.com).* We were happy to endorse this book because it was much like something we would write on a subject dear to our hearts. When I received a thank you from Claudia she said, *"I know you don't know me, and I hope you don't think it rude to ask, but would you ever consider doing a sort of pen-pal thing with me? The old- fashioned letter type? I would simply love to pick your brain about many more things on marriage/children/family/business* *and balancing them all. I truly love and respect your creativity, depth, and passion to create a 'haven of peace' within your home and yet still pursue that which fulfills your heart. I long for a connection with someone whom I know is successful in these areas."* Wow! How could I resist? Looking back at all the people Daniel and I asked for advice and counsel through the years, giving back to those who value our input after decades of experience is the least I can do. But combine that with actually putting pen to paper? *Oh, yeah!*

Letter writing has become a lost art, having been replaced with all the current email and texting technology. I admit to doing the bulk of my communicating electronically too, but I have never forgotten the value of receiving a hand-written note, card or letter. How often do you go to the mailbox only to bring home a stack of totally junk mail or bills? Rarely is there any personal correspondence. So here's a creative idea. How about standing out by being in the minute minority of old-fashioned letter writers? Reviving the old excitement of having a pen-pal or two or reconnecting with a friend or relative.

Now, I am definitely not sitting around watching daytime TV and eating bon-bons. I keep mighty busy. But when something comes up that ignites excitement because it resonates with what I love to do and is another creative outlet, I can carve out time.

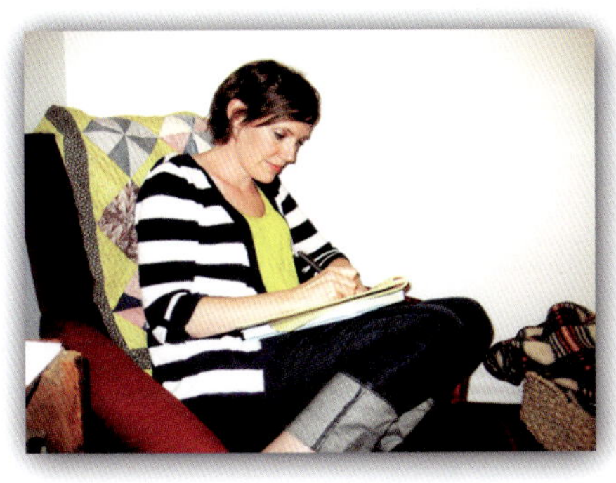

photo of Claudia Good writing to me

Claudia lives in Pennsylvania and I have not yet met her face-to-face. She is the same age as our daughter, is an artist and very creative. Bonus! We immediately started writing back and forth, both of us so eager to do this that as soon as we get a letter, we usually write back within the week! In Claudia's first letter she said, *"Here is my question for this letter....When you first set out on your journey to live a purposeful life did you struggle to find women friends who desired the same thing?"*

She went on to ask several more questions and our letters to each other are usually five to six pages long. In her most recent letter she wrote, *"So, Joanne, as a highly imaginative lady how did you find creative outlets while being a mom?"* And in the next paragraph, *"Also, how did you create a 'haven of rest' in your home?"* Great questions that stimulate my thinking; helping me appreciate the importance of mentoring to a younger generation. I am keeping each letter and copies of my responses. It could be fodder for another book *(the Art of Communication? Creative Mentoring?).*

When my father-in-law was confined to assisted living and then nursing care, I wrote to him at least twice a month. Just a nice update on what we were doing and an inquiry of how he was spending his days. Once in a great while I would get a letter back with his shaky handwriting and I knew it took a lot of effort for him to respond. He cherished those letters. Kept them all and often told people how much it meant to him. We were both blessed by the effort. I write because I enjoy it and I love to give others the thrill of going to their mailbox and receiving a personal card or letter. I don't expect or require a response. I do it from my heart and it is a small way to give back to others in a unique way.

I once challenged a group of women to be more diligent about sending a card or word of encouragement to others. One lady spoke up and said, *"Well, Joanne, that is your gift. Some of us don't have that gift!"* I stewed on that one awhile. She wasn't wrong in what she said. In fact she was very right on. But the underlying message I heard was, *"I don't want to learn to be a better communicator. I don't want to work harder on my relationship skills. I don't want to make the effort."* It really doesn't require much to buy a card, sign it and address an envelope but it says volumes to the recipient of that effort about how much you care.

I have only made this letter longer because I have not had the time to make it shorter.

Blaise Pascal (1623-1662), French mathematician, physicist and philosopher and child prodigy

Awaken Your Senses

1. Make a list of what is important to you.
2. Is there something on that list you might want to revisit that has fallen asleep?
3. What steps can you take to rekindle that love?
4. Can you find a pen pal or a virtual coorespondence and develop a new friendship?

More than kisses, letters mingle souls.

John Donne (1572-1631), English poet, preacher

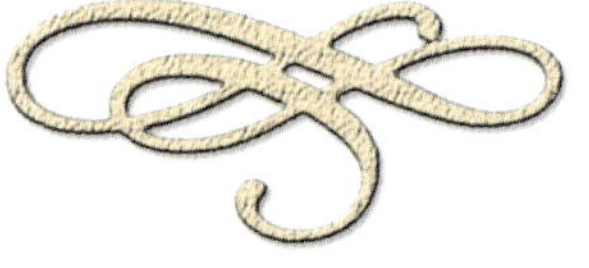

CREATIVITY CAN BE GOOD FOR YOUR HEALTH

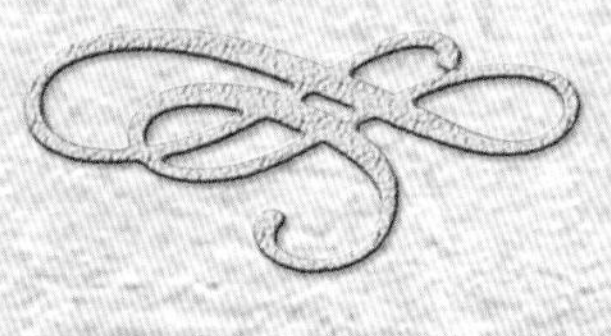

(Creatives) experience depression simply because they are caught up in a struggle to make life seem meaningful to them.

Eric Maisel, PhD, author of ***The Van Gogh Blues*** *and* ***Coaching the Artist Within***

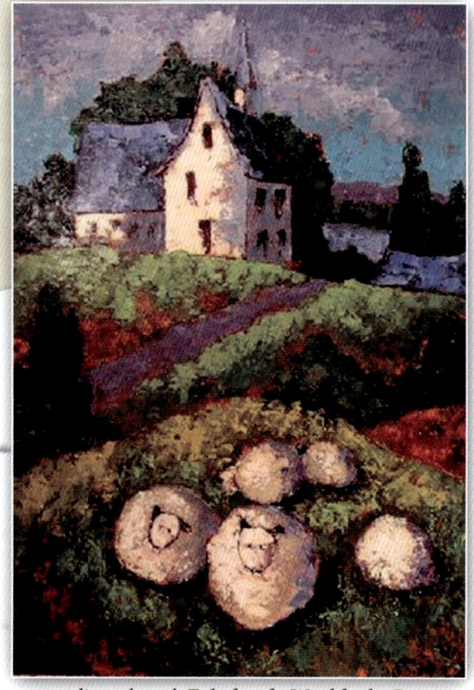

acrylic on board, ***Fabulously Wealthy*** *by Dorsey*

A Healing Salve To The Soul

Dorsey McHugh

A few years ago, on a trip to Carmel, CA. I saw the fattest sheep I had ever seen. On the plane home, I did some quick sketches of sheep and this painting came out of those sketches. **"Fabulously Wealthy"** was the first of many sheep paintings. Sheep appeal to me for many reasons. This image eventually became part of a fundraiser for the non-profit, **Feed the Children**. A new friend told me that her mother had asked for her poster of **"Fabulously Wealthy"** to be brought into her hospital room to encourage her during her pre- and post-operation hospital stay. I feel honored by all of this. Art gets the credit, in large part, for physical and emotional healing in me, if for no other reason than the stress relief it has provided.

can be good for your health

Occasionally I lead worship services and classes at a large women's prison nearby. A few times I have talked to the women about their creative natures. Most of them agree it is their creativity that landed them in prison. It always surprises me how many of them love to write, draw, paint and express themselves artistically through makeup, hairstyle, etc. I hope I help them recognize there are more positive and rewarding ways in which to use their talents and that a better understanding of their own uniqueness could help them pursue more admirable and legal results.

If we believe in a Master Creator and that we are made in His image, then it follows we, too, are inherently creative. When we ignore or suppress that part of us many consequences can occur. We can become unhealthy mentally and physically.

It would be safe to speculate that the majority of children with an autism spectrum disorder are left-brain dominant. The left-brain deals with details, planning, and organizational skills and is very analytical and logical. You can best see this among the people with Asperger's and the savants of the world; whereas the right side of the brain deals more with creativity, intuitiveness and interpersonal skills. Which is very interesting when you look at our culture and the rising rates of autism. In practice I have seen some children improve socially and emotionally just by adding arts and creativity into their lives.
Shannon Skye, DC www.SkyeChiropractic.com

Joanne's Personal Journey

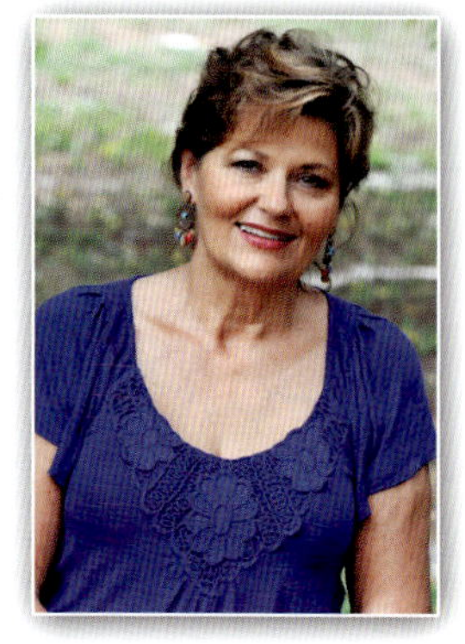

In 2004 I faced a deep depression from which I was unable to escape. I began to experience numbness on my right side that began at the back of my neck and radiated down into my shoulder. It was like I had been shouldering a heavy purse that was pinching a nerve. But it was persistent and after awhile I started researching what might be going on. This search for answers led me to fear I might have Multiple Sclerosis. I made an appointment with Greg Skye, my trusted holistic chiropractor.

Dan and I were to fly the next day to California for a visit with friends and I needed to find out what was going on fast. Maybe just a pinched nerve? But instinctively I felt it was more than that. I had experienced some other weird things going on in my body that made me suspicious. I told Greg I wanted him to tell me I did not have MS. We talked and he examined me; did some tests that revealed a severe loss of strength in my right arm and hand. He looked at me gravely and said he couldn't tell me what I wanted to hear. He suggested that as soon as I got back from my trip I should see a specialist.

Dan and I flew to California and by the time I got there the numbness had spread to my waist. By the next morning I stepped out of bed on a numb leg and foot. My abdomen and scalp even felt numb. I was literally numb from top to toe. Just on my right side. I could walk but had a hard time with lifting my leg. I tried to brush my teeth and my hand slapped the side of my face with a toothbrush full of paste. I couldn't even get my hand to my mouth without helping with the other hand. I was frightened. My thoughts raced with dire possibilities.

We finished our time in California with dear friends who were understanding and patient with me as I tried to keep up. I couldn't even get in the car without assistance. When I returned home I made an appointment for a checkup with my Internist who said the same thing......he was afraid he didn't have good news for me. He suggested I see a neurologist he knew of at Vanderbilt who specialized in MS. I couldn't get in to see himfor a couple months. I made an appointment but wasn't willing to wait that long for answers so I found another neurologist who took scans and confirmed I had MS-like lesions on my brain. I went to my gynecologist. She too gave me the same story. I then kept my appointment with the Vanderbilt specialist. All the doctors confirmed I had the classic symptoms of MS.

I began to research everything I could about a disease that is, so far, incurable. I read voraciously and watched videos. I was into about two months of coping with profound weakness and numbness totally on my right side. I was not incapable of walking but maneuvering was tedious and slow for me. I still battled the depression and chronic fatigue but now I knew the cause.

We can let circumstances rule us,
or we can take charge and rule our lives from within.
Earl Nightingale (1921-1989), motivational speaker and author, ***The Strangest Secret***

Friends and family prayed for me. I learned depression is a common symptom of MS and so, for a while I took anti-depressants. At one point I had continual pain and was on anti-convulsion medication because nerve pain requires a different regimen. I refused to be on the typical drug treatments for MS because I couldn't bring myself to believe I would be like this forever. I didn't want to commit to a life-long medical dependency.

I attended classes and seminars and even a weekend retreat for patients with MS where I heard a speaker who helped me put into perspective what might lie ahead for me. She was an actress/comedienne who had advanced MS and walked with a cane. She said defiantly to the audience that she had decided she would not let Multiple Sclerosis define who she was. That one bit of advice stuck with me and changed my thinking. How many times had I heard my husband teach and write about what you are thinking can become your reality?

In time, over a few months, I began to regain strength and the numbness dissipated. Six months after the initial onset of the symptoms I was "in remission" and pretty much back to normal with only slight tingling and weakness in my right hand, pain in a few areas and a knowledge that I needed to rest more.

Without belaboring this issue, I will say that for years I have occasionally had recurring symptoms, pain, cognitive blurring, and other issues to deal with but one thing that rang true to me during this period was I did not have to let MS dictate my state of mind; to define who I am. But I had to come up with a plan.

I was in my early 50s and I began to put my life back together. Not only was I dealing with health issues that were very real, but our youngest, Ashley, was going off to college and I was finding it very difficult to deal with an empty nest. Now that is not an insurmountable issue for most women but combined with the ever-present depression that clouded my mind I was simply unable to cope. Like so many mothers, I had the erroneous belief that my duties as a mother had ended and I had no earthly idea what to do next. In my mind, I had been let go of my job; my job that I had invested every bit of me into and now I didn't have a clue who I was supposed to be; what I was supposed to do with the rest of my life.

During those dark days I would look in the mirror and see the ravages of aging and remember the days when I was a young, attractive model for department stores, newspapers and brochures. More fuel for the consuming fire of depression. Where was I going with my life? Who was I? What was my purpose?

Our life is what our thoughts make it.
A man will find that as he alters his thoughts toward things and other people, things and other people will alter towards him.
James Allen, author, As A Man Thinketh

It is surprising how when you can't get your head around the changes in your life, those changes can eat holes through the very fabric of your existence like a cancer spreading; leaving dark malignant stains on your everyday activities.

I had put my heart and soul into being a superb mother and a supportive spouse through some very difficult times of financial to support our family of five with very meager resources. It was hard on me. I had difficulty understanding how we got to this place when we had worked so hard to live a good moral life, raise good Christian children, were deeply involved in church, gave to others, blah, blah, blah. If my heart was in the right place and I was working so hard why were we struggling so hard and for so long? Where did we go wrong?? *(I'm sure no one else has ever asked those same questions!)*

"Life isn't fair!"
Joanne's mother

"Life's hard!"
Dorsey's mother

It was also during this time that our middle child, Jared, in his early teens and a struggling "creative", was trying to find himself and in so doing, delved heavily into addictions that several times almost ended his life. It certainly was detrimental to his and our family's well being. As his mother, I wanted to shield him from harm. I was beyond heartsick. It was just another worry to add to my already depressed state of mind. When did helping cross over to enabling was a question ever-present in my thinking.

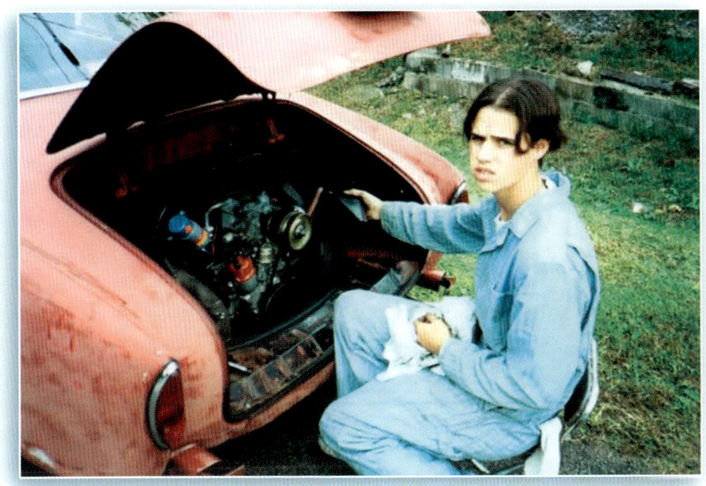

photo of Jared during the drug years working on a ***1968 VW Karmann Ghia*** *he and Daniel restored together to bond and learn*

Our oldest son, Kevin and his wife, Teri, tried intervention with Jared and helped in every way they could but those years were very difficult for our family.

Trapped in the restrictions of our financial downfall and our struggles to keep a roof over our heads, a son needing rehab and continual watch to make sure he didn't kill himself or someone else, my depression and health concerns, our last child going off on her own and my inability to sort out where my place was in this world, I knew I had to come up with a plan but I lacked the strength to do it alone. I leaned heavily on Daniel for support, encouragement and direction. He helped me understand that the very skills I had used as a mother and supportive spouse to an optimistic entrepreneur could be translated into a new season of exciting opportunities.

I tell you my story because I think it is important to recognize I am not by nature an unrealistically optimistic Pollyanna. I have not lived a storybook life with no real problems or setbacks to take me down. I live in the real world with all the dysfunctions and malfunctions most families endure to varying degrees. I could actually add more drama to my story but will spare you all the gory details. I think you get the picture of my state of mind at that time in my life. I certainly had strong ingredients for a storm to develop in my physical and mental health.

Got Stress?

Everything I read and hear about stress suggests that it is impossible to avoid and sure to cause illness in some form or fashion if not given an outlet. More than a decade since my initial struggles with MS I am convinced peace of mind is directly linked to many (most) of the raging illness and disease that is taking over our bodies.

Worry and stress affects the circulation, the heart, the glands, the whole nervous system, and profoundly affects heart action.
Charles W. Mayo, M.D., The Mayo Clinic

Christiane Northrup, M.D., author of the best seller, **Women's Bodies, Women's Wisdom** dedicated her huge tome to "......*all who believe that it is possible to flourish, regardless of our present or past circumstances......it is for those who yearn to be well and know that there is something more to healing than simply external substances or techniques.*"

Northrup goes on to say in her excellent health manual for women, "*.....if the intensity and the frequency of the stresses in your life, from either inside yourself (such as your perceptions about your life) or outside yourself (such as having surgery or working the night shift), become too great, then over time your adrenal glands will begin to become exhausted—not unlike a horse that continues to be worked or runs too much without adequate rest, food, and water. Eventually your body will produce many different symptoms in an attempt to get you to pay attention and change some aspects of your life—just as a tired horse will sooner or later stop working, no matter how much you whip it.*" *(pg 533,)*

Learn to enjoy every minute of your life. Be happy now. Don't wait for something outside of yourself to make you happy in the future. Think how really precious is the time you have to spend, whether it's at work or with your family. Every minute should be enjoyed and savored.

Earl Nightingale, Motivational speaker and author, ***The Strangest Secret***

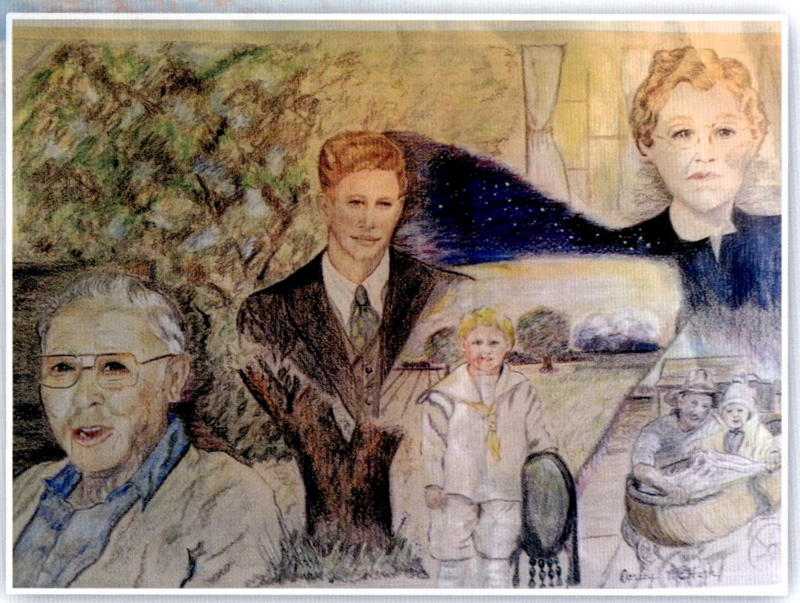

Drawing of Dorsey's father, Peter Livingstone Edwards. Dorsey's grandmother is in the top right corner.

Dorsey McHugh When we let something outside ourselves define us, in a negative way it becomes a myth. We often let the myths define us. Our lives become inauthentic because they are written by someone else.

Julia Cameron refers to people like me as "shadow artists". I stayed in the shadows. I designed and made quilts which, for awhile, I sold to help with our family income. It did not occur to me to take seriously this aspect of myself. My awareness of my own artistic side was waiting for the key to release me from the stone barrier which was erected around my artist self in early childhood. Some time after I was given a book by Betty Edwards, **Drawing on the Artist Within**, my Dad died.

He was very dear to me, and as the process of mourning began, I sketched him and other members of our family using old black and white photos as reference. It took me hours to carefully draw his face. While doing this, I remembered him. I understood him better. I was stunned to see this side of me growing rapidly. My artist self was making up for lost time.

All the amateur psychology I had developed along the way began to assert itself in the choices I made artistically. These were the first steps of my artist journey home. The lovely surprise of being introduced to art was an intense one.

This all happened over 20 years ago. I have been showing and selling my work since those first few years. It has caused me to think differently. Artists train their brains to "see" an object from all angles, to study what it is. Art also generously gives one a real sense of adventure. It has kept me on target with purpose.

Art has been my meditation in stressful times. It has calmed me when sorrow, fear, or anxiety tried to interrupt my life. I am very thankful for all art has given me! Not to mention it has fed, clothed, and kept me warm for years. It is, without exception, the most transformative adventure I have experienced.

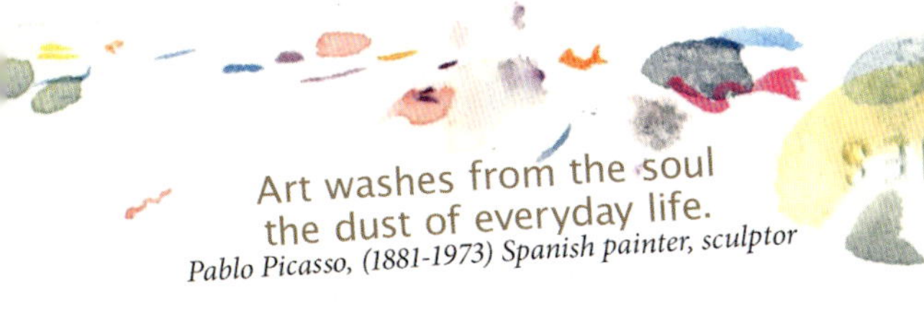

Art washes from the soul
the dust of everyday life.
Pablo Picasso, (1881-1973) Spanish painter, sculptor

(Because Dorsey has a whacked sense of humor, she wanted me to inject one of her favorite quotes by Woody Allen, which could be his paraphrase of Picasso's words.)

I love the rain.
It washes memories from the sidewalk of life!

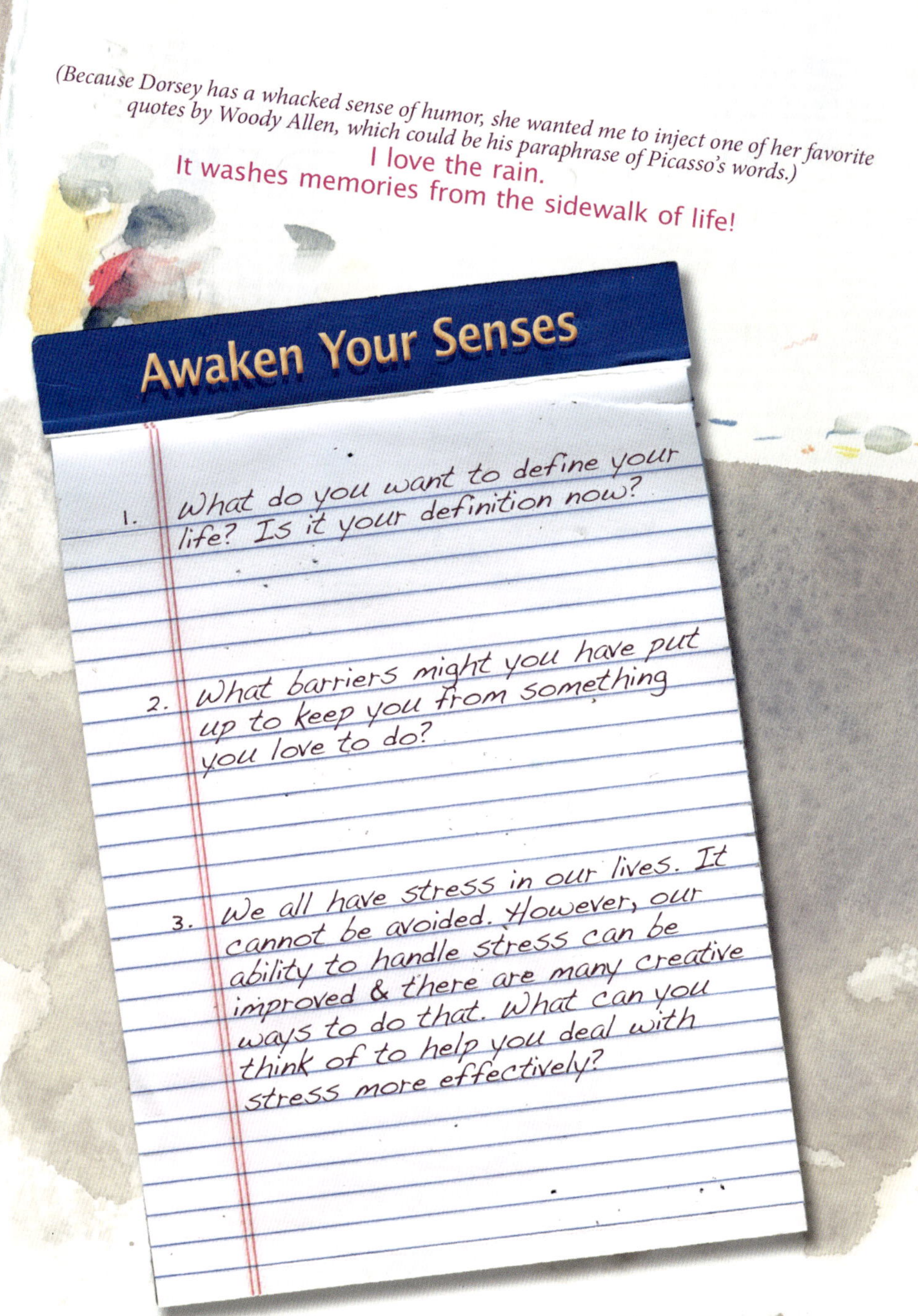

Art As Therapeudic Discovery

One of the best things I did on my road to inner healing was to answer an ad in the newspaper for an art class. It was based on Betty Edwards' book **Drawing on the Right Side of the Brain**. It was a six week class, led by local artist Melanie Jackson.

I had never drawn before and found the class to be very difficult at first but I felt compelled to stick with it. I knew I needed the discipline and I needed time for me. I studied with Melanie for over eleven years. Through her teaching I began to see the world with different eyes. I saw beauty I had long overlooked. I saw light and shadow with new interest. I learned how, as in life, light and dark work together to weave beauty in unexpected ways.

I read books on creativity and as I began to tap into my right brain I saw how life parallels art. I became less depressed; more aware of the importance of taking time for myself each week to balance out the realities of life with the awe of fantasy, imagination, and dreams. One thing about inviting fun and laughter into your life is that it is very hard to stay depressed.

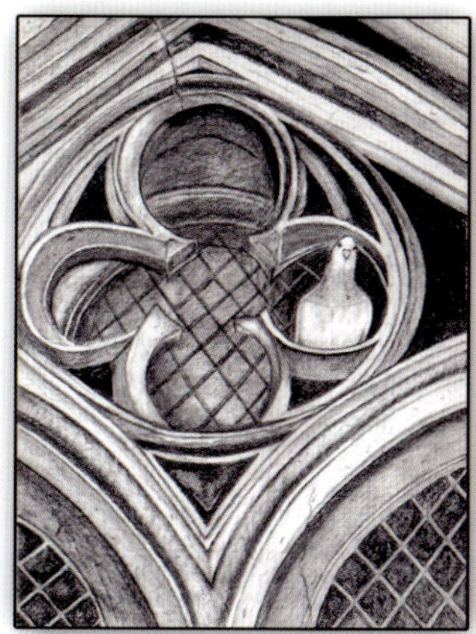

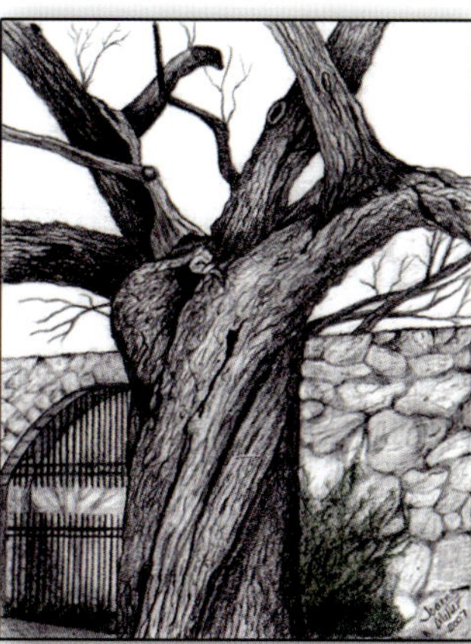

Joanne's graphite drawings, ***A Peaceful Perch*** *and* ***Tangled Treasure.***

Good humor is a tonic for mind and body.
It is the best antidote for anxiety and depression.
It is a business asset. It attracts and keeps friends.
It lightens human burdens.
It is the direct route to serenity
and contentment.
Grenville Kleiser, (1868-1935), inspirational author

I have gained more self confidence and direction and definitely more joy by increasing my creativity level. When I sit down to write, draw or paint, I experience a peace and excitement that transcends all the chaos that may seem to whirl around me. Taking time to tap into your creative side doesn't mean denying the realities of your life. It helps to make your problem solving skills better, your ability to cope with unpleasantries increase, your thinking capacity broaden and you find beauty where you didn't see it before; joy where you might have before only seen darkness. By increasing my right brain power, I have found I have more trust in my gut instincts. More confidence in my ability to make better decisions.

Why should we all use our creative power...?
Because there is nothing that makes people
so generous, joyful, lively, bold and compassionate,
so indifferent to fighting and the accumulation
of objects and money.
Brenda Ueland, (1891-1985) author,
If You Want to Write: A Book About Art, Independence and Spirit

It has been many years now since I declared I would not let MS define my life. I am on no medications whatsoever, have lost a considerable amount of weight. My art class is the highlight of each week. It provides the therapy and medicine I need to make my life sing! I have also been more creative about my health and well being by changing some poor eating habits and getting a weekly full-body massage and plenty of rest. I call this preventive medicine.

Tapping into one's creative nature can eliminate a lot of angst and sometimes even pain. I am much more creative and intentional in everything I do. I begin each day wondering how I will impact my world in new and beautiful ways. One of my art friends said it well when she said she now wakes up *"scanning my day with excitement!"* What a wonderful way to start EVERY day! Thanks to Melanie Riekena for reminding me to do that!

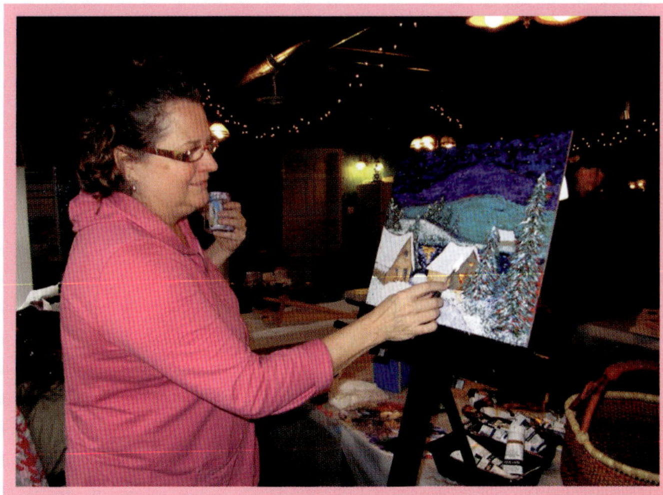

Melanie Riekena in art class.

Dorsey McHugh

A few years ago, I saw a television special documenting research into why some people live to 100 years old or beyond. There was a lot of speculation as to what the common denominator might be. In the final analysis the group encompassed health nuts, vitamin freaks and those who abused their bodies by smoking, drinking to excess and living on junk food. All lived to 100 or more. The common thread appeared to be all were engaged in living; performing in something which they loved. They couldn't wait to get to work in the morning!

One 73-year old woman worked in a museum and broke her hip, looking forward to a long convalescence. A broken bone at this age would usually be the beginning of the end for any senior. But, she loved her work and was so determined to return to her job, she healed rapidly and was back in the museum far earlier than doctors said was probable. She wanted to be back into her life. This is how art has given me better health. When I am engaged in a creative process, I wake in the morning with it on my mind, eager to get into my studio to work. I use the word 'work' while feeling it not labor at all. I love doing what I do. It is certainly more like play than work. I am often rejoicing that I get to do this to earn my living. I can say without any doubt art has eased my stress level, given me unexpected adventures and hope, often in the midst of anxiety. Whether you put paint to canvas, words on paper, or apply creativity to your left-brained accounting career, you will find joy and satisfaction in the process.

A Change In Direction

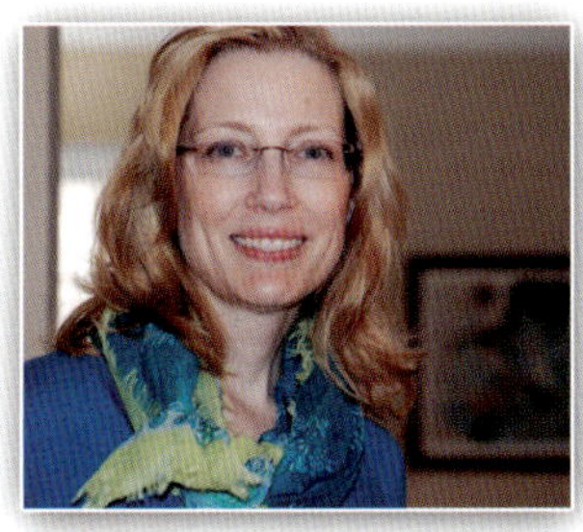

Nancy Bowron is a student of Dorsey's and a talented Nashville artist (*www.npbstudios.com*). Nancy was managing a knit shop, creating and publishing knitwear designs and teaching, when a shoulder injury halted her activities. She tells how she regained a love of art she had forgotten:

After physical therapy, I could only knit for very short periods of time and was rather depressed. My sweet husband saw that I needed a creative outlet and purchased for me a series of oil painting classes. I hadn't painted since the 9th grade. I remembered I had won an art contest back then. I realized I had some talent. Being "an artist" gives me a tribe - a group of like minded people. I remember walking into my first workshop and realizing that every one there was a Creative like me. In no other group was I as comfortable as I was with these people. I remember being excited about this artist whose work I loved. The colors and subject matter spoke to me. It was Dorsey! I am so grateful to have the opportunity to walk some of this artistic road with her.

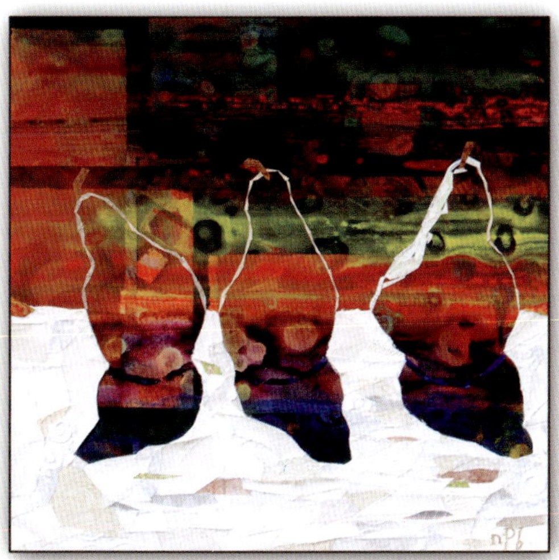

***A Pear of Three** by Nancy Bowron*

A Healing Touch

Dorsey McHugh

My friend, Consuelo Mathews, has hands that heal. She is a massage therapist. She is also an artist. I count her as one of my students, though we have been friends since long before she began doing either of these professions.

A few years ago, my assistant, Susan and I went to Hawaii to meet my gallery representation in person. *(I know, I know…….somebody had to do it!)* While we were on Maui, our rep met us and had planned a two mile, two thousand foot hike up a mountain trail. We were used to walking about three miles in an hour at home. Piece of cake. Our view from the narrow, rocky, uneven path was breathtaking. Unfortunately, I tripped and twisted my ankle quite badly on the way back. It was sprained, but not broken. It took several months to get it back to normal. During my healing process, I walked differently. One morning, I awoke with my back seizing up in pain. I could barely move, let alone stand up straight.

Consuelo came to my home with her massage table and spent 2 hours doing SacroCranial massage on me. It is an unusual and thoroughly creative form of massage which resulted in me standing up, completely pain free after 2 hours. Consuelo is creative and gifted in her approach to healing and to art.

Daniel and I have been consistent about getting full body massages at least three to four times a month for many years. Several years ago we bought a nice massage table on-line and our massage therapist comes to our house needing to bring only her cream and her healing hands. In an effort to take control of our health we consider massage to be part of our preventive health regimen and a great way to eliminate stress. Here is a suggested activity from Dorsey's therapist, Consuelo, to release creativity and reduce stress that you can do at home. It may help you deal with pain, stress, unrest…..and the chaos in your head:

One way to awaken creativity in you is a breathing exercise. Find a comfortable position. Not so comfortable that you fall asleep. Rest your hands on your abdomen and begin to breathe. The goal here is to distinguish between the left and right side of the brain. Breathe and observe. How much do you hear yourself thinking? How much are you feeling? Most of us think too much. After a few moments like this, begin to quiet the left brain by saying, No thinking. Just feeling. Take notice how you feel. Maybe have a pen and paper ready without disturbing yourself. The more you practice feeling the more your creativity can flow.

A Creative Touch To Dentistry

In 1998, Dr. Karen O'Donnell of Homewood, IL was in a funk. It was December and she wasn't feeling very cheery. Her mood ran more along the lines of getting through the holiday and on with life. She missed her mother, Mary Wright, who had died in 1985

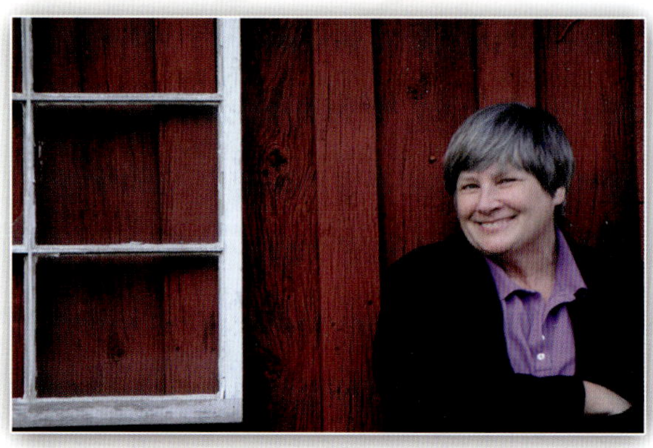

at the young age of 55 years old. A Christmas tradition Karen had grown up with was her mother's christmas fudge. She emailed her good friend and priest, John Cusick about missing that holiday tradition and he responded with, *"Karen, go ahead and make the fudge. I don't think she will mind."* That little nudge of encouragement changed her perspective and helped create a tradition of her own. She tells her story:

"Growing up the aroma of chocolate permeated our home during the holiday, as our family joined in the process of making Mom's Christmas Fudge. We eleven kids got to lick the spoons and eat the broken pieces. But this was not family fudge. It was Mom's special gift to her special friends. We weren't allowed to eat much because it was very expensive to make.

Mom wrapped her fudge in tin foil and ribbon, like a sacred gift. We all went from house to house as she hand delivered her fudge. Smiles were huge on the faces of those who received the special gift."

So that December in 1998 Karen contacted various family members and found the beloved recipe for her mother's fudge. One

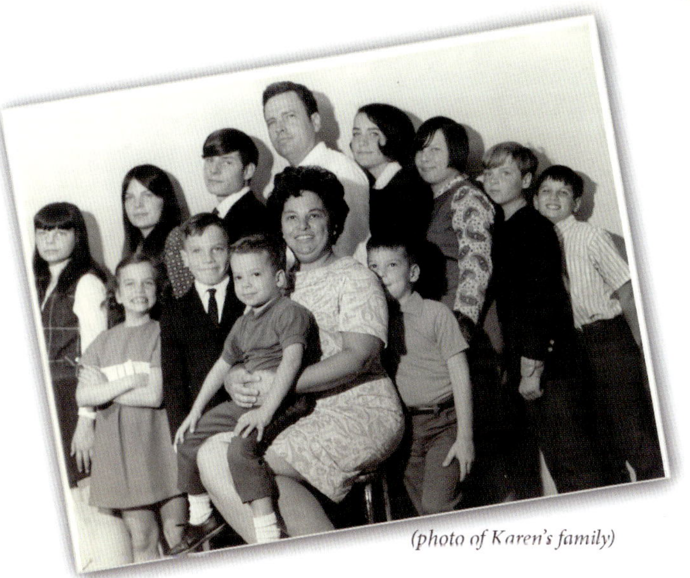
(photo of Karen's family)

day she placed a picture of her mother on the kitchen counter and turned on soft music as she began to melt together the ingredients for that wonderful fudge she had sorely missed. As the delicious aroma of the blended ingredients began to awaken her senses she could actually feel her mother's arms around her six-year-old shoulders as she helped her mother stir the pot. She could hear her brothers and sisters fighting over who got to lick the spoon and who got to lick the pan.

After Karen finished making her Christmas Fudge she emailed Fr. John and thanked him for helping make her Christmas more meaningful. She remembers that at the same time she sent Fr. John that message she heard a song on the radio she had never heard before called **Mother, I Miss You**, and wondered how God got into her radio!

Fr. John responded back to her, *"Karen, perhaps now you will understand what we mean when we say —Do this in memory of me."* But that isn't the end of Karen's story:

"On Christmas eve I sang in Fr. John's midnight mass. After mass I gave him a gift of the fudge I had made. His eyes welled up with tears as he said, 'This isn't about the fudge. This is about your mother's love.'

The following year I invited my nephews, who had never met Mom and we made the fudge together. Through the stories, the memories, the aroma and the taste, they came to know my Mother's love. They told me, 'She must have been a very special lady.'

Oh, yes, she was. And long after she is gone, her love remains visible through the fudge I make regularly and give to my patients each time they come to my office for an appointment. They won't leave without their little box of Mom's fudge. I like to think I continue to spread Mom's love throughout the world by giving her Special Fudge to special friends...."

Karen's story is a great example of being creative in showing her patients she cares. Karen is a dentist and, unfortunately, most people do not rate going to the dentist high on their list of fun things to do! But Karen's patients don't feel that way. They know they will be treated with love and care. Not just by Karen but by the loving memory of Karen's mother.

Creativity is a doorway in which we connect with what is larger than ourselves.

Dorsey

Do You Really Need This Illness?

Dorsey McHugh

There is a rainbow in the morning sky. The sun is shining, but it's still raining. In this place, in this moment, I am particularly aware of the strangeness of these juxtapositions. It's easy to see the metaphor. The exciting, joyful, lovely parts of life happen often in the same season as the sad and difficult. All mixed in together. This is certainly why art can have such a voice in our souls. Music, visual arts, movies, poetry, etc can all touch us deeply. The voice of art is often like a surgeon's hands. Hands that, in their skilled way, get deeply inside us. Healing us. Art plays the role of a rainbow……A promise. A still small voice whispering to us "Love is still real and Hope is still alive".

JM

Dorsey and I want you to think about being creative in every area of your life. One of the best ways to take back control of your life is to take inventory of your physical and mental health. What medications are you taking and why? Do you get up in the morning thinking:

I have the measles and the mumps,
A gash, a rash and purple bumps.
My mouth is wet, my throat is dry.
I'm going blind in my right eye.
My tonsils are as big as rocks,
I've counted sixteen chicken pox…

From the poem ***Sick (Where the Sidewalk Ends)***
Shel Silverstein (1930-1999)
poet, singer, songwriter, author

If you are distressed by anything external,
the pain is not due to the thing itself
but to your own estimate of it;
and this you have the power to
revoke at any moment.
Marcus Aurelius (121 AD-180 AD), Roman Emperor, philosopher

We agree with Stephen Pressfield (**The War of Art**): *"How many of us have become drunks and drug addicts, developed tumors and neuroses, succumbed to painkillers, gossip, and compulsive cell-phone use, simply because we don't do that thing that our hearts, our inner genius, is calling us to?"* We highly recommend reading his book, by the way.

When I was a teenager and into my early 20s, I was plagued by bouts of colitis. (Do you see a pattern of poor stress management here?) I was often ill and looked it. I was having a terrible time trying to break away from a controlling mother who demanded a lot from me. Pretty much, she made me sick. No, let me rephrase that. I allowed her to make me sick. (I read Dr. Wayne Dyer's book, **Your Erroneous Zones** back in the '70s!) I have learned that to process and handle well the trials of life and the stress of our everyday existence. It is a crazy game of Whack-A-Mole. You think you have finally got coping with one stress and then another pops up and you have to learn how to place that mallet over the current load of crap so you don't lose the game totally.

I find that learning to creatively deal with stress is not a one-time event and you are cured! I take great measures to recognize when stress is beating at my door. I was once asked by a group of incarcerated women, *"How do you stay looking so young and vibrant?"* I smiled and told them, *"I'm happy!"* And it is true. I am happy because I have creatively learned to take better care of myself and in so doing, am better able to care for the world around me.

The way you process stress is unique to the individual. For some people it is easier just to succumb to it. It becomes a comfortable misery. And truth be told, it is hard work to learn to deal with stress in a healthy way. Easier to self-medicate with nicotine, pain meds, hitting the bottle or illicit sex. Some just get a disease. Some just die. By their own hand or by a socially acceptable illness or accident.

Daniel once worked with a client, a highly paid doctor, who hated his career to the extent he took up ultra light aviation because he thought it would be a socially acceptable way to check-out and he would no longer have to face his everyday self-loathing.

Every stress leaves an indelible scar, and the organism pays for its survival after a stressful situation by becoming a little older.

Hans Selye (1907-1982) Austrian-Canadian endocrinologist, ***The Stress of Life*** *(1956)*

Getting To The Root Of Creativity

Pei Kang-Boggess *(www.findingyourvoiceradio.com)* is an endodontist by profession. She and her husband, Joel, are also certified life coaches and she is a registered yoga instructor. She is professionally trained to get to the roots of teeth, but her real joy is helping people get to the root of their own authenticity. When I interviewed her she offered some wise insight into the mind-body connection:

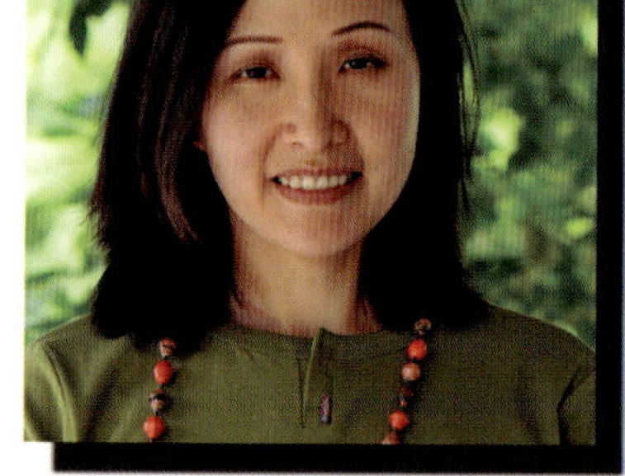

"I am rarely ill but when I have been, I have found my illness is accompanied by negativity in other areas of my life. Illness seems to take away my ambition to tackle other major roles or accomplishments or to make wise decisions. Physical health affects one's mental health.

When we talk about our 'gut feeling' it is for a reason. Our digestion does affect our health. There is a similarity in the looks of the brain and the looks of one's digestive system. And, similarly, the digestive tract has its own process of 'thinking'. Good digestive health is important for good overall health.

Each of us is unique in every way. It is important to tune into how food affects you. When you feel ill or fatigued, ask yourself, 'What have I done to my body that might have caused me to feel this way?'

I have a routine in yoga that includes several simple deep stretches that open up the meridians to vital organs--kidneys and bladder and others. In Chinese medicine it is believed the kidneys and bladder are related to the emotion of fear. So many of our life decisions are based on either love or fear. When we are fearful, we can't be very creative because creativity comes out of the heart—out of love. When you open up those channels, you unblock creative energy. Similar to pulling weeds after the soil has been softened by a rain, the stretches help me generate new ideas and creativity. I think about how grateful I am when I am stretching and that brings on more positive energy and better health."

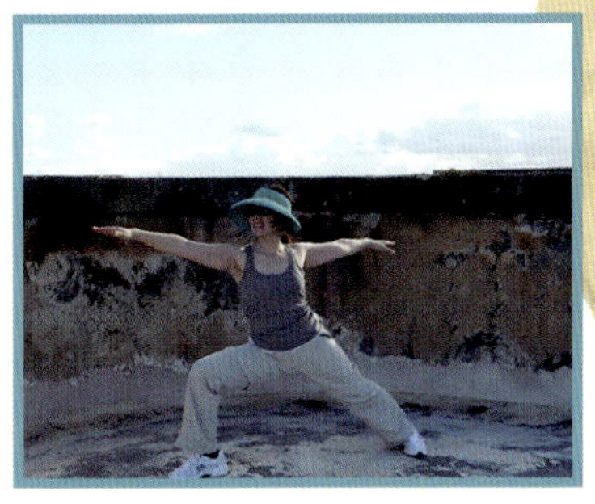

I promise you nothing is as chaotic as it seems. Nothing is worth your health. Nothing is worth poisoning yourself into stress, anxiety, and fear.
Dr. Steve Maraboli, Behavioral Scientist, Peak-Performance Coach, Speaker, Author

Bernie Siegel, MD, wrote an amazing book titled **Love, Medicine and Miracles**. It should be recommended reading for anyone suffering from disease, illness or stress. No, let me restate that. It should be read by everyone before they encounter disease and stress-caused illness in their lives; anyone who wants to take control over their health. I figure that covers about everyone. (Dorsey admonishes me when I "should" on people but we both agree on this.) There is no one totally immune to stress. In America it is so pervasive that we almost pride ourselves competing with others as to how much stress we can endure.

Dr. Siegel relates a time when he became the patient due to a severe staph infection that landed him in the hospital. It was an invaluable learning experience for him. *"When we play the role of a saint with one-word answers, we don't help people. We help when we listen and share our pain. We must live the sermon, not just deliver it."* he wrote.

This illness came at a time when Dr. Siegel had a lot of changes in his life. We must recognize that even positive events can cause stress.

Stress Inducers
A Wedding
A Divorce
A Birth
A Death
A Challenge
A Deadline
An Earthquake or Hurricane
A Threat
A Vacation
A Holiday
A Lost Job
A Family Reunion
A Child in Trouble
A Fight or Argument
Some events on this list are fun and exciting......and stressful.

While being the patient, Dr. Siegel began to realize the importance of listening to his patients and asking questions that told him a more complete story about why a patient may have fallen ill or contracted a disease. Interestingly, he discovered his patients were shocked he would ask questions that were spot on

The greatest discovery of our age is that people can alter their reality by altering their states of mind.
Wm. James (1842-1910) American philosopher and psychologist

about changes and stress in their lives. Dr. Siegel believes that if everyone took more control over their own healing there would be far fewer deaths. He and his patients make decisions together and create a relationship based on trust, truth and empathy. Now isn't *that* a novel idea? This is a doctor who is being very creative in treating his patients and is reaping amazing results.

I highlighted many pages in Dr. Siegel's book but this part really jumped out at me: *"Part of the mind's effect on health is direct and conscious. The extent to which we love ourselves determines whether we eat right, get enough sleep, smoke, wear seat belts, exercise, and so on. Each of these choices is a statement of how much we care about living. These decisions control about 90 percent of the factors that determine our state of health."* He goes on to talk about self love and how it *"has come to mean only vanity and narcissism. The pride of being and the determination to care for our own needs have gone out of the meaning........Self-esteem and self-love are not sinful. They make living a joy instead of a chore."* He goes on to say we tend to make self prophecies by our negative remarks…such as *"this problem is eating me alive."*

I promise you nothing is as chaotic as it seems. Nothing is worth your health. Nothing is worth poisoning yourself into stress, anxiety, and fear.
Dr. Steve Maraboli, Behavioral Scientist, Peak-Performance Coach, Speaker, Author

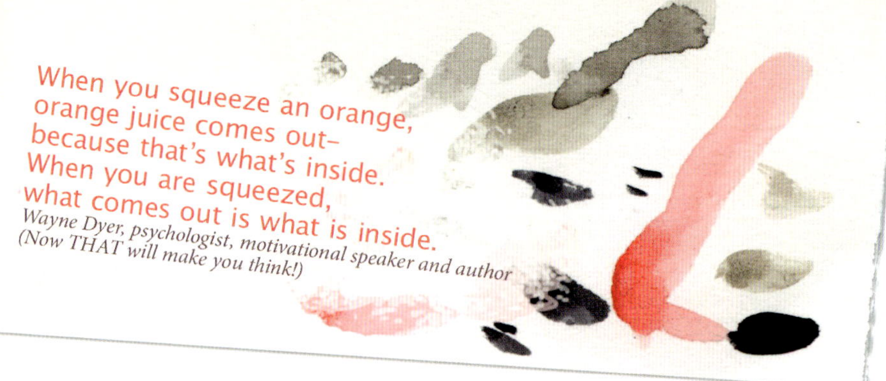

One important fact I learned in reading Dr. Siegel's book is that living with tension and anxiety (stress) on a continual basis lowers our resistance to disease. Another example of how our state of mind has an immediate and direct effect on our *state of body.* We can change the body by dealing with how we feel. One's attitude towards oneself is the single most important factor in healing or staying well. Those who are at peace with themselves and their immediate surroundings have far fewer serious illnesses than those who are not……..When we don't deal with our emotional needs, we set ourselves up for physical illness……..Those who can give vent to their feelings yet continue with their lives generally stay well.

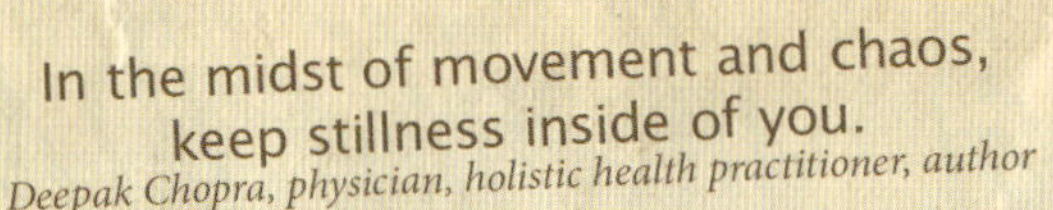

Creativity can be good for your health

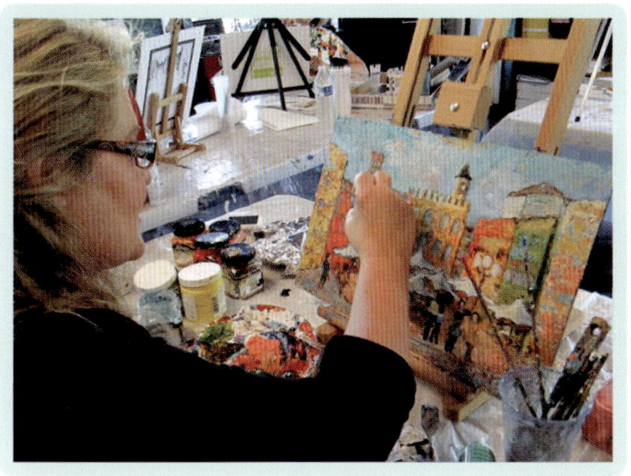

Redefining Her Voice

Sometimes physical problems come out of nowhere and leave us baffled as to what to do to compensate.

My very creative friend, Deby Dearman and her husband, Kirk have been leading worship services all over the world for decades. They have written many worship songs you would likely recognize. But in the last couple of years Deby has found she has been losing her voice. Literally and figuratively. Her singing and speaking have been greatly hindered by a severe problem with her vocal chords that often makes speaking difficult for her, much less singing. In the last year, she became one of Dorsey's students and has surprised herself with a talent she didn't know was there. One day she told Daniel she was shocked to find she could paint. She said she wondered what other talents she has never delved into might be lying dormant inside her. Wow! What an interesting way to look at what most would perceive as a serious career diversion!

Deby has been having art shows and selling her work and being commissioned to do more. She has definitely found a new voice. And interestingly, she is finding her speaking/singing voice is getting better in the process! *www.ComeToTheQuiet.com.*

Now is a good time for a personal disclaimer. *Please do not misconstrue what I am saying to imply that if you have an illness or malignancy you are only imagining it or that you caused it. My goal is to impress on you the importance of taking your health and well being to more creative levels to overcome some of the manifestations of stress in your life. And as a by-product you may become your own best physician!*

Give sorrow words;
the grief that does not speak
knits up the o-er wrought heart
and bids it break.

William Shakespeare (1564-1616),
English poet and playwright, ***Macbeth***

I have talked with many people who have found being creative, in whatever form, to be emotionally healing. C.S. Lewis said, *"Sorrow...turns out to be not a state but a process."* When he lost his wife, Joy, he wrote a lot about sorrow and grief. His writing helped him express his deepest feelings and getting them out on paper, I suspect, was therapeutic.

Creativity is a rare part of living. It's fundamental.
None of us can squelch our creativity without feeling
less than whole, incomplete and depressed.

Lynn Weiss, PhD, ADHD expert, author and consultant

Creativity can be good for your health

The Pain Of Divorce

Jeanne Bilbo has been an avid journal writer for decades. Her journaling and foray into art helped her through the pain of divorce. Here is part of an entry from her journal in 2007:

"Over the years, I have had pictures in my head that have enabled me to categorize or explain my own heartache and suffering. I have generally assumed they were God's way of speaking to me; His way to enable me to find where I had been and where I was, and where I was going. For those of us who are in a life transition like divorce....where we have been and where we are is the easy part. Where are we going? That question seemed like an almost impossible quest for me. So, I journaled and whenever I had a picture in my head, I drew it in my journal, and sometimes put it on canvas with splashes of paint. I have kept a journal on and off since I was twenty-one years old.

Writing, drawing, and painting enabled me to grasp the reality of my overwhelming emotions. My own creativity explained and categorized where I had been and where I was in that moment. It also gave me a better understanding which enabled me to leave it behind and create space to move into a more positive future."

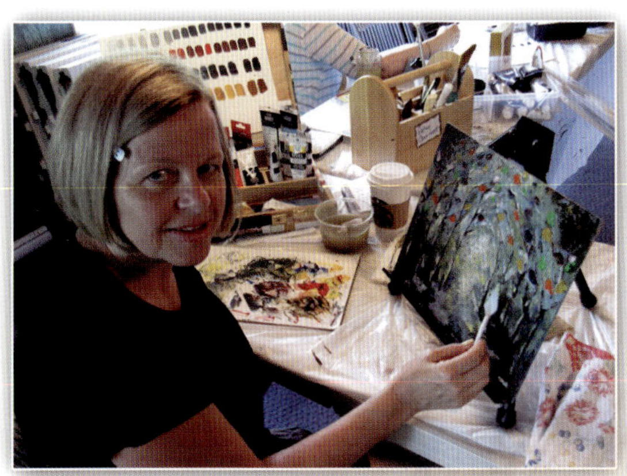

photo of Jeanne in Dorsey's art class

Walking Through Grief

I asked my niece, Rhoda Marie Miller to tell how her creativity has helped deal with the painful death of her older sister in 2000. You may remember I mentioned SaraLisa in Jared's telling of his imaginary friend, Cathy. Here is what Rhoda wrote:

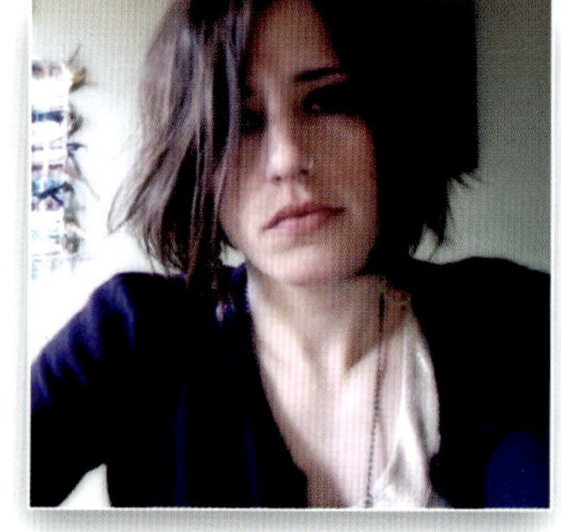

"I don't know if creativity is an innate or cultivated characteristic. I do know that what creativity I was born with was nurtured from a young age by my parents and an influential art teacher I was blessed to learn from for eleven years throughout my childhood. I also know that at the lowest, darkest times of my life, I have clung to my creativity and art like a life preserver in the middle of a raging ocean, and without fail, it has held me up every time. I've often heard people talk about having pets for their ability to love unconditionally, and it may sound silly, but that is what art has done for me. Art has always given back to me in a way no human or pet ever could.

Art pulled me from the depths of what could have been a vast depression after my sister, SaraLisa, ended her life when I was 19. A sophomore in college and having recently changed my major to art, I poured myself into creative expression as a form of healing for the first time in my life. For several years after SaraLisa's death I was very resistant to traditional counseling; I have later come to realize that I am a very internal processor, one who can sit on my thoughts and emotions for weeks without being able to make sense of them. In the early stages of grief, often my only moments of great clarity were found through creating art. In the lowest times following my sister's death, I sank deep into myself and was often only pulled out through visual expression, writing, and the sheer determination to continue living.

Throughout the years, many people have told me that something good would come of her death. Life events of such enormity are never able to be quantified, nor would I ever begin to find equal the exchange of my sister's life for my expanded artistic repertoire. What I do know is, while my loss has brought me great pain, my pain has inspired multiple facets of creative expression that I may never have otherwise experienced.

I credit art more than any other thing in my life for bringing me great healing. Art has taught me to be gentle with myself, as nothing ever comes out on canvas in the way I imagine it. I have learned vulnerability by sharing my work with others. It has also sparked countless conversations and thus forced me to add external processing to my coping skills, ultimately leading me to be comfortable speaking with a therapist. Healing never happens in a vacuum or through one mode of processing alone, and I believe the winning combination of these pathways is different for each person. Art is something I take with me wherever I go and I know as long as I have the ability to create, I will feel like a whole person with a world of possibility at my fingertips."

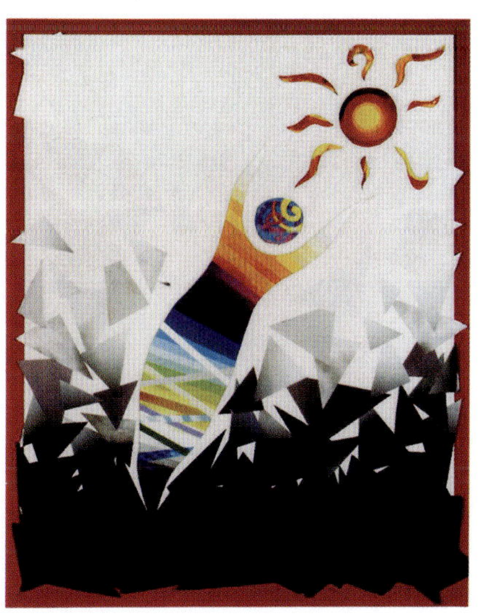

Rhoda's art will never take the place of the sister she loves but she recognizes the power in using her creative energies to bring her inner peace.

A month after SaraLisa's death, Rhoda submitted this piece of art as a final project in her college art class. Her mother, Viola, took it to a conference on Suicide Prevention in Canton, Ohio where she was to be part of a panel discussion of survivors. The Director of the Ohio Suicide Prevention Foundation saw the piece and ultimately it was chosen as the state logo and is used in many OH county suicide coalitions statewide. Visit Rhoda's website at *www.rhodarts.com.*

Those who do not weep, do not see.
Victor Hugo (1802-1885), French poet and novelist, ***Les Miserables***

Health From Within

When I met Shannon Skye, a young chiropractor and a self-described "healthy, happy hippy", I knew she was one healer who understands how the mind can control the body. What follows is a brief interview with Dr. Skye:

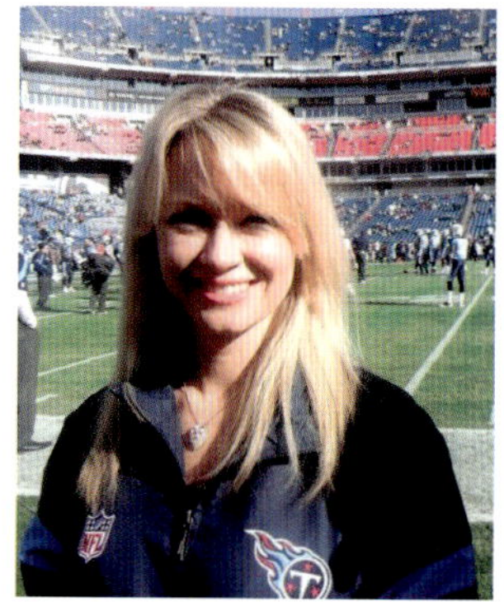

"In chiropractic we believe that health comes from within. If we take two people with similar genes from the same environment, one gets sick and the other does not, we have to ask why?

The answer lies in how we relate to our environment, and we do that through the nervous system. Is there something interfering with the neurological pathways that prevents them from properly adapting to their environment? Things that could be interfering with that pathway are stress, thoughts, trauma and toxins.

So if we accept that health starts in the mind, then it is critical to examine our thoughts. Sometimes you don't choose a thought that comes into your mind, but you do have a choice in what you invite to have a cup of coffee with you. If your thoughts are not as kind, forgiving, loving, or patient as you hope, change your mind. Remember your body is listening to the conversation going on inside, and responding to it.

Anxiety, anger and fear stimulate the Sympathetic Nervous System, (fight or flight response) which increases your heart rate, breathing and adrenal glands. The feeling of worry activates the Parasympathetic System, stimulating the digestive glands. If there is no food present, this is a negative response and can lead to ulcers, colitis, IBS, and gastritis.

Additionally, the subconscious is where the majority of the activity takes place in the mind. Imagine background music that is always playing. If your life has not been full of trauma (emotional, physical or spiritual) the music is soft and, most likely, pleasant. But if you, like the majority of adults, have grown up in an imperfect world filled with imperfect people, there is likely a lot of static playing in the background. That static becomes an irritant in the mind which will eventually be expressed as physical symptoms."

www.skyechiropractic.com

The components of anxiety, stress, fear, and anger do not exist independently of you in the world. They simply do not exist in the physical world, even though we talk about them as if they do.
Wayne Dyer, psychologist, self-help speaker and psychologist.

There are many benefits of positive self-talk and taking time to rest when needed. Confining my worry to only those things for which I have control eliminates a lot of stress. You can reduce negativity by restricting media input. In doing this, your energies can be better spent taking inventory of your assets and finding creative outlets for using them.

My Mentor

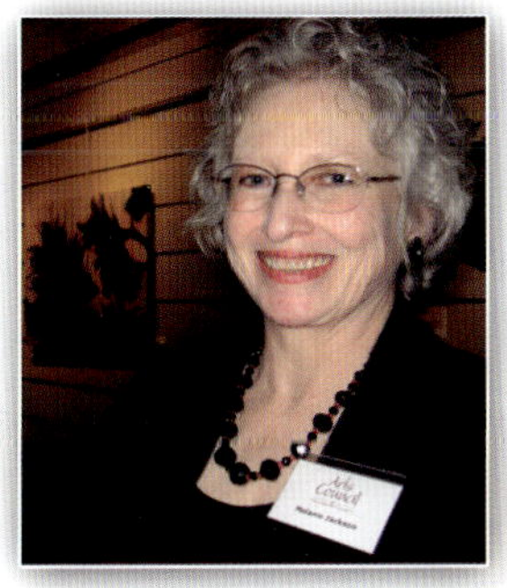

What a difference those hours of art with Melanie Jackson made in my life. I learned to see my world very differently. I also received the gift of better problem solving through learning to draw. Ten years ago I had no idea I could draw. I had certainly never considered myself an artist. I have since been in numerous art shows (*thank you, Melanie!*), taught art classes, spoken on creativity and honed my skills as an artist. Art has made me more confident, more authentic and more content. There was a new world out there for me (new glasses!) I observe more, notice more, see more clearly and listen better. And I continue to learn. Yes, I wear rose-colored glasses and carry a bouquet of happy thoughts most of the time. Art is a part of my health regimen.

A lot of what we think of as neurosis in this country is simply people who are unhappy because they're not using their creative resources.
*Julia Cameron, author **The Artist's Way***

I know when I am being creative I am happier and more excited and energized than I am otherwise. Because I have taken time to develop my artistic side, I am more in tune with the world around me. I can't help but be. When engaging your right brain you develop a whole new dimension to life. And you become healthier, happier and more fun to be around.

My friend, Mattie DiBona has been plagued for many years with serious illness, sometimes quite debilitating. She often talked about her love for writing and being creative so I encouraged her to take art classes. She began to take Drawing From the Right Side of the Brain from Melanie Jackson and has been diligent about attending class even when she is not feeling her best and in spite of the over thirty miles one way she has to drive. Mattie says this about her new-found creative energy and excitement:

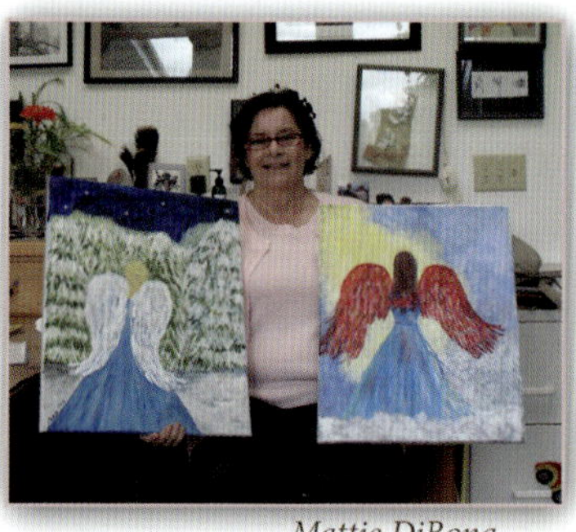

Mattie DiBona

"All my life I have been interested in the arts - drama, music, writing, etc. Several years ago I had a brain aneurysm. I developed other serious illnesses and in fact was bed-ridden for two years. Enrolling in the art class was one of the best therapies I have done to make sure I get healthier. My life is so much richer and fuller for this and my stamina and self-esteem have increased since starting the lessons. I have many more good days now than bad. I feel art has given me a sense of purpose. I have now enlisted two of my friends and we all ride together, enjoying the beautiful scenery along the way."

Artistic expression helps us to resolve our angst through paint, paper, etc. Art is like blood in the body. You can take a sample of blood and find out all sorts of things about a person. The value a person, organization, etc places on art reflects who they are; how healthy they are. Art is the overflow of a heart filled with LIFE.

Dorsey

Awaken Your Senses

1. Is there something creative you could incorporate in your work that would make that environment more unique & welcoming?

2. Can you take a realistic look at why you might be ill & how you could be creative in your own healing?

3. Can you be honest with yourself about how you relate to your environment & the people in your life?

4. In what ways can you be more creatively intentional with your physical & mental health regime?

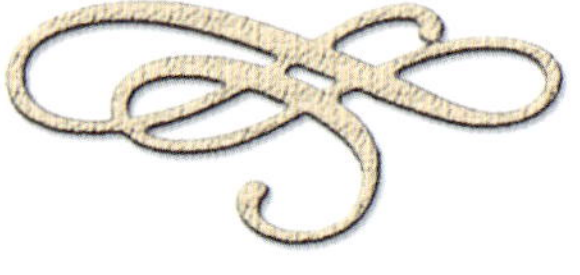

WHAT'S
KILLING
YOUR
CREATIVITY
?

Teaching and learning should be a joy!
Rita F. Pierson, Ed.D, Education and anti-poverty advocate since 1972

Make Your Own Coloring Book!

Daniel and I took our second son, Jared, out of school in the middle of sixth grade. It was a scary and revolutionary thing to do in the 1980s. Our family of five was making a major move to a neighboring state and having to uproot Jared in the middle of a school year was going to be a major ordeal. We had been having a rough time dealing with his acting out in school and I knew from the time he began first grade we had a *square-peg-in-a-round-hole kinda situation* trying to fit Jared into a traditional classroom setting.

It had been hard enough with our first son, Kevin, who had difficulty understanding why he had to go to school to learn coloring inside the lines when he really wanted to make his own coloring book. He was smart and enjoyed learning until going to school killed his enthusiasm. In a Christian kindergarten class, Kevin got his hands slapped (they could do that then) because he said *"poop"* in school. When we went to pick him up early one day and saw how the children were forced to stand in a straight line and not speak a word while waiting for lunch we decided we weren't paying to put our preschooler through military camp. We promptly unenrolled him.

When we begin studying the person,
the real child,
we must serve who he is,
not fit him into our schedules or plans.
Part of this is allowing him play.
Susan Schaeffer Macaulay, ***For the Children's Sake*** *published in 1984*

What's killing your creativity?

Another incident that stands out as a real winner is when a fifth grade teacher told Kevin he should listen to her and not rely so much on his parents because she was the one who had the degrees and his parents were idiots. Seriously? You can imagine the stir that caused in our family.

While visiting Kevin and his family in Colorado he brought out a copy of the letter Daniel wrote to the school superintendent during that fiasco. I was again incensed reading what that teacher actually told the students about her superiority over their stupid parents.

Daniel (who, by the way had more education than she did, if you want to get down and dirty) began a ritual of going to the school and observing her class. We tried to get her ousted from the school because that was not the first time she had told Kevin he was listening to too much Christian teaching. Getting her fired was impossible. We were told she had "tenure". Give me a break. The woman was a disaster in the classroom (they didn't deny she was out of line) but the best they could do was pack her off to another school to be a poor teacher there. Sad, discouraging and totally unacceptable.
But in the '70's, as young, naïve and inexperienced parents, we really didn't think we had a choice in educating our children outside the traditional norm.

When faced with moving to another state as a result of a devastating business crash that left us without a house, without automobiles *(we had to borrow one. The IRS wanted to be paid now!)* and no money,

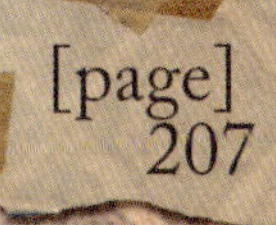

we were confronted with pulling Jared out of school in the middle of an already difficult academic year.

Being the enterprising man that my husband is, he knew he had to revert back to his skill of being a good salesman to dig us out of the financial hole we were in. In a sort of cleansing-our-palates kind of way, we chose to move from the area where we had the business crash and move to Nashville, TN, a city we had loved each time we visited. Due to the good fortune of networking and finding a house available we could live in while it was being readied to sell, we moved to Nashville without checking out the school situation much.

When I realized Jared was going to have to catch the school bus an hour early (before light in the winter months), be bused to a huge inner-city school, my mother's heart did a complete nose-dive. I could not allow my son to sink further into trouble and I knew that the scenario I was putting him in would not foster a good educational experience for him. But what to do?

Homeschooling Jared, as suggested to me by others, presented me with an option that seemed scary at best. I thought the idea laughable, which is the response I hear a lot when I mention this possibility to other parents who have children struggling in school.

One day Daniel brought home a book by Susan Schaeffer Macaulay called **For the Children's Sake**. I reluctantly read the book

When a baby is picked up, spoken to, and loved, he is starting his education as God planned it. For all our lives we are human beings, in an active state of learning, responding, understanding. Education extends to all of life. In fact, an educational system that says, one bright summer's day in the dawn of my youth, 'There. Now you are educated. This piece of paper says so' is doing me a gross disfavor. The truly educated person has only had many doors of interest opened. He knows that life will not be long enough to follow everything through fully.

Susan Schaeffer Macaulay~ ***For the Children's Sake***

and it began a mindset change that unleashed the creativity our family now so avidly embraces.

The closest thing to teaching I had ever done in my life, or so I *thought*, was standing in front of my dolls and stuffed animals as a young teacher wannabe or helping my mother grade test papers when she was a high-school English teacher. After reading Macaulay's and similar books, I realized the importance of being a *living* example of the education you want your child to have. I hadn't recognized I was teaching my child every day by everything I read, spoke, experienced and acted upon. I began to see possibilities for educating my child(ren) in a very non-traditional way that probably changed the trajectory of his life (and mine) in profound ways. So I *timidly* said yes to home-schooling Jared. And no to continuing the path of traditional schooling I suspected would destroy his will to learn.

With a high school diploma, average grades, a year and a half of college where I majored mainly in dating, and a degree from a business school in retailing and fashion design with some modeling thrown in, I didn't have much confidence in my teaching skills.

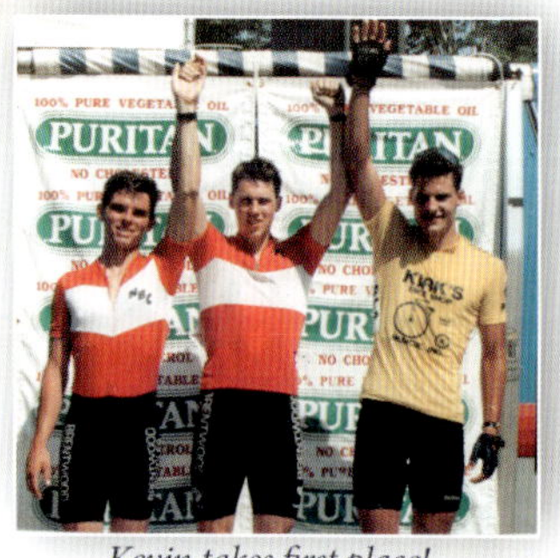

Kevin takes first place!

Kevin had graduated from high school, by passed college and was burned out on formal education. He was living in Europe as a professional bicycle racer. His dream was to find his own form of education in the real world.

Our youngest, Ashley, was in third grade and since I was very intimidated at first, I figured home-schooling one child (one active, think-outside-the-box, non-conformist, adventure-seeking sixth-grader) was all I could handle starting out. We put Ashley in a grade school within walking distance where she finished out her third grade year totally bored with the program because she was so far ahead in her academic skills.

Homeschooling Jared was wonderful! It was **amazing!** My fears of not being able to teach, not being able to handle being one-on-one with this child with whom I so often butted heads, not being able to get him to sit still long enough to learn quickly dissipated. I think we both felt the richness of the one-on-one interaction and I got the privilege of getting to know my son in a way I never would have if we had continued the more traditional path. I soon regretted I had not taken this path with Kevin. But, I simply didn't know I had options. Today's world is different. We have so many options for educating young minds from Internet resources to homeschooling to private schools. All of our grandchildren are, in some form, homeschooled and attend small private schools for some subjects.

That first year went so well that when Ashley asked to be homeschooled, I took her out of school after her 3rd grade experience. Because she was academically gifted and easy to teach and because Jared was dyslexic, ADHD, bipolar *(you pick the label ...he was diagnosed with them all)* and a poor reader, I pretty much taught them together rather than differentiating grade level. When they got to high school I put them in group classes with other homeschooled teens. They had certified, retired or substitute teachers to cover my limitations.

I learned quickly how creative my kids were. They loved art much like most kids like recess! When they were creating they got in a "zone" that made any lesson more palatable. In discovering this style of teaching I also discovered my own passion for being creative. When we studied history, math or language we made art projects that went along with what we were learning. That technique made learning fun and exciting for them. They began to want to learn and have continued to be lifelong learners.

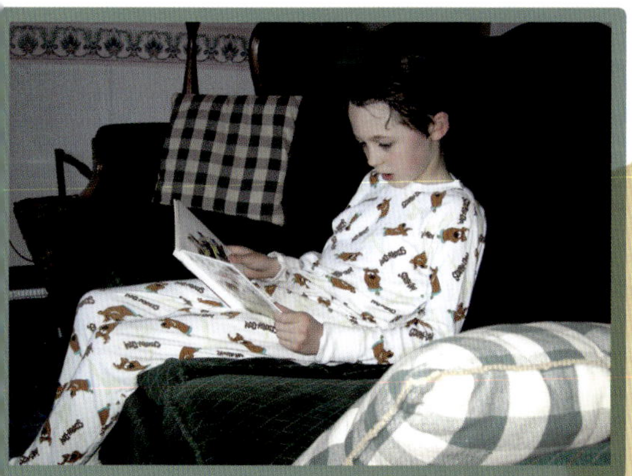

Every child deserves a champion—an adult who will never give up on them, who understands the power of connection, and insists that they become the best that they can possibly be.

Rita F. Pierson, Ed.D,
Education and anti-poverty advocate since 1972

Creativity Birthed From Expectation

By Kevin Daniel Miller, Woodland Park, CO (Oldest son of Joanne and Daniel)

"Children are expected and encouraged to be outrageously creative. Social media today is filled with proud parents rabidly posting pictures and testimony of their kid's creativity run wild. It's not only expected, it's assumed and lauded.

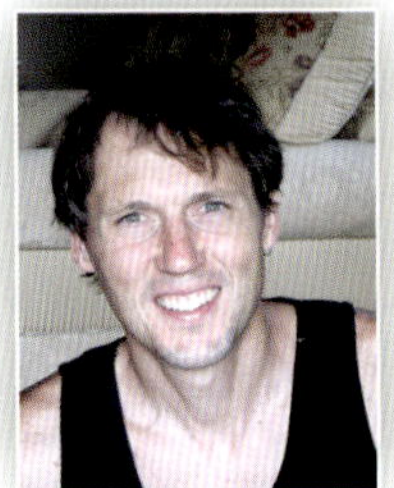

Until school, where often creativity is squelched and conformity and performance gain priority. Grades and academic accolades are the new goal and measuring stick for applause. One must not only get the grade, but stifle creativity in the achievement of the grade. If the correct answer is not accepted with a creative or intuitive approach to the conclusion, kids must showcase getting to that answer through the accepted steps.

My parents allowed/expected me to be creative right through school and into adulthood. School grades were not the measuring stick my parents adhered to, and questioning the norm was an expectation.

Family and meal times were not wasted on grilling me about my grades, but discussing the complexity and wonder of real life. If school and culture didn't add up, I was allowed, and even expected to question and ponder it. Debates were the norm in our family and this helped me to formulate my own beliefs.

When other kids were getting grounded for a poor grade that equaled mine, I was applauded for earning an income with a business endeavor or winning a bike race after countless months of disciplined training. When other kids and their parents were fretting over college applications, sometimes ignoring their 'bent' and natural inclinations, I was given the opportunity to tour the nation and globe on adventures that gave me true life and insight and a priceless education.

Today, the proud father of seven children, I am continuing this philosophy of providing for them a creative, thoughtful, intentional life of purpose. Grades and cultural benchmarks can be won by rote memorization and rule following. Creativity, wonder and glory are won by being given rein and encouragement to pursue them."

FreeAgentUprising.com

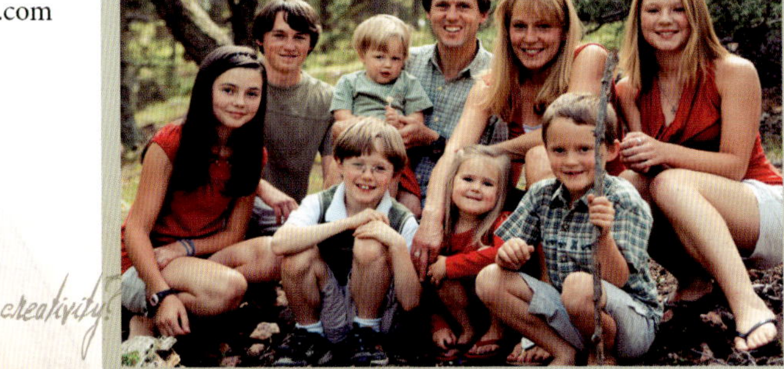

Teaching for creativity aims to encourage self-confidence, independence of mind, and the capacity to think for oneself.
Sir Ken Robinson, English author, speaker

Create A Learning Environment

The role of teacher should be to *facilitate* learning. To make learning such a part of everyday life that the child hardly knows when she is *in class.* This makes learning fun. Traditional schooling is not working for creative kids who quickly become labeled as "disruptive", "slow learner", "hyperactive", "inattentive" or "trouble maker". I began to recognize that over twenty years ago, before it became a popular notion. It didn't work for my creative right-brained children and I know others who struggle to fit into a system that often undervalues creativity as being frivolous, impractical and nugatory.

Dorsey and I encourage you to listen to Sir Ken Robinson or read his speeches on education and creativity. He is an British author, speaker and international advisor on education in the arts. In 2006 he gave an impassioned and rather humorous speech at a TED conference (Riveting talks by remarkable people, free to the world) about how schools kill creativity. Last time I viewed this talk it had been listened to over 19, 800,000 times. Pretty significant interest, wouldn't you say?

Creativity is as important in education as literacy and we should treat it with the same status.... We don't grow INTO creativity; we grow OUT of it... or rather we get EDUCATED out of it."
Sir Ken Robinson, Ted Talk in 2006

Sir Ken says human life is inherently creative but often lies dormant waiting for the seeds underneath to be given the opportunity to sprout. Children are natural learners. They learn from the people of influence around them, good and bad.

Our educational system is archaic and outmoded in the world we live in today and parents are becoming alarmingly aware of the need for change. Homeschooling, Unschooling and other terms are being used by parents who are striving to make learning a more positive experience in our changing and more right-brained world.

Create a climate of possibility!
Sir Ken Robinson, English author, speaker

People are becoming more open to alternative approaches to learning than ever before. And we are starting to understand that the college diploma does not carry all the promises with it that we have been led to believe for decades. In fact, many courses our children are taking now are quite possibly going to be outdated by the time they graduate! Now that is an interesting thought.

100% College Admission - How Sad

Last Sunday on a leisure drive back from lunch Joanne and I passed one of the most prestigious private high schools in our area. A sign was proudly posted at the front entrance stating: "100% College Admission for our Seniors – again."

I'll have to admit I cringed on seeing that. Now I know that any high school principal who doesn't claim this as his/her goal is likely to be accused of not having the student's best interests at heart and would also likely be run out of town by indignant parents. But personally, I think there is a major elitism at play here. And ultimately, a lot of those students suffer as a result. Is our goal really to prepare every student for life in a cubicle? In looking at my grandchildren I see those who would weep at such a prospect.

The elitism is in believing that every occupation pursued by a path outside of college is somehow "lower" and not a worthy pursuit for our students. We have become a culture that looks down on labor and craftsman positions. So, really, in this graduating class we will have no Ferrari mechanics, no sculptors, no HVAC specialists, no one I can contact to design another water feature, no skilled carpenters, no stone masons, no welders and no piano tuners?

If we consider our children to be smart and really want the best for them, should we not consider a broad range of occupational possibilities?

I must admit I've made a very good living working with people who at 45 years of age admit they are living someone else's dream. As we unpack that incongruity and begin to move toward an authentic life, all kinds of things come to the surface as meaningful work possibilities. Pastors have become artists, dentists forest rangers, and doctors organic gardeners.

Having the ability to go to college is not enough reason for doing so. There must be more of an alignment with a person's values, dreams and passions. I have worked with countless professionals who have proven their academic ability to create a life they detest.

Let's stop depriving our children of their best options. I'd like to see that sign say – 60% college, 10% trade school, 10% continuing family business, 10% entrepreneurs, and 10% world travel to further clarify a career path. That would make me want to send my child there.

From a blog posted by Dan Miller, www.48Days.com,
100% College Admission—How Sad, June 11, 2013

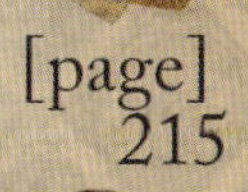

Preparation For Life?

It is interesting how our public school systems devalue life skills as no longer important enough to include in their curriculum. Many schools can no longer "afford" to teach home economics and mechanics but Heaven help us if someone suggests they eliminate the football program.

I remember how incensed the office staff would get over our trying to take Kevin out of school to experience new areas of the country with his bicycle racing or to hear his dad speak on motivational topics of work and relationship. More than once we told these well meaning academicians to go ahead and give him Fs for the time away if necessary (their policy) but our child would be going with us so we could further his education in the way we felt best.

Ironically, when Kevin graduated high school it was not uncommon for our friends to ask if he was going to college. Daniel would chuckle and say, *"He's living in Europe; too busy getting an education to be in college!"*

Teaching by example, travel, exploration and adventure was how we began to approach educating our kids and we learned as much as they did. Educating our kids creatively has taught us so much about the excitement and importance of continued learning. We have redefined education to include life skills.

Live as if you were to die tomorrow.
Learn as if you were to live forever.
Mahatma Gandhi (1869-1948), Indian civil rights leader of non-violence

Examples of creative education for us included going to a bakery and watching how donuts were made from start to tasty finish. As a family we went to a Hutterite community in New York to stay a few days to expose them to an alternate lifestyle. We took them to libraries,to museums, to the English Cotswolds, to plays and speeches, and to hear motivational speakers they grew to love and quote.

Each of our children went, as youngsters, to hear and personally meet popular motivational speaker, Zig Ziglar. His book, **See You at the Top**, became one we studied in its entirety. Dave Ramsey's Financial Peace is a far better Economics class for life preparation than most textbooks. I became quite creative in molding their curriculum so they remained interested and eager to learn more. I adapted each subject to include artistic expression that has kept them eager for learning and seeking new adventures into adulthood.

Here's a creative tip we used when one of our children needed to be disciplined. From the time our kids were around 8 years old, they would receive time outs by taking 10-30 minutes listening to a Zig Ziglar motivational tape (back when we had cassette players!) and then telling us what they learned. Zig was a family favorite.

You are what you are
and you are where you are
because of what has gone into your mind.
You change what you are and you change where you are
by changing what goes into your mind.
Zig Ziglar (1926-2012) motivational trainer, teacher and author

Zig died in 2012, a sad day for the Miller family. He had become not only an icon in the world of business and speaking but he had become a friend, a trusted adviser and mentor for all of us. He appealed to all ages. Here is a popular Ziglar-ism that our kids particularly liked:

Don't Get Cooked In The Squat

"Many times individuals will indicate with a nod of the head that they already know or have heard the information as I start to cover a point in a talk. I'm often tempted to stop and ask what they've done about it. Unless and until you do something with what you have learned, you might as well not have learned it. ***The person who won't read is no better off than the person who can't read.*** *The person who knows but won't use success principles and information is no better off than the person who doesn't know them. You intend to "do something," don't you?*

Success is not a destination, it's a journey, it's the direction in which you are traveling. *Not only have you started, but you're headed in the right direction.*

Most people wait until everything is just right before they do anything. They refuse to go out on a limb where the fruit is. They are the people who end up like the cook's biscuits.

Let me explain. When I was a small boy in Yazoo City, Mississippi, we lived next door to some rich folks. I know they were rich because they not only had a cook, but the cook had something to cook. In the 1930's that was a sure sign of wealth. I was there for lunch one day, as I tried to be most every day. On this occasion, the cook brought out a pan of biscuits. Since they were no thicker than a silver dollar, I asked, "Maude, what happened to those biscuits?" She reared back, laughed, and said, "Well, those biscuits squatted to rise, but they just got cooked in the squat."

Zig Ziglar, **See You at the Top**, 1974 Pelican Publishing Co, Inc.
Ziglar.com

The expiration date of pharmaceuticals specifies the date the manufacturer guarantees the full potency and safety of a drug. Why don't universities specify the length of time a degree will be fully applicable and useful? When I graduated from Ohio State University I was required to take a computer course to be eligible for a BA degree. I took FORTRAN. Developed in 1958, it was an early version of programming. Today it's right up there with the rotary phone in terms of usefulness. My diploma should have estimated the value of that to expire in perhaps 1979.

From a blog posted by Dan Miller, www.48Days.com, ***Your Diploma Has Expired****, April 29, 2013*

Awaken Your Senses

1. Are you open to alternative forms of learning for yourself & your family?

2. Can you envision a learning environment in your home that is stimulating & creative?

3. Your inner voice is going to learn to speak. Are you willing to listen? Are you willing to trust it?

Are You Stifling Your Own Creativity?

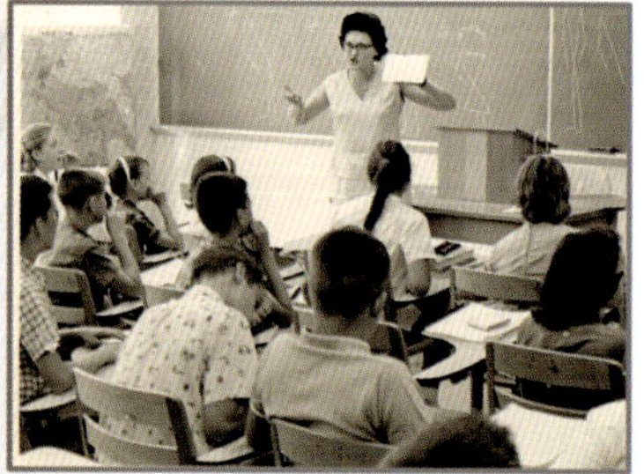
photo of Polly Fairchild, teaching

Writing has always come easy for me. My English teacher mother was my most ardent critic. It is safe to say she seemed overly enthusiastic in her criticism, often telling me what was grammatically or structurally wrong with my efforts. I would rework and rework till finally my finished writing would end up being hers, not mine. I stopped writing for many years.

Though my mother was a good English teacher, she was not well-versed in how to break the rules to be a good writer. Through my love of reading, it became apparent to me the rules could be broken. My illustrious art teachers have pointed out that when you know the rules you can break them successfully and make it work. Lots of good writers do. Good writing, as in all art forms (and sometimes life) doesn't have to obey all the rules.

My love of writing resurfaced when I was in my mid-forties. That desire to put my heart and soul on paper has grown immensely since I started taking art classes and discovering the joy of creativity.

What keeps you from being creative are the limitations you have put on yourself! Limiting your creativity is usually caused by one of 3 things; **1.** FEAR, **2.** SELF DOUBT, **3.** UNSolicited CRITICISM!
Since you are created by God in His image–the God who created Heaven and earth, all the creatures, plants and even man and woman–that makes you creative by the nature of your creator.
No Fear! No Doubt! And you can let go of that negative criticism and let that creativity show through!
Paula Foster, Executive Director, The Gathering Nashville, TN (www.thegatheringnashville.com), artist, speaker

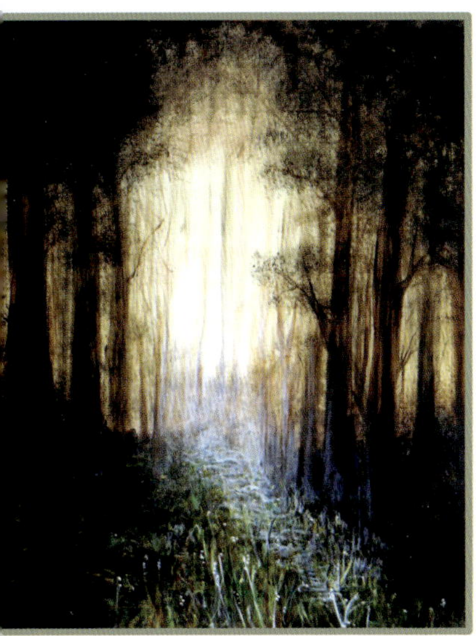

Acrylic on paper, ***Peace****, by Jean Clark*

Rekindling An Old Love

Jean Clark is my sister. Just thirteen months younger than I, she lives on Hilton Head Island and is a part-time dental assistant. She was creative as a youngster; loved art and sometimes worked in clay. Our mother was convinced Jean was going to end up behind bars and made Jean's life miserable in many ways. Often she lived with our grandparents and used her creative nature to enter horse shows with Bay Bonnie, her beloved horse, given to her by our grandfather.

As an adult she put away her creative interests, devoting time as a single parent raising two sons and pursuing a career in dentistry. Now Jean is in her early sixties and her boys are happily married. Jean has dear friends, who opened up an IDEA art studio (www.scartstudio.com) on the island and enlisted Jean's help from time-to-time while encouraging her to paint. Jean's first painting of a huge sea turtle was amazing! It was a piece worthy of praise! In the past year of painting Jean has turned out some incredible pieces. She finds painting relaxing and a great challenge. Being creative again has opened up an old love that brings joy and beauty into her life.

I have observed many men and women in midlife return to an

abandoned creative love, even developing a new career around their rekindled passion.

Dorsey McHugh

Possibly you will be able to relate to this experience. My mid-life "crisis" came in the form of art. No one was more surprised than I. School required me to take art in 7th grade. We were shown how to do a pastel still-life. Our art teacher gave us the formula for every object, leaving no room for individual creativity. This was perfect for me. Art held no appeal yet. This was not the beginning of my estrangement from art however.

At about age four my closest friend from childhood was my double cousin, Tim. We were 6 months apart, so Aunt Betsy, who wanted her own little girl, borrowed me most weekends. Betsy gave me a thorough idea of how a pampered little girl would feel. She is still one of my top ten favorite people. I loved her. So it is ironic she was the one who reacted so strongly to my color crayon rendition of 4 yr. old genitalia.

Like most young children, Tim and I were allowed to bathe together. After dinner and a bath one evening, we were lying on the floor, sharing a coloring book. Tim was doing a perfect job on his page (It makes sense. He is an electrical engineer now).

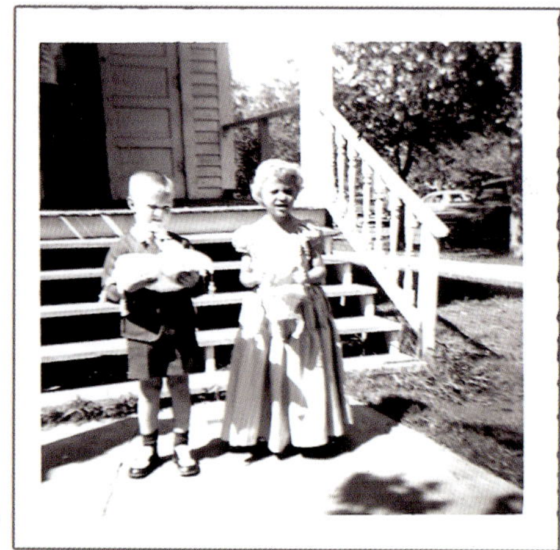

photo of Timmy and Dorsey

Coloring between the lines bored me, so, having just come from the bathtub, I saw nothing wrong with drawing penises all around the edges of the page. I must have been somewhat talented because when Aunt Betsy walked by, she …………freaked out! My shame became directed towards my creativity, and I never drew again unless forced. I needed Betsy to like me. It was years after my re-introduction to art that this memory emerged. It is cool to observe the power in creativity. It found a way to come out though I set up every road block I could.

Have you ever felt embarrassed or ashamed by your creativity? These stories aren't unusual. Thomas Edison only attended three months of official schooling because his teacher called him "addled". He was then homeschooled by his mother. Many times labels such as dyslexia, ADHD, Asperger's, etc. can crush a child's confidence to pursue creative endeavors. Yet, we know of many creatives who have become well known names in spite of their "labels". Richard Branson, Charles R. Schwab, Pablo Picasso, Tom Cruise, Whoopi Goldberg, and a long list of others were all considered "slow" due to their learning labels.

A Budding Artist

Dorsey asked her cousin Tim Edwards to write a bit about their adventures into creativity when they were youngsters. Perhaps this gives a bit of insight into this artist's imagination.

Children must be taught how to think, not what to think.
Margaret Mead (1901-1978), Anthropologist

"My dear cousin Dorsey asked me to discuss the evolution of the creative mind and whether or not a creative person resides in all of us. I might add that this type of discussion with Dorsey is typical of numerous other discussions we have engaged in over a lifetime of self- discovery and a quest for a logical explanation of who we are and how did we get here.

The unfamiliar reader must understand our unique genetic bond of being "double cousins" with fathers that were brothers and mothers that were sisters. With this in mind, it is reasonably accurate to state that our gene makeup is nearly identical. In our adolescent years we were commonly mistaken as twins while in fact, she is the elder by a few months. During our early childhood years we were nearly inseparable and exposed to essentially the same environment. Why, then, did these 'two peas in the pod' (one male-one female) evolve to such different careers; she the artist (right brain) and me the electrical engineer (left brain)? Or, perhaps we aren't so different after all!

Two memories from our early childhood years might shed some light on the evolution of the artist (Dorsey). The first invokes vivid images of an apple orchard located in the back yard of the farm house where Dorsey lived with her family. It was a somewhat magical place to us and we spent countless hours there creating what we called 'spitza', commonly known as mud pies. While some may have labeled our creations mundane, we saw things quite differently. Dorsey was the creative genius of this play and I was merely along for the ride because I enjoyed playing in the mud.

Another activity we enjoyed together on the farm was gathering eggs. Mind you, this was the good old days of free range farm chickens that were likely to lay eggs nearly anywhere around the barn yard. The work of gathering eggs was also a game of hide and seek. We became quite adept at finding the eggs as the chickens usually returned to the same location. On one such excursion I recall we discovered a new art form of creative expression by taking the eggs we had diligently gathered and hurling them against the weathered barn boards where they would break and leave a glistening yellow pattern as they slid down the boards. Recrimination for our act would follow but that is a subject for a different story on child rearing.

I truly believe this imaginative child's play was a precursor to the wonderfully creative person Dorsey has become. As for me, I continue to solve the world's electrical problems and still can't draw worth a hoot!"

Do not then train youths to learning by force and harshness,
but direct them to it by what amuses their minds
so that you may be better able to discover with accuracy
the peculiar bent of the genius of each.

Plato (427-347 BC) Classical Greek philosopher, mathematician

Awaken Your Senses

1. Who or what might be stifling your creativity?

2. If you are a parent, how can you help your child reach his/her potential by embracing how he/she is wired?

3. Do you harbor fear, doubt, or past criticism that has kept you from enjoying your creativity?

Creative Educating

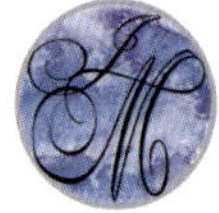

Here is an interview with my friend, Theresa Lode

(www.TheresaLode.com, Rants, riffs and resources on kids, school and ADD)

who always has a humorous outlook on life and who looks creatively at education:

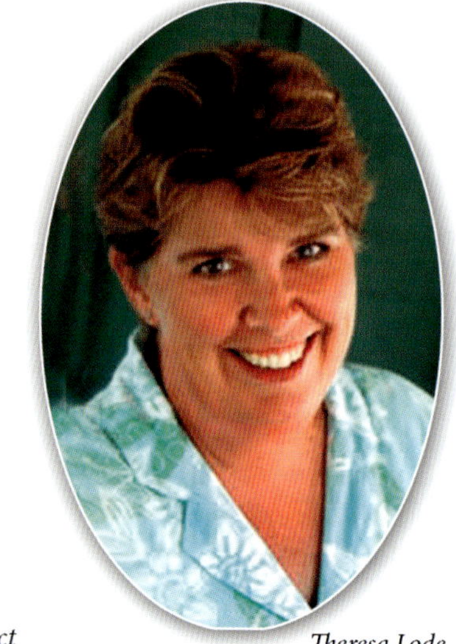

Theresa Lode

"Over thirteen years ago I faced a decision about educating my three children. And I, like Robert Frost, chose the road less traveled. I decided to home school Molly, Caleb and Daniel.

I had a curriculum. I had a plan. My kitchen may have even been clean the day we started homeschooling. So with great focus and enthusiasm...

My plans unraveled quicker than a math speed drill.

It started when my oldest was diagnosed with ADHD. I immediately began to question as suspect a diagnosis whose basis is rooted in a classroom setting. I knew I needed to rethink "school".

I began by asking myself the question: What is education? Being a product of the public schools myself, my knee jerk reaction was: A set course of instruction in certain subjects at certain times. And don't forget the good grades to validate the process. Creativity? Ha! Who has time for such frivolity when there's work to be done?

I was conflicted. My son was obviously bright. He learned the basics of electricity and plumbing by the time he was two. At age four, he could have a cogent discussion with a plumber. (That was amusing!)

Forcing him to 'do school' would extinguish the light that sparkled in his inquisitive eyes. So, starting with a crash course on education and learning styles, I began homeschooling him.

The more I learned from education experts and the latest research, the more I tossed curriculum aside. It was clear I wasn't alone in questioning the status quo of the educational system. I grew more confident in the educational value of play and my children's extraordinary capacity to direct their own learning.

By the time my youngest was school age, we embraced unschooling or what I like to call, Free Range Education. Aside from plenty of reading together, I encouraged my kids to follow where curiosity led them. Class was in session anywhere. At anytime. From anybody.

We explored science museums, cooked together, calculated savings at the store and practiced giving a good handshake. (What good is education without equally good people skills?)

As my children grew and matured, I watched their confidence, creativity and self-awareness grow. (How many 40-year-olds do you know who are clueless about their identity and their passions?)

Not that I didn't have fits of fear regularly along our journey. Rejecting the typical metrics used for education in a culture that values standardized testing is swimming against the current.

But I knew that following the commonly accepted cow-path would be doing a disservice to my kids' future, given the changing economic and workplace models.

Thinking creatively and embracing a compass versus a road map approach to education means trusting that each child has an innate ability to learn things for which they're naturally inclined.

It's foundational to learning and I believe, key to a bright future."

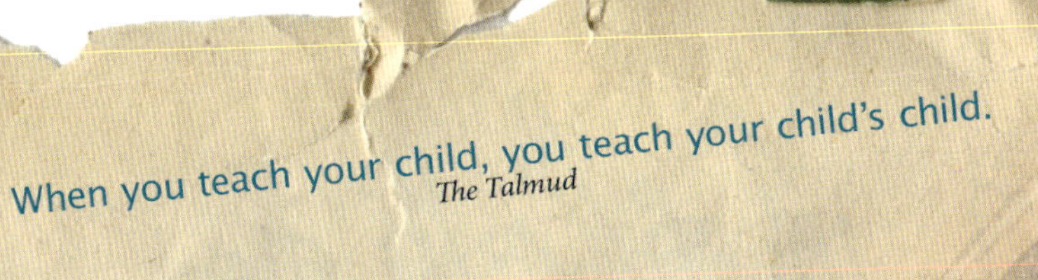

When you teach your child, you teach your child's child.
The Talmud

I have always referred to Theresa's humorous writing-style as another Erma Bombeck. In typical Theresa-style, she ended her piece with this:

> *Theresa is amazing (just seeing if you're still reading) and writes and speaks on family, education and small business topics.*
> You can connect with her at *www.themotherlode.com*

Incidentally, Theresa wrote a wonderful eBook, **A Parent to Parent Chat on ADHD, The Book I Wish I Had** that makes understanding the label in layman's terms and takes much of the fear out of dealing with the diagnosis. She is currently working on another eBook called **Free Range Education, Learning Beyond the Coop.**

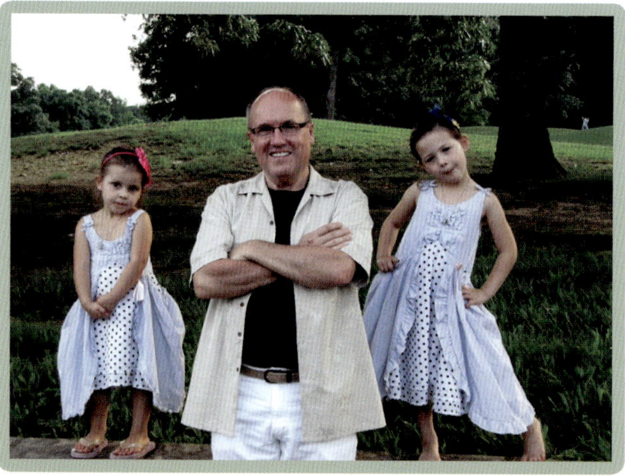

Here's an example of a creative conversation our five-year-old granddaughter, Clara had with her Papa (Daniel) recently that conveys the need to think outside the box with kids these days:

Papa: ***"So what did you learn at school today?"***

Clara: ***"Nothing; we just play." (Insert shock at him for thinking they actually learn).***

Papa: ***"How do you learn all the things you know about then?"***

Clara: ***"From Mommy and Daddy and making things up."***

Papa: ***"What do you mean 'making up'?"***

Clara: ***"I make things up in my head and then I figure out how they work."***

I asked my son-in-love, Nathan Logsdon (Clara's brilliant Daddy) to give me his perspective on educating his girls who are totally high-spirited and curious. I can't imagine a home more conducive to creating an exciting learning environment than the Logsdon home in Nashville. Their fenced-in back yard has a dog, a cat, chickens and baby chicks, tadpoles in the water feature, raised gardens where the kids (all vegetarians) freely pick what they want to eat at any time. What follows is what Nathan has to say about teaching Clara, Ellie and Juliet:

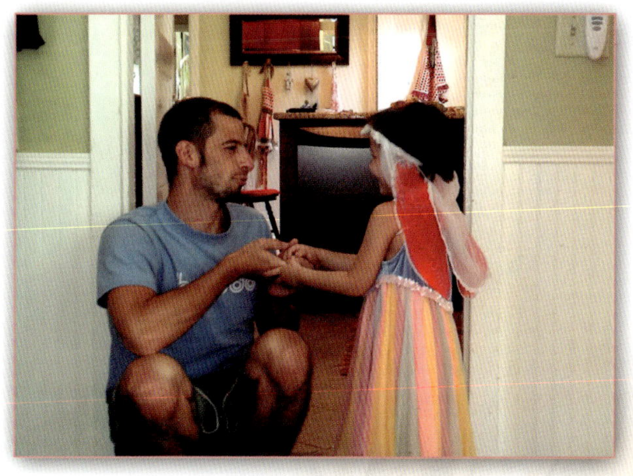

Creative Parenting 101

"Being a creative parent is one of the most rewarding jobs I have ever had but it takes some skill and practice to get good at drawing the line between the role of playmate and disciplinarian. Here are 4 ways to keep the fun alive in your relationship with your kids.

1. Just say…Yes! *I can't tell you how many times my wife and I have looked at each other and said, "What is so bad about it"? My girls are free spirits and I want them to feel free to explore all areas of their life and experience the world around us. We often go on walks as a family in a park near our house where there are creeks, trees, mud, and the occasional baby rabbit. We let them get covered head to toe in mud right before we would normally be putting them to bed. While your gut might be saying, "now is just not a great time for you to jump into that creek…" see what happens when you say "Sure, go have fun…". You will be thankful you did. Besides, what parent doesn't remember the joy of squeezing cool mud between bare toes?*

2. Follow the Leader. *Time and time again, I have had profound conversations with my girls just by simply keeping my mouth shut and letting them talk. You will have a chance to discuss such advanced topics as botany, chemistry, sexuality, astrology, biology, math, English, economics, etc. This hunger for knowledge is something that helps children draw their own conclusions and foster an environment of learning that is missing in our school system. When asked, my 6-year-old will tell you she learns nothing in school, but rather learns from her parents, and making her own ideas (hypothesis) and then tests them to see if they are true. I am simply a sounding board for my kids' exploration of this world, and I hope to always play that role in some small way for the rest of their lives.*

3. ***Play Peter Pan.*** *Remember that Uncle or Aunt who got down on all fours and played with you like an equal? Yep, your kids will have that same memory, so why not let your parental wall down and be creative yourself? I have been a prince, a blob that eats toes, a lion trainer, a witch, and a hunter to name a few. Role playing is a great way for kids to explore who they are and test their social limits so get down on all fours and act like a kid.*

4. ***Listen and if necessary, use words.*** *Creativity is about feeling safe and comfortable in your own skin. After all, a self-conscious creative sometimes never lets their light out long enough to brighten the world. Don't discount your child's feelings, even if they have difficulty articulating themselves. My 3-year-old stutters, as many children do. While having a conversation with her feels like practicing Zen- like patience, she has a voice and deserves to be heard completely, no matter how long it takes. Sometimes, treating your child's opinion as if it were that of an adult will make you privy to the most profound statements you have ever heard. After all, truth comes from the mouth of children, and we should never forget that.*

We only have one crack at this parenting job, and we all want the best for our children. Sometimes being a creative parent means having to learn how to color outside of the lines ourselves. So enjoy your parental responsibilities, for that season will not last forever. Treat every day as the most important day of your child's life. Meet your children in that place of imagination and let yourself relearn the wonders this world has to offer. I guarantee you will see a creative blossom open up and proudly share their unique light with the rest of the world."

Are You A Dreamer?

I once attended a seminar given by Dana Spears and Ron Braund, authors of a book called **Strong Willed Child or Dreamer.** They defined the creative-sensitive dreamer. I wept openly because they were describing my frustrated son, Jared, who had been labeled everything in the book. Only this time Jared was being described as a creative-sensitive dreamer ...not ADHD. Not Dyslexic. Not Bipolar. Like any concerned parent, I had to ask myself, "Why didn't I know these things sooner?" It was a defining moment.

Reading that book and talking to the authors helped me put into perspective Jared's learning method and his inability to follow traditional educational and societal expectations. These doctors said that dreamers are very imaginative, sensitive, idealistic and compassionate. That certainly described Jared. I began to see him in a new light. Not the disobedient, hard to handle child but the curious, creative and compassionate child he truly was.

Looking at my son with new eyes opened up a whole new world for both of us. Why did I so readily accept the opinion of others defining all that was wrong with Jared rather than embrace the amazing person he was and accept that he learned and viewed the world differently than others? Why do we often accept the

Dreamers don't get their security from specific limits like drivers do. They can feel as if they risk being destroyed when the limits are too rigid. Dreamers feel a desperate need to survive with emotions and imagination undefiled by the earth.
*Spears/Braund, **Strong-Willed Child or Dreamer**, 1996, Thomas Nelson Publishing, pg 15*

diagnoses and labels of well-meaning "professionals" and mistrust our own instincts? Who knows a child better than the parent? I learned that Dreamer children are full of passion and compassion. I learned to embrace Jared's creative nature and, through him, I have learned to be far less judgmental of others and of other parents.

We now accept the fact that learning is a lifelong process of keeping abreast of change. And the most pressing task is to teach people how to learn.
Peter Drucker (1909-2005)
Management consultant, educator and author

It's A New World Out There!

In 2005 Daniel Pink wrote a popular book, **A Whole New Mind: Why Right-Brainers Will Rule the Future**. He predicted that we were heading in a new direction from left-brained, analytical "knowledge workers" into a more right-brained workforce. Pink said, "…..the future belongs to a different kind of person….creative and empathetic right-brain thinkers whose abilities mark the fault line between who gets ahead and who doesn't." It seems pretty obvious he was on the right track.

In 2008, Oprah Winfrey purchased 4500 copies of Daniel Pink's book and presented them to the graduating class at Stanford University. She said she wanted to ensure they were prepared for the enormous challenges they were sure to face, one of those being the diminishing significance of degrees. Our world is getting smaller and smaller and America no longer holds the title of smartest and most competent. Now America is competing with India, China, Russia and other countries where out-sourcing is cheaper and often better.

So what makes a person stand out in the glut of degreed graduates today? One key element is the ability to be creative and not just statistical, intellectual and text-bookish; tapping into your right brain is essential to getting ahead in today's market. No longer are we faced with only options A or B, but we have a *zillion* other options available to us if we learn to see them.

Hamburger-A Or Hamburger-B?

Do you remember the 1989 television commercial for Wendy's that had a guy dressed in a suit with two hamburgers on a table in front of him? Hamburger A was twice the size of Hamburger B because it had all the special condiments and sauces that made Wendy's famous. Mr. Suit asked a passing good ole boy in a flannel shirt and ball cap,

> *"Sir, would you choose hamburger A, a Wendy's hamburger that is made fresh, or hamburger B that's premade so it sits around? Mr. Flannel Shirt, says, "B, 'cause it sits around. I'm a trucker and I need something for the long haul. That baby looks like it would hang around for six, maybe seven states."* Mr. Suit says in awe, *"But wouldn't the fresh Wendy's hamburger taste better?"* to which Mr. Flannel says, *"It might. But I can eat this B burger in Shakeytown and still be tasting it in Salt Lake."* At that point the announcer says, *"Most people prefer the taste of fresh hamburgers like Wendy's. The best burgers in the business."*

That commercial has become a family joke when there's a choice to be made... *"Umm, hamburger A or hamburger B?"* Gotta hand it to Mr. Flannel. At least he made a decision! I know people who have become totally incapacitated because indecision has derailed their ability to think straight. I hear *"I have a choice of staying in this miserable job (relationship or city) and hating every day or quitting (breaking up or moving) and both choices do not seem like good options."* Putting this in "hamburger perspective", do you think perhaps there might be a more *creative* solution? What about a hamburger that isn't either A or B but perhaps a variation? Maybe even a chicken sandwich? Something completely "out of the box" perhaps *creating your own sandwich?*

We live in a country where the options are myriad. Being more creative about finding solutions has helped me get through many stressful situations. Knowing it isn't always just a choice of hamburger A or hamburger B is comforting and enlightening. Our children know that in our family we don't have *problems,* we have *opportunities for solutions*! And we can get mighty creative in how we deal with these opportunities!

When any man holds 'twixt chin and hand a violin of mine, he will be glad Stradivari lived, made violins and made them of the best. If my hand slacked I should rob God, since he is the fullest good, but he could not make Antonio Stradivari's violins without Antonio.

Antonio Stradivari (1644-1737) Italian crafter of string instruments

Thinking Outside The Box!

Here's a story from a friend, Don Roulo, a pastor in Indiana. He visited us in Tennessee and on his way home had quite an adventure ending with a creative twist I thought was pretty impressive. His attitude about it was even more impressive. Perhaps his story will help you think more creatively next time you have an "opportunity for a solution!"

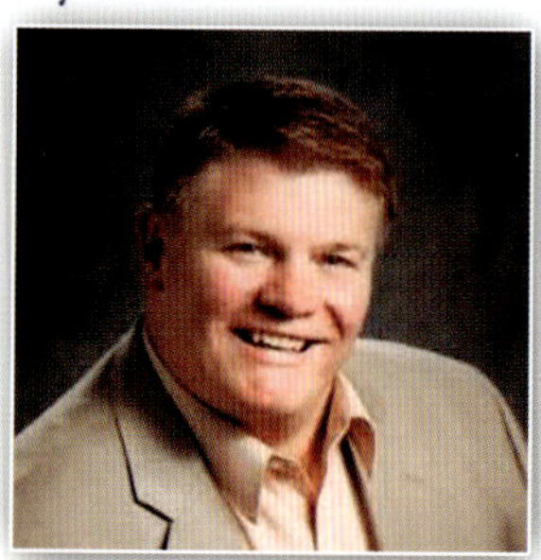
Don Roulo

"Funny ending to the travel home...Have to tell you there must be something BIG going to happen for me! I left Franklin at 2:30 AM anticipating getting home by 11:30 AM local time here. I needed to be home to pitch a workshop to a small group of pastors. About 90 minutes from home the alternator decided not to 'alternate' anymore. After the car dying three times and getting a jump I finally pushed the car, by myself, into a grocery store parking lot about 150 yards away. I did not have time to get the alternator fixed and still make it to the meeting, so I bought a new battery and ran my jumper cables from the battery in the engine compartment to the new battery which was on the floor of the passenger seat inside the car. Battery cables from under the hood to inside the car...maybe some of the Tennessee 'hill' culture rubbed off on me. I made it home in time to speak to the pastors for a brief period of time. Something REALLY good is going to happen!"

I wrote back to Don, "Oh my gosh! I think that is the most ingenious 'think outside the box', problem solving I have heard in a long time. How many people....even GUYS....would just give up and conclude they couldn't make it to the meeting? Most people would consider it too hard to figure out. YET.........YOU found an opportunity for a solution and got there in time to make the meeting. Now I don't call that another episode in a string of bad luck....I call that a stroke of genius that turned lemons into lemonade and will be the impetus to creating MORE great solutions to your difficult and trying circumstances now and in the future!! This is what sets whiners apart from winners! In my book, Don...YOU are a WINNER!

There is a video circulating on the Internet of a TED talk by artist, Phil Hansen called *Embrace the Shake*. Daniel wrote a blog about it:

In a TED talk Embrace the Shake, Phil Hansen shares how, as an art student, he developed nerve damage, causing a tremor in his hand. Devastated, he dropped out and lost his way..........until a neurologist suggested he "embrace the shake." That kind advice tweaked his point of view and spurred him to find different approaches to making art. Hansen challenged himself to create art using karate chops with painted hands, large murals with painted feet, and even using his torso as the canvas. His art stopping tremor simply redirected him from "normal" art to something distinctively creative. I just ordered his book, ***Tattoo a Banana.***

Many of you know the story behind Laura Story's song titled Blessings. A few years ago her husband was diagnosed with a brain tumor and she wondered, "Why didn't you just fix it, God?" After mentioning her desire to return to normal, her sister said, "You know, I think the detour is actually the road."

So here's my question: What is your shake that you think is holding you back? Could you embrace the shake and release your greatest art?

Blog by Dan Miller, www.48Days.com , May 29, 2013

I encourage you to Google Phil Hansen's Ted Talk. It is extremely inspiring. He discovered that by embracing his limitation, he could actually be MORE creative than ever. It was a whole new approach to his creativity that changed his artistic capabilities. He encourages everyone to become creative within the confines of their limitations.

We all have an opportunity to paint a beautiful picture on the canvas of life if we choose to take the reins and be deliberate about it.
Jared Miller Angaza, ***Wisdom Meets Passion***

Tommy Hollenstein, the Wheelchair Artist is another inspiring story of embracing limitations. Tommy has sold paintings to the likes of Joaquin Phoenix and Ringo Starr. At age 24, Tommy had a mountain bike accident that left him paralyzed from the chest down. As a child he enjoyed art but when he tried to paint with a brush in his mouth (like Joni Erickson Tada), he didn't like that so he didn't create for awhile. Two years after his accident he got a service dog that led him into painting with his wheelchair. It is a story you will want to hear. Google *Tommy the Wheelchair Artist* and watch the two minute video. You will hear him talk about how he lives with pain but when he is in his studio creating he seems pain free.

Be Your Finest Art

Dorsey and I hope that by the time you get to this point you are brimming with ideas, looking for new ways to play and recapture JOY in your life. We have both become healthier in our journey into creativity. Every day is a new adventure, seeing, hearing and imagining more clearly.

On the last page of Steven Pressfield's book, **The War of Art**, are a few paragraphs which summarize how Dorsey and I feel about the importance of embracing your authentic self.

If you were meant to cure cancer or write a symphony or crack cold fusion and you don't do it, you not only hurt yourself, even destroy yourself. You hurt your children. You hurt me. You hurt the planet... Creative work is not a selfish act or a bid for attention on the part of the actor. It's a gift to the world and every being in it. Don't cheat us of your contribution. Give us what you've got!
Steven Pressfield, ***The War of Art****, Grand Central Publishing (Hachette Book Group), 2002*

I have read that part of Pressfield's book to many budding artists but it is applicable to everyone, not just artists. If we can't be comfortable being authentic then we need to ask ourselves, *"Why not?"*

And if you are thinking that one day you might revisit an old passion or delve into exploring your creative possibilities, let me quote another friend and author/speaker, Ken Davis:

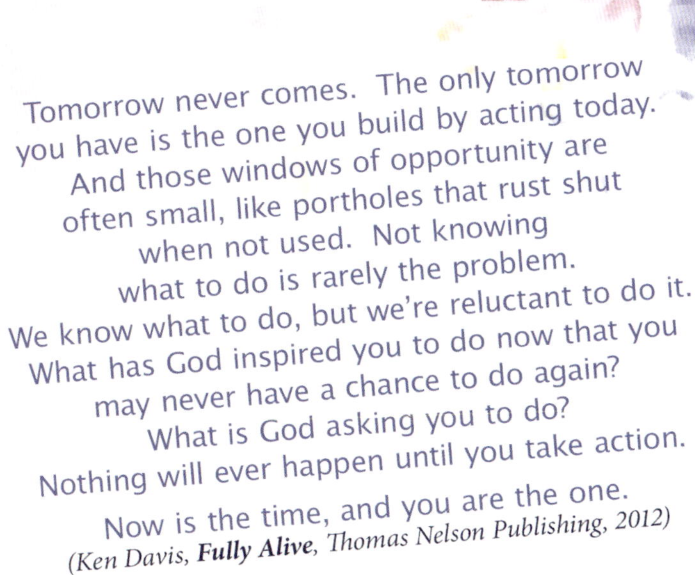

(Ken Davis, ***Fully Alive****, Thomas Nelson Publishing, 2012)*

Taped onto the bathroom mirror in Jared and Ilea's (son and daughter-in-love) bedroom is a prayer they composed and has become their family mission statement. It is a great synopsis of how to **Be Your Finest Art**:

Angaza Family Mantra

I thank you, our Creator, for my health, strength and passion. I am grateful for my family, friends, and the beauty of this world. I am grateful for abundance and the many blessings in my life. I am grateful for this journey, and the struggles that bring me wisdom. Let me value nothing above relationships or human life. Let my choices not be swayed by lust for power, money or recognition. Give me strength to choose love over ego in all I do. Give me understanding, wisdom and strength to serve and protect. As a symbol of gratitude, I regard my body as an instrument for altruism. Make me a vessel of love and a force for peace. Keep me aware. Keep me grateful. Let my life be your art.
In Nomeni Patri Et Fili Spiritus Sancti.
(In the name of the Father, Son and Holy Spirit)

There are many ways to add art to your daily life.
Begin by listening to yourself when you wake in the morning.
Dress creatively. Dine creatively.
Design your environment to reflect your authenticity.
Find a way to make your relationships more creative.

Dorsey

A Final Note From Dorsey

Dorsey McHugh

When our class begins on Wednesday mornings, I remind my students to calm themselves. I tell them to approach art as the holy calling it is. We develop a respect for the gift we have been given. It is a gift worth protecting. In this environment, we see differently. We become more imaginative about our relationships, about Love.

A fun exercise is to ask what color you would paint yourself and others, if that were the only language you had. Then ask what lines could you add to this picture? Another fun metaphor is to ask yourself, *"If I were an animal, what would I be?"*

Give yourself time to remember who you are. Go back to your childhood memories. What did you enjoy doing? How did you play? What made you laugh or cry?

Use your imagination to visualize where you want to be. What would your ideal day be? What would your home look or feel like? Imagine in as much detail as you want. Write a whole story about you.

Art is fueled by truth. I often use a photograph I have taken as the inspiration for a painting. The painting rarely ends up as an exact likeness. I embellish the painting as my inner landscape inspires me. Tell the truth about yourself. Tell the truth about yourself poetically. Leave out as much as you can, to enable the viewer to insert their own story into your image or your writing. You don't have to justify yourself to anyone.

Creativity is a lifestyle. It is not a band-aid or cure. It is a change in how you live. If you can begin the first steps and continue walking you will find yourself becoming your finest art. Expect that you will not always know where your journey may lead you. Listen for and learn to follow your own inner voice.

Six Tips For Unlocking Your Creativity:
Joanne Miller and Dorsey McHugh

1. ACKNOWLEDGE THAT YOU ARE A CREATIVE BEING.

We are reflections of God's Glory (Genesis 1:26)… which is a good basis for our self-worth and for our own creative nature we inherited from the greatest Creator of all time. (In the beginning God CREATED…….Genesis 1:1)

Exodus 31:3-5 gives an example of God's instilling the gifts of craftsmanship and artistic abilities in Biblical leaders.
To deny yourself the JOY of creating is to limit God's beauty in your life and the world around you.

You need courage to be creative. You need the courage to see things differently, courage to go against the crowd, courage to take a different approach, courage to stand alone, if you have to, courage to choose activity over inactivity.
Jim Rohn (1930-2009), entrepreneur, author and motivational speaker

2. KEEP LEARNING, KEEP GROWING

Painting, computer graphics, drawing, sculpture, stained glass, landscaping, writing, poetry, dance, voice, acting, directing, floral arranging, whittling, wood carving, cooking, building, etc. are all ways in which you can release right-brained energy. We are sure you can come up with many wonderful ideas.

You can find classes through local recreation centers, community colleges, computer stores, art stores, libraries, news and media publications, and civic organizations. Perhaps you can create a new hobby or turn your passion into an income producing business.

3. TRY NEW THINGS! TAKE WALKS IN UNFAMILIAR PLACES. SIT IN A PARK AND OBSERVE . REDECORATE.

Learn to live in the moment. Don't be so quick to turn on the iPod, the boom-box or stereo. Close your eyes and listen. Concentrate on your senses and how they are stimulated.

Treat your senses to new experiences. Try a new ethnic food or culture. Travel to a different part of your state, your country, the

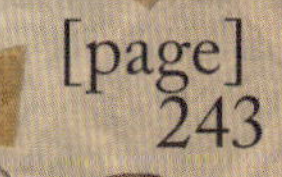

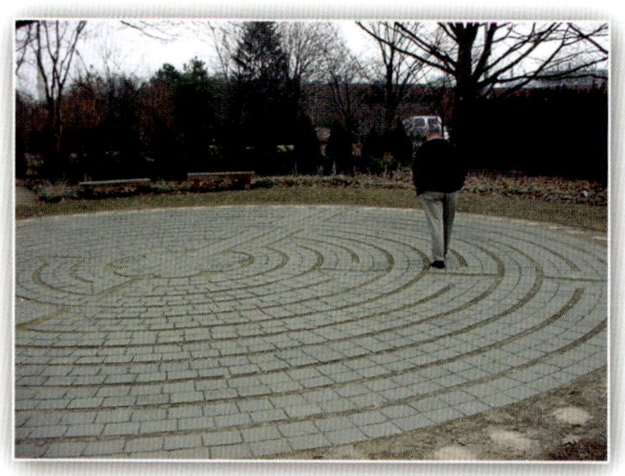

Dan Miller walking a Labyrinth

world. (If your finances don't afford you this opportunity, watch documentaries on other cultures and experiences on DVD or TV) Go to a concert or listen to an album of music you haven't explored before. Go to an art museum and study works by a variety of artists and determine what you like or dislike about each one.

The most potent tool for contacting
inner guidance and creativity is walking.
*Julia Cameron, **The Artist's Way***

Daniel and I love labyrinths. So, often when we visit a new city, we check on-line first to see if there are any labyrinths in that area and we seek them out. We have found some beautiful hidden-away labyrinths where we can walk, meditate, pray and just BE.

Another suggestion for getting creative and lifting your spirits is to sit in a room of your house and redecorate it in your mind. Then play with colors, textures and design and have fun redoing it. You will find it to be addictive. You'll find all kinds of things to redecorate!

4. BE IMAGINATIVE, PLAY GAMES, AND LAUGH!

The best memories are made playing games together! And these days, playing games is very portable. Daniel and I play each other on our Smart Phones when we are caught waiting somewhere. We may be sitting next to each other in an airport, playing SkyWords or whipping out our Quiddler cards at a favorite restaurant. We are known around town as the couple who plays cards. Dorsey and I love challenging each other in WordFeud on our SmartPhones.

Playing games helps you think more creatively about situations and problems. But the best part of playing games is that it helps you laugh more. We often included games in our family nights as the kids got older. We have memorable stories of laughing till we cry.

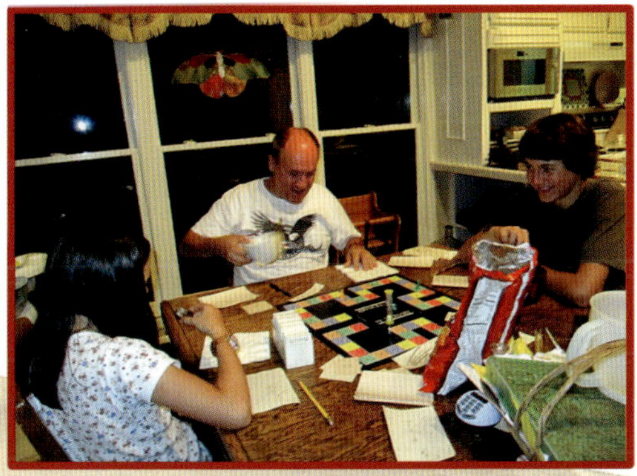

Eliza Miller, Dan Miller, & Caleb Miller

If we couldn't laugh we would all go insane.
Robert Frost (1874-1963) American poet and Pulitzer Prize winner

5. VISUALIZE YOURSELF AS A BLANK CANVAS. SLAP ON SOME COLOR!

If you look in the mirror and don't like what you see, change it! Just as you can change a painting you don't like or a room that seems drab by slapping on new color or redecorating you can do the same with yourself.

Start with a smile. I am a people watcher, often dismayed by how few people smile regularly. Dorsey and I have this theory that smiling will make our faces less likely to droop in old age (of course that is waaay in the future)so we are doing it a lot these days. Have you noticed how hard it is to be critical, angry, upset and judgmental when you have a big smile on your face? I love to smile at people as I pass them and say a big, *"Hello!"* Sometimes it takes them by surprise if you don't live in the South. But in Tennessee, it is expected! I like that.

Don't tell me you can't afford a new wardrobe. Dorsey and I both love shopping at thrift stores, consignment stores and

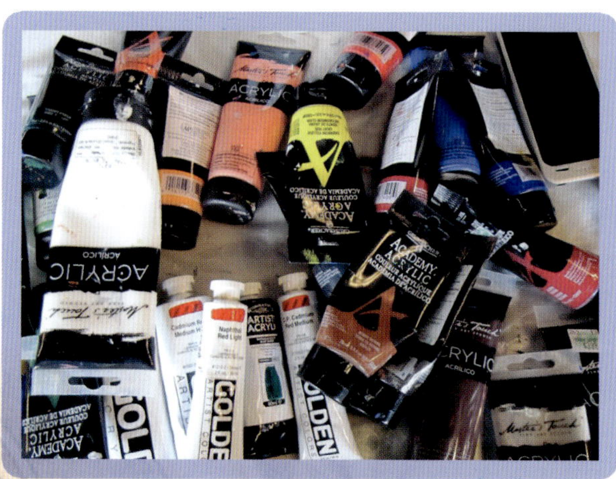

Goodwill. Stopping at garage and yard sales runs in the veins of all our family members. On a fun thrift store outing with Dorsey I spent $75 and got a designer dress, several new tops, a gift for a grandchild and some other little treasures.

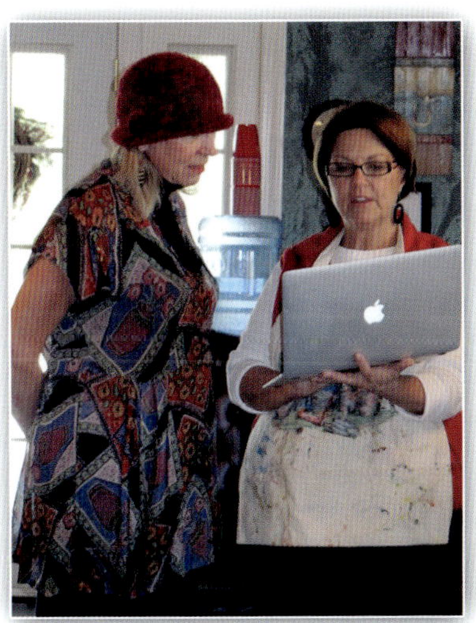

talking with Gail Hyatt

If you still sport the same hairstyle and makeup you had in 1950, 1990 or even 2000…it might be time for a makeover! (Men, the hairstyle goes for you too…makeup is optional!) Times are a'changin' and you should be too. Ask your children or a good friend what they would like to see changed in your appearance. Sometimes they can see things you don't because you are too familiar with the reflection in the mirror. In recent years, Daniel is often seen sporting a cool scarf around his neck to set off a great outfit. There are no rules saying you are required to look your age!

I am an artist at living—
my work of art is my life.
D.T. Suzuki, author and essayist

6. **TAKE RESPONSIBILITY FOR YOUR HEALTH & WELFARE.** Please do not take an ostrich-approach of sticking your head in the sand when your health is involved. We hope we have given you good input on being in charge of your welfare. Pick up a copy of **Love, Medicine and Miracles** by Bernie Siegel, MD. YOU are responsible for taking care of you, not your doctor, counselor or psychiatrist. Those professionals can certainly help but you have to be willing to work on changing and growing. They can't do it for you. Remember to ask yourself, "*Why do I need this?*" when you feel illness, anger, depression or frustration overshadowing your JOY! Think of creative ways in which to redirect the negative so you simply don't have time to be sick, angry, etc. Be truthful to yourself about the root causes of those emotions and if you are in situations where change is necessary, take the steps to follow through. The pushing through may be difficult but the result will give you a new release of energy and creativity you will want to embrace!

Create your own illness-blocker by getting into the zone of creativity!

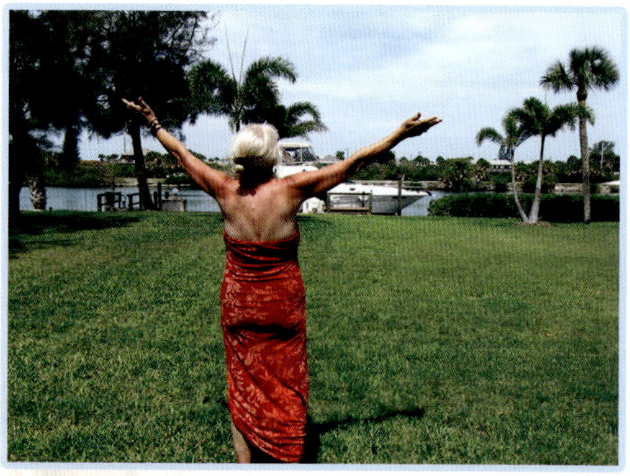

Dorsey McHugh in Nokomis Florida

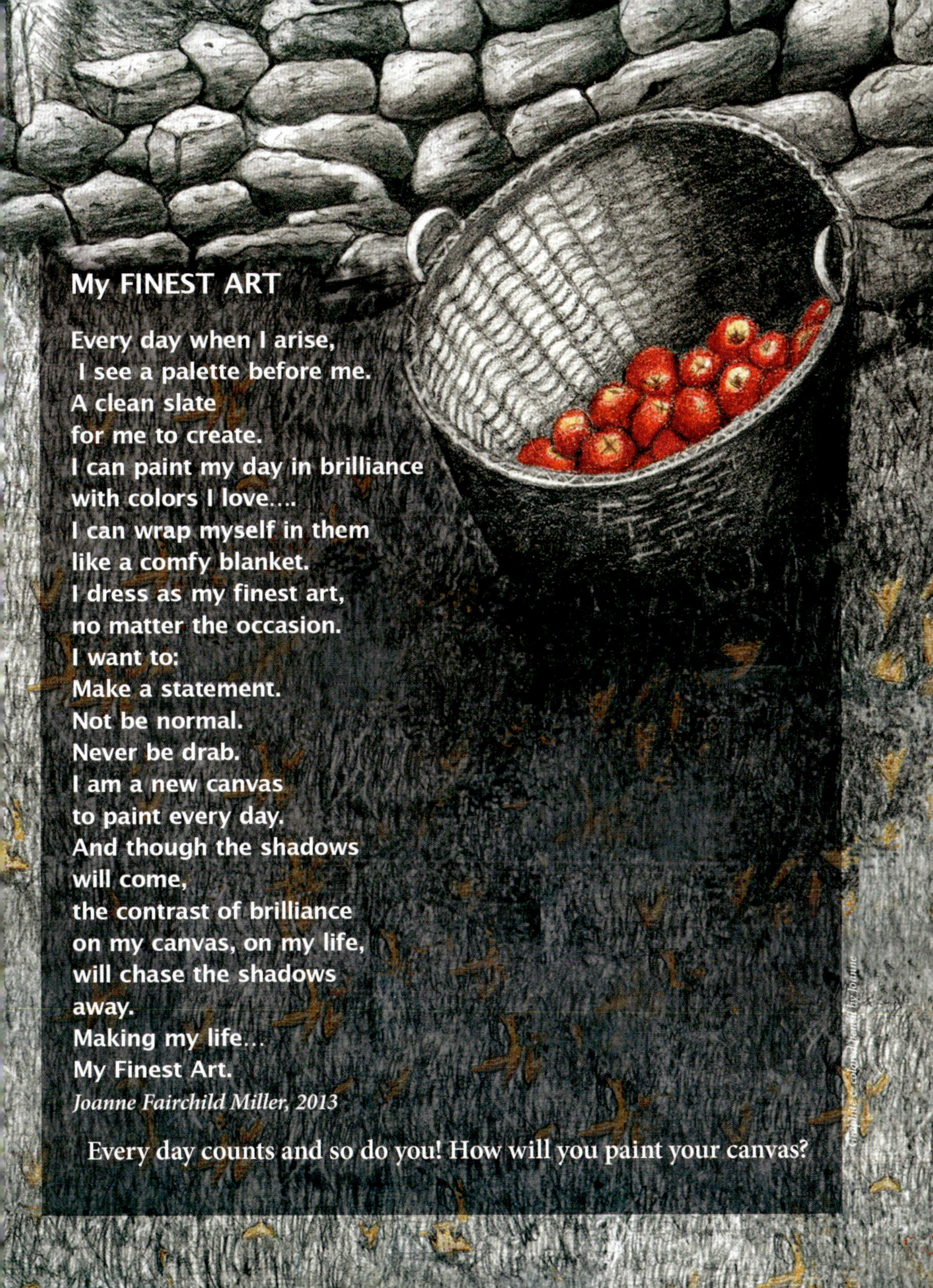

My FINEST ART
Every day when I arise,
I see a palette before me.
A clean slate
for me to create.
I can paint my day in brilliance
with colors I love....
I can wrap myself in them
like a comfy blanket.
I dress as my finest art,
no matter the occasion.
I want to:
Make a statement.
Not be normal.
Never be drab.
I am a new canvas
to paint every day.
And though the shadows
will come,
the contrast of brilliance
on my canvas, on my life,
will chase the shadows
away.
Making my life...
My Finest Art.
Joanne Fairchild Miller, 2013
Every day counts and so do you! How will you paint your canvas?
Graphite & colored pencil by Joanne

And when you have CREATED YOUR FINEST ART,
please contact us and give us your story.
You just may be in our next book!

Joanne Miller
Dorsey McHugh
ART@48Days.com
PO Box 681381
Franklin, TN
37064

For art sales, please contact Susan Macke Miller, 615-293-3623 or hisusan@gmail.com

Books You Might Enjoy

Wisdom Meets Passion *by Dan Miller and Jared Angaza*

Drawing With Children *by Mona Brookes*

The Success Strategies *by Deb Austin Brown*

The Millionaire Messenger *by Brendon Burchard*

The Artist's Way *by Julia Cameron*

The Artist's Way Every Day *by Julia Cameron*

Awakening the Artist Within *by Julia Cameron*

Claiming Your Creative Self *by Eileen M. Clegg*

Fully Alive *by Ken Davis*

The Creative Call *by Janice Elsheimer*

The Draw Book:Creativity Boosters and Art Lessons *by Rose Gauss*

The Icarus Deception *by Seth Godin*

When Pleasing Others is Hurting You *by David Hawkins, PhD*

The Art Spirit *by Robert Henri*

Leaving a Trace: The Art of Transforming a Life into Stories
by Alexandra Johnson

Bird by Bird: Some Instructions on Writing and Life
by Anne Lamott

Coaching the Artist Within *by Eric Maisel, PhD*

Will I Ever Be Good Enough? *by Karyl McBride, PhD*

Living Beyond Awesome *by Jen McDonough*

Stirring the Waters: Writing to Find Your Spirit *by Janell Moon*

Writing From the Heart *by Leslea Newman*

Women's Bodies, Women's Wisdom, *by Christiane Northrup, MD*

You Can Sleep In Your Car, But You Can't Drive Your House To Work
by Sutton Parks

The War of Art *by Steven Pressfield*

Do The Work! *by Steven Pressfield*

The Resiliency Advantage *by Al Siebert, PhD*

Love, Medicine and Miracles *by Bernie Siegel, M.D.*

The Way They Learn
by Cynthia Ulrich Tobias Focus on the Family Publishing, 1994

If You Want To Write:A Book About Art, Independence and Spirit *by Brenda Ueland*

A Tree Full of Angels *by Macrina Wiederkehr*

Blue and Yellow Don't Make Green *by Michael Wilcox*

The Art of Possibility
by Rosamund Stone Zander and Benjamin Zander

Raising Positive Kids in a Negative World *by Zig Ziglar*

See You at the Top *by Zig Ziglar*

On Writing Well *by William Zinsser*

Recommended Podcasts, Videos, Blogs, Websites, Etc.

www.DorseyMcHugh.com
Dorsey's website
www.HiDorsey.wordpress.com
Dorsey's blog

www.48Days.net
Dan Miller's business/entrepreneur based social network
www.48Days.com
Live events and Dan Miller's blog link, podcast link
www.48Days.net/profile/JoanneMiller
JoanneMiller, Joanne's profile and blog

www.berniesiegelmd.com
Dr. Bernie Siegel's website for taking control over your health

www.nashvillemuse.com
Doak Turner, Nashville Muse, editor, marketer and artist advocate.

www.jaredangaza.com
Jared Angaza's blog site for discovering the extraordinary

www.findingyourvoiceradio.com
Joel & Pei Boggess, Life Coaching out-of-the-box.

www.RoseGauss.com
Rose Gauss graphic artist and children's book illustrator.
www.theDRAWpage.com
Her ***Draw Book*** *is amazing and available on her website*

WANT TO MEET JOANNE AND DORSEY IN PERSON? COME TO THIS LIVE EVENT IN FRANKLIN, TN!

INNOV48

Artist
Thought-leader
Singer
Poet
Free-Thinker
SPEAKER
Writer
MUSICIAN
Free Agent
ACTOR
Dancer
Rule-bender
Creative
...Eaglepreneur

If any of these words describes you, you are in the right place. Are you sick of being labeled a "starving artist" because of not being able to make money doing what you are most passionate about? Are you ready to have "Wisdom" meet your "Passion?"

Can you clearly state...

- What do you truly love doing?
- What are your skills and abilities?
- What is your Economic Model?

Lacking clarity in any of these will cause you to fail. **So how do creatives take their unique passion and make it profitable?**

JOIN US AT ONE OF OUR INNOV48 EVENTS AT THE SANCTUARY IN FRANKLIN, TN. This is a two-day intensive event focused on unleashing the creativity within you to create a life where wisdom meets passion.

www.48Days.com/liveevents/inov48

WWW.48DAYS.NET

48Days.NET is the **Idea Networking** site for people who are committed to finding - or creating - work that is meaningful, purposeful, and profitable. That includes entrepreneurs, artists, authors, musicians, those working from home, small business owners, BIG business owners, franchisees, independent contractors, reps...etc. as well as people who have found that fit as an employee. People who work on their own terms. We're honored to have you here with us!

Our mission is to enhance the process of imagining, dreaming and introspection to help people recognize their calling and true path, and to translate that into meaningful, purposeful and profitable daily work – in **48 Days.**

Note to self:
Get connected!

WITH OVER 14,000 MEMBERS, THIS FREE ONLINE COMMUNITY IS A GREAT WAY TO CONNECT WITH OTHERS - THERE ARE GROUPS FOR EVERYONE - ARTISTS, SINGERS, MUSICIANS, WRITERS, ECOMMERCE AND TECH GROUPS, ETC!

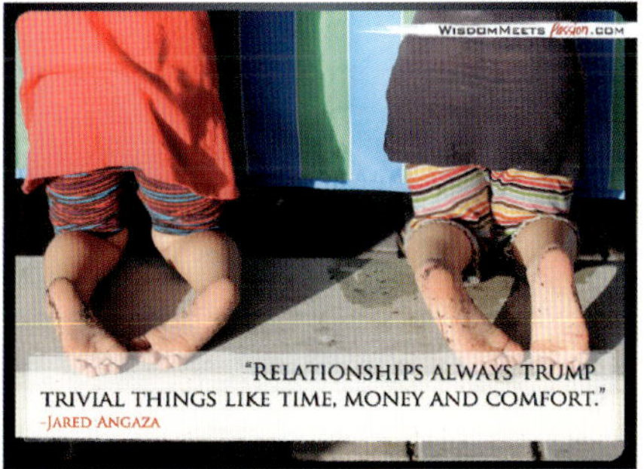

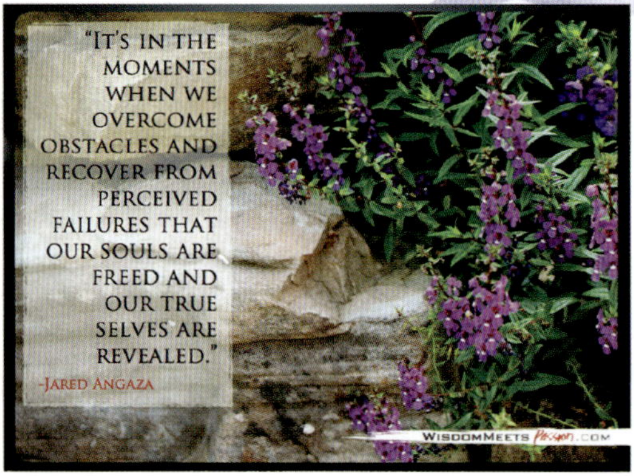

"It's in the moments when we overcome obstacles and recover from perceived failures that our souls are freed and our true selves are revealed."

-Jared Angaza

WisdomMeetsPassion.com

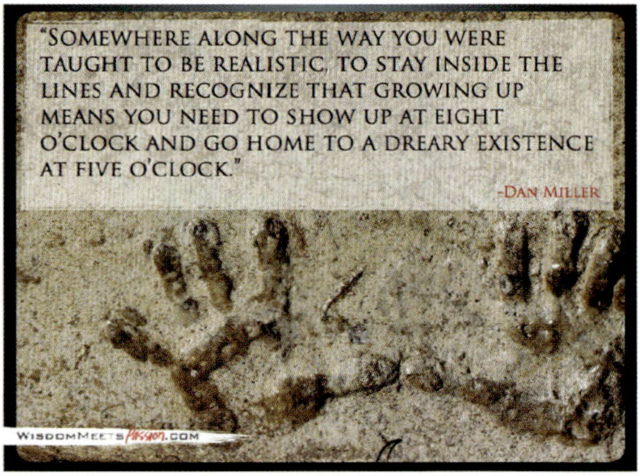

"Somewhere along the way you were taught to be realistic, to stay inside the lines and recognize that growing up means you need to show up at eight o'clock and go home to a dreary existence at five o'clock."

-Dan Miller

WisdomMeetsPassion.com

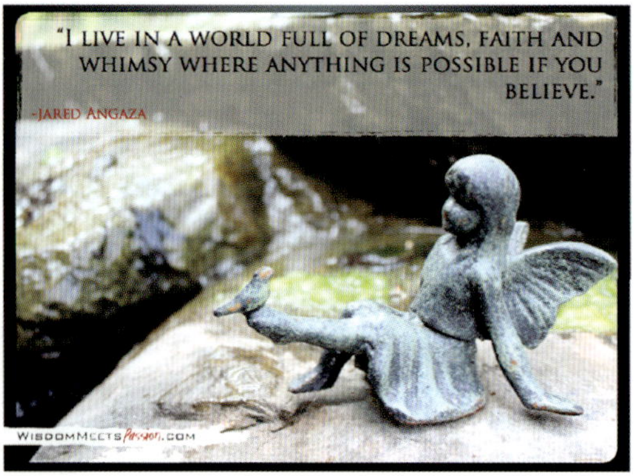

"I live in a world full of dreams, faith and whimsy where anything is possible if you believe."

-Jared Angaza

WisdomMeetsPassion.com

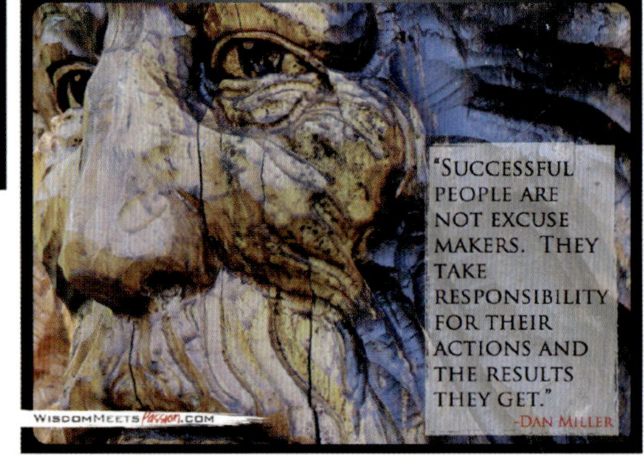